Heart of Africa

HEART OF AFRICA

Centre of my Gravity

Sihle Khumalo

UMUZI

Published by Umuzi 2009
P O Box 6810, Roggebaai 8012, South Africa,
an imprint of Random House Struik (Pty) Ltd
Company Reg No 1966/003153/07
80 McKenzie Street, Cape Town 8001, South Africa
P O Box 1144, Cape Town 8000, South Africa
umuzi@randomstruik.co.za
www.umuzi-randomhouse.co.za

First edition, first printing 2009
9 8 7 6 5 4 3 2 1

ISBN 978-1-4152-0081-0

Cover design by mr design
Cover image based on an image from
Alan Moorehead's *The White Nile*, 1960,
and on a photograph supplied by Sihle Khumalo
Map by John Hall
Text design by William Dicey
Set in Minion and Journal
Printed and bound by CTP Book Printers,
Duminy Street, Parow 7500, South Africa

This book is dedicated to Sifiso "Bru" Sibisi,
a confidant who almost was my best man

"To be independent of public opinion is the first formal education in achieving anything great."

Georg Wilhelm Friedrich Hegel
German philosopher, 1770–1831

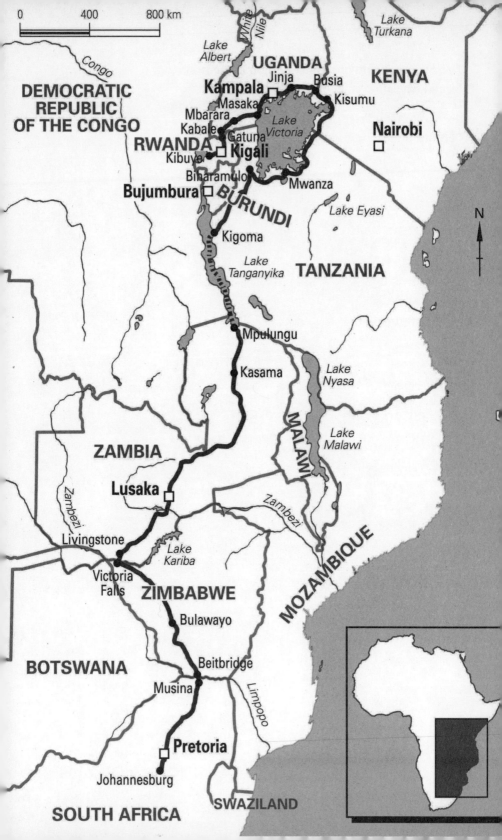

Contents

Ready, steady ... eish!

One of the greatest mysteries of the nineteenth century, geographically speaking, was the mystery of the source of the River Nile. It was something that had intrigued people for a very long time. The ancient Greeks and Romans, not to mention the Egyptian pharaohs, all wondered where the mighty river that ended in the Mediterranean Sea near the ancient city of Alexandria – where my first trip through Africa also happened to terminate – sprang from. By the middle of the nineteenth century it was very much on the agenda of the European explorers. The interior of the "dark continent" was still an enigma to the rest of the world (not that Mama Africa is an open book now!) and explorers were competing to see who could find what first. They disagreed about many things, except that finding the source of the Nile would be first prize.

The source of the Blue Nile, the main tributary of the Nile, had been discovered in 1770 by a Scotsman, James Bruce, who traced it all the way to Lake Tana in Ethiopia. But where did the White Nile spring from?

Another Scotsman, the well-known medical missionary David Livingstone, who had been beating about the bush in Africa since 1840, became so obsessed about finding the source of the White Nile that he completely disappeared from sight for over four years. Sixteen years before he was found, in 1871, by a Welsh-raised American journalist-turned-explorer named Henry Morton Stanley, he'd "discovered", among other wonders, the Victoria Falls, which he named after the reigning British monarch, Queen Victoria.

In 1854, on their first expedition, two British explorers, John Hanning Speke and Richard Francis Burton, managed to discover a few things about the course of the Nile – before Speke was stabbed several times by locals in present-day Somalia. He managed to free himself and got away; Burton escaped with a spear imbedded in his bum (both cheeks pierced).

After recovering in England they were back for more, two years later. Luckily for them the local tribes were not as hostile this time round, but the two encountered endless problems. Speke became deaf at one stage after a beetle crawled into his ear and had to be removed with a knife.

Another time he turned partially blind due to some disease. But their persistence paid off: it was on this expedition, in February 1858, that they discovered Lake Tanganyika (which Speke couldn't see properly because of his partial blindness).

Later that year it was Burton's turn. He became so sick that he couldn't travel. So Speke left him behind and went on to discover the biggest lake in Africa, which he also named after Queen Victoria. When he returned to England (without Burton), he claimed that he had discovered the source of the Nile.

Burton, however, did not accept his former travelling companion's claim, so Speke had to go on a third expedition in 1862, after which he insisted that he had found conclusive proof that Lake Victoria was indeed the source of the Nile, one of the longest rivers on planet Earth.

The controversy was finally put to rest by Henry Morton Stanley, who had been sent to look for the lost Livingstone. By the time Stanley confirmed Speke's claim in 1874, both Speke and Livingstone were dead.

To cut this long story short: it is fair to say that, despite some further discoveries, the source of the Nile was found by Speke in 1858. I was aware, however, of contesting claims as to the river's real source. After all, Lake Victoria is itself fed by several rivers and lakes.

In 2008, exactly 150 years after Speke, I decided to commemorate the discovery of the source of the Nile and head for Central Africa to see for myself what the fuss was all about.

My job in the Exploration Division of a global mining company based in Johannesburg involves a lot of travelling, and the only preparation I could manage to make for my intended trip was to phone my wife from Namibia a week before I was supposed to leave and ask her to book a seat on the Johannesburg–Bulawayo Greyhound bus for me. My intention was to travel northwards from there by road and rail.

Once back in South Africa with less than three days to go, I phoned my company's travel clinic to enquire which malaria prophylaxis to take. I was informed that Mefliam, which you must start taking a week before you get to a malaria area, continue to take once a week while in the malaria area and for four weeks after you've left, is ideal. This posed a small problem: I had to leave in three days' time. So Doxytab was recommended, which must be taken daily while in a malaria area, plus for twenty-eight days after your return. Taking daily medication on a full stomach, especially when doing a trip of this nature, is almost impossible. I therefore settled for Mefliam, even though I was four days late. That meant that I would arrive in Zambia – the first malarial country on my itinerary – not properly protected against *omiyane* (as mosquitoes are called in Zulu).

The aim of my trip was to see a few key places visited by some early European explorers, but it did not have a real destination. All I really wanted to do was travel through Central Africa and along the way do six things:

— take a ride on a ferry on Lake Tanganyika;
— stand on the equator in Uganda;
— bungee jump at the official source of the Nile in Jinja, Uganda;
— get up close and personal with some mountain gorillas in Rwanda;
— visit the remote source of the Nile at Nyungwe forest in Rwanda;
— visit the Kigali Memorial Centre in Rwanda.

"Travel is a brutality. It forces you to trust strangers and to lose sight of the familiar comfort of home and friends. You are constantly off balance. Nothing is yours except the essential things – air, sleep, dreams, the sea, the sky – all things tending towards the eternal or what we imagine of it."

Cesare Pavese
Italian poet and novelist, 1908–1950

North with Greyhound

On the day of my departure, Friday, 3 October 2008, I did not go to work since I had spent the previous weekend away from home in Namibia. So I decided to do some running around, accompanied by my wife and four-year-old daughter Nala.

I still had to decide which route to take. As I would once again be travelling by public transport, I had, broadly speaking, two options: travel to Mwanza in Tanzania through Zimbabwe and Zambia, and from there go west to Rwanda by the main road that skirts Lake Victoria in the south before proceeding north to Uganda, and fly back to Johannesburg from Nairobi, Kenya. The second option was to go north from Mwanza to Kisumu in Kenya, proceed to Uganda by the main road that runs just north of Lake Victoria, finish the trip in Kigali and fly home with Rwandair Express, Rwanda's national carrier.

I preferred option two, which meant travelling in an anticlockwise direction, starting on the eastern side of Lake Victoria and finishing off on its western side. There was, however, a tiny, little, last-minute stumbling block: Rwandair Express had not flown on its Kigali–Johannesburg route for a couple of months. According to their website the flight was going to be relaunched on 12 October – only nine days away.

So I decided to give Rwandair Express a call. The lady on the other side of the line did not sound convinced that the airline would be flying from Kigali to Johannesburg in nine days' time. In fact, she told me straight that they had not even started taking bookings for that route. The news was definitely not comforting. One thing I did not want was to travel all the way to Kigali only to discover that I could not fly back to Johannesburg direct.

Why had the Kigali–Johannesburg flights been cancelled in the first place, and where were they going to source the new plane at this late stage? With these unanswered questions in mind I decided that, much as I preferred the second option, I had to go for the first: travel in a clockwise direction from Mwanza, through Kigali and Kampala, the capital cities of Rwanda and Uganda respectively, to the capital of Kenya – even though the prices of the direct Nairobi–Johannesburg flight were exorbitant. Kenya Airways charged more than R8 000 and South African Airways asked about R6 000. According to Rwandair Express's website, a one-way flight from Kigali to Johannesburg would have cost less than R3 500. So the higher airfare from Nairobi was going to mess up my budget.

Because airline tickets are usually more reasonable when you buy them well in advance, I decided – after endless phone calls and repeatedly checking the internet – to book the Nairobi–Johannesburg flight on SAA. It was a huge risk because it meant I had to get to Nairobi by 2 November, whatever happened on the way.

With my flight back to South Africa sorted, I could start worrying about other things. I still had to buy some toiletries. Just when I was about to do that, my wife suggested that we have "a proper lunch as a family on your last day". Without any argument I obliged. The meal took almost two hours. Once that was done, and after buying R15 000 worth of US dollars at the then R8.70 exchange rate, my wife (again) made a suggestion – that I have a haircut. It had never entered my mind to have my hair cut as I still had not packed my bag. But the last thing I wanted was a fight with Lulu, considering that we were not going to see each other for about a month.

It is worth mentioning that less than a month earlier she had had an ectopic pregnancy, which necessitated an operation during which her Fallopian tube and ovary had been removed and which halved our chances of having another baby. So for the past weeks she had not been her 100-per-cent self and now, barely four weeks later, I was going to be away from home for a month.

It being a Friday afternoon, people were getting ready to go out and the hair salon was packed. I suggested that we drop the haircut, but Lulu insisted. After an hour of waiting and twiddling our thumbs, she decided we'd better leave. We had to go home via the gym, I said. No, not to exercise – I wanted to weigh myself. I knew that, with the stress of travelling on my own and having irregular meals (less food), I was definitely going to shed some kilos, and in order to measure the exact weight loss during the trip it was necessary to know my current weight.

I clocked a hefty but very healthy 94.3 kilograms, which meant that if I were a boxer, I would be in the heavyweight division (over ninety kilos).

Weighing that much reminded me of a T-shirt I had seen a few days earlier: *I am in great shape and that shape is round.*

Finally we rushed home. I packed my backpack and less than an hour later we were ready to make a beeline for Park Station, as Johannesburg's railway-and-bus station is often referred to. As we were about to leave home I discovered – while quickly glancing at *Voetspore* on SABC 2 – that with all the running around I had left my sunglasses somewhere – probably in the banking hall. We nevertheless checked the car, the lounge, the bedroom. To no avail. I was resigned but somewhat disappointed that I would be without a good pair of sunglasses, which is an essential item when embarking on an African expedition.

Then, just as we were about to leave the house, Lulu suggested that we pray. I was so shocked I almost cancelled the trip. She, like me, is not into praying but, I guess, having a husband going on a Central African adventure on his own was enough to make her welcome any type of intervention from Above. All three of us held hands whilst Lulu led us in a mumbled prayer. In less than a minute she was done. It was time to leave. By this time Nala was not feeling too well.

We drove from the south of Johannesburg (living there instead of the leafy northern suburbs is a sure indication that we are not wealthy), and getting through the CBD was not easy as some roads had been closed off for construction work. While rushing to Park Station, Lulu asked me one of those so-you-think-you-are-clever-stupid-man type of question: "Don't you think you should leave your wedding ring behind, considering you are going backpacking?"

To be honest I had thought about the very same thing while packing my bag, but decided removing my wedding ring just then could be interpreted wrongly and cause a lot of disharmony. However, now that she was the one suggesting it, who was I to argue with the madam?

We made it to Park Station only fifteen minutes before the scheduled departure of the bus. As we were going down the escalators I was surprised to see so many people at the Greyhound check-in counters. Even more surprising was the amount of luggage passengers were dragging along – mostly white-red-blue-striped bags, which in rural KwaZulu-Natal we used to call *umhlab'ungehlule* – the world has conquered me.

It was absolute chaos with loads of people pushing and shoving and babies crying all over the place. With all this confusion it was clear that it would take at least thirty minutes to check in. As Nala seemed to be coming down with flu, we decided it would be best if she and her mother left.

It was not the most appropriate way to say goodbye to your loved ones, but I reminded Lulu to take the ring. Amidst people pushing and pulling and shoving around us, she tried, unsuccessfully, to remove the ring from my finger. Quite a few people looked amazed at the woman forcefully trying to remove the wedding ring from a guy's finger in a packed bus station, with him calmly looking on. Finally, the silver band slipped off.

With that the moment arrived for them to leave. A very sombre and solemn moment. Everyone except Nala knew full well that dangers and challenges would be my companions on my month-long mission. After some hugs and kisses they left. I looked at them, my daughter in my wife's arms, as they took the escalator to the parking area. They were both waving, Nala smiling sweetly.

Lula and Nala had not been gone for a minute when a tall guy came up to me and said, "Look, my brother, seeing that you only have one bag, will you please take one of my bags as if it is yours through the check-in point, please?"

It was at that moment that I noticed posters on the wall saying, "Warning: Each passenger is allowed a maximum of 30 kg only. Anything above that will be charged at R4.00 per kilogram."

I turned down the tall guy's request. No sooner had he disappeared into the crowd than a woman approached me with the same plea. Again I politely turned her down, saying, "No, I cannot."

It took me and some other passengers, who were carrying bags that looked like they weighed less than thirty kilos, more than half an hour to go through the check-in point and get our luggage stickered. The rest of the passengers were made to queue on one side while their bags were weighed to determine how much they had to pay for excess weight. Only after they had paid the correct amount were stickers attached to their luggage.

As I approached the bus, thinking everything had been done according to the rules and that we were ready to roll, I was surprised to see stacks of striped bags lined up next to the bus, ready to be loaded. While waiting in the queue to have my name added to the passenger list, I saw that quite a few people had managed to pass the check-in counter without their big bags having been weighed and without the necessary stickers. Now they were pleading with the driver to load their bags anyway. One of them, a young girl in a tight pair of jeans and short, belly-button-showing vest, was pleading with the driver, who must have been in his mid-fifties, *"Asikhulume njengabantu"* – let's talk as people. Whew, I thought to myself, driving a bus heading for Zimbabwe can come with blood-pressure-raising-and-very-tiring additional benefits.

Our queue was moving very slowly and soon another brother approached me and told me that he would appreciate it if at the South Africa–Zimbabwe border I could take one of his bags as mine because "the customs officials are very strict". With a bit of a smile to show some empathy, I turned him down too.

At last seated towards the back of the bus, I noticed, even though not even a fifth of the passengers had boarded, that the overhead storage was almost full, mostly with 36-unit egg containers, ten-kilogram bags of potatoes, five-kilogram bags of apples and five-litre containers of cooking oil. I leaned back in my comfortable window seat as I watched a never-ending queue of people with white-red-blue-striped bags pleading their case with the bus driver.

After all the drama and once all the bags, bicycles and car batteries had been loaded into the belly of the bus, we left the station at 10 p.m. – one and a half hours late. Under a dark, cloudless African sky we headed north on the M1. I had a perfect view of the office blocks in Parktown, Killarney and Melrose as they slipped by. I watched the distant, slowly drifting Sandton skyline and wondered about the journey ahead.

People will always find a way of beating the system. At our first stop on the N1 in Midrand, four people embarked with twelve bags. The bus did not carry a scale to weigh bags picked up en route. The bags, obviously weighing much more than the 120 kilos they were allowed, were loaded without a single question being asked.

On the way to pick up more passengers in Pretoria/Tshwane (depending who has won the latest round of the name-changing legal wrangle), I glimpsed the Voortrekker Monument on my left, a huge square granite structure inaugurated on 16 December 1949 to honour the discontented

Voortrekkers who left the Cape Colony with their wagons and livestock around 1836, a few years before Livingstone started his wanderings further north. Soon thereafter I spotted, on my right, the magnificent piece of architecture that is the University of South Africa (Unisa) building. I must confess that I am not into architecture, but every time I look at that building, especially at night, I appreciate how truly creative some people can be.

At Pretoria/Tshwane station we picked up one passenger, a middle-aged woman with two massive striped bags, which went into the bottom of the bus, and a 36-unit egg container, which she carried with her.

Immediately after the first toll gate on our way north, there was a roadblock where traffic officers and policemen and women seemed to be on the lookout for overloaded bakkies and overcrowded vans, many of which had already been pulled off to one side. After a few seconds' chat with our driver, the traffic officer sent us off on our way to Bulawayo.

However, our trip was soon interrupted again. About thirty-five kilometres before Bela-Bela – né Warmbad – our bus had to go over a weighbridge.

Considering all the striped bags that had gone into the hold of the bus, I thought this was going to be very interesting. And it was. After being weighed, the bus, instead of turning right and back onto the N1 North, was instructed to turn left into a holding area where it stopped in an inspection zone under the directions of torch-bearing officers.

The inspectors opened the luggage doors and had a long chat with the driver, who then stepped into the bus and instructed the passengers seated in rows one to six to go and stand at the back of the bus as we were going for a second round of weighing. I had thought such things only happen in Tanzania. Three years earlier, on a bus from Mbeya to Dar es Salaam, I had witnessed exactly the same procedure when passengers seated in the front of the bus were instructed to move to the back "to balance the load". Well, in Tanzania it worked. I was now going to see whether the same method of screwing the system would do the trick in Mzansi too.

After queuing behind a line of trucks, the bus went over the weighbridge again. And again, instead of turning right, we were instructed to turn left past the holding area into the inspection zone. This time no inspector came close to the bus; the driver knew exactly what to do. He instructed that over and above the passengers in the first six rows – who were still standing at the back – those in rows seven to ten should join them. Thank goodness I was in row twelve.

In the tight squeeze at the back I could hear an elderly sounding man inviting a young lady (presumably), *"Sondela"* – come closer.

The second time round the balancing of the load worked. We were given the green light to turn right and rejoin the N1 North. The whole rigmarole took more than an hour, and by the time we reached the Bela-Bela offramp it was already after one o'clock in the morning.

The event sparked a conversation between myself and Michael Khumalo, the guy sitting next to me. Apart from a basic greeting we had not spoken to one another. According to African tradition any person with the same surname as yours – even if he is from another country, as was the case with Michael – is your brother. Needless to say, I had found myself a brother from another father. He told me that the extremely high inflation rate and economic meltdown had resulted in many businesses having to close down in Zimbabwe; people had no choice but to buy their groceries, including basic foodstuffs, in South Africa. That explained why people were carrying so much luggage. It was nothing other than their monthly groceries.

It was a warmish night (11 degrees to be precise, according to the screen I'd seen at the Tshwane University of Technology) and I did not need my sleeping bag. I dozed off, still pondering the Zimbabweans' plight, and only woke up when the bus stopped for a comfort break at the Polokwane – né Pietersburg – Ultra City. As I disembarked I realised that comrades from the Jacob Zuma camp must have taken a break here as well in December 2007 on their way to unseat Thabo Mbeki as party president at the ANC's 52nd national conference.

In my view Thabo Mbeki made a serious blunder in accepting nomination for re-election as party president for a third term. After all, the man is credited with spearheading the implementation of the New Economic Partnership for African Development (NEPAD); he is also seen as having been instrumental in promoting a new breed of leaders in Africa. Yet, when he had to put his money where his mouth was, he, not unlike the dictators who rule in different parts of the African continent, found it too hard to let go of power. Well, the more things change the more they remain the same ...

Within half an hour, and with everybody back on board, we had left the Ultra City. With most people fast asleep we drove through the town of Polokwane towards Makhado (né Louis Trichardt). We made another stop soon after sunrise at Musina (né Messina). Most passengers disembarked to buy bread and returned with an average of four loaves per person. Needless to say, the convenience store at the garage ran out of bread very quickly. That created space for on-the-spot entrepreneurship, and people lucky enough to have bought bread started selling one or two loaves to their fellow passengers, obviously at an inflated price.

Business must be booming in Musina. Besides the high demand for bread, almost all vehicles going to Zimbabwe stop at the Ultra City, not only to fill up but also to put additional fuel into twenty-litre drums. Our very own bus did the same. It was then that I noticed, not far from the petrol station, several people selling empty plastic drums to the passers-by.

After about thirty minutes we were at the South Africa–Zimbabwe border, better known as Beitbridge. It was daytime now and there were already five buses in front of us in addition to many bakkies pulling trailers; but nothing could have prepared me for the long queue I was about to join. It was one of those take-a-deep-breath-and-accept-it-as-is-because-there-is-nothing-you-can-do-about-it moments.

The endless queue of people consisted mainly of jolly Zimbabweans going home. Whilst waiting with them under the African sun, which was getting warmer and warmer, and observing the dozens of bakkies and vans stopping and parking next to us, it became clear that Zimbabweans were not only buying foodstuffs in South Africa. They were also buying building materials and household goods. Most bakkies were, in addition to being loaded to the brim, pulling trailers stacked with corrugated-iron sheets, door frames, doors, microwave ovens, sofas, stoves, mattresses and sound speakers. I was very tempted to take photos of the incredible loads.

The thing I hate most about standing in long queues, besides my patience being tested to the limit, is that some (or is it most?) people do not have a sense of personal space. They stand right behind you and breathe into your neck while every now and then touching you with their big stomachs. It is irritating and nauseating, but what can you do but breathe in turn into the neck of the person in front of you?

Moving my head for a breath of fresh air, I noticed why we were moving so slowly: people were jumping the queue, joining it right at the front.

"It's all about the money, my brother," the young man whose neck I was warming told me. "Taxi drivers pay the police officers who are supposed to monitor and control the queue; that's why taxi passengers are allowed to go to the front of the queue just outside the immigration office entrance." He was a student at Wits University in Johannesburg, he told me as we shuffled slowly forward.

After slightly over three hours, I was eventually stamped out of South Africa. During the time we spent in the queue, two truckloads full of Zimbabweans went through; they were being deported back to their country.

"It is all a joke," another passenger from our bus said. "Some of those people on the trucks will be back in South Africa within an hour from now. All they have to do is pay a thousand rand to the police officer driving the truck and he will bring them back and drop them off just outside Musina. If the police truck is from Johannesburg and you have two and a half thousand rand, the police officer takes you all the way back to Gauteng."

Much as I was aware that some police officers might be getting paid to turn a blind eye, this came as a surprise to me.

In conclusion, the gentleman who was giving me this classified information stated the obvious: "It is a vicious circle which is costing poor Zimbabweans a lot of money, while corrupt South African policemen are making a quick buck."

Once all the passengers were back on the bus, it was a short hop across the Limpopo River – the second largest river in Africa in terms of volume, draining into the Indian Ocean. The thought of standing in another long queue on the Zimbabwean side of the border was very depressing, but I assumed that returning citizens and visitors would not, as happens in most countries, share the same queue. I further assumed, considering that not many people would be visiting Zimbabwe, that I would be the only person in the visitors' queue. I was wrong. Both returning citizens and visitors were standing in one and the same queue.

That notwithstanding, the queue moved quickly and smoothly. In record time I was inside the immigration office. I read the Department of Immigration's vision on the wall: "To build an Immigration Department which will be the pride of the country and of Africa and rank amongst the best in the world."

I must confess I was very proud of the Zimbabwean Immigration Department. They were living up to their ideals, and within twenty minutes I was stamped into their country. Perhaps the officials were so efficient because no computer system was being used. You simply handed in your completed entry form and passport, and voilà! – your passport was stamped. Easy peasy.

I was thrilled when the bus started moving again with everyone on board. But I had forgotten a small, little, minute but very important hurdle when crossing a border: clearing customs. The bus drove approximately twenty metres and then stopped at a mandatory customs checkpoint. All passengers had to disembark because, according to the driver, "customs officials are not happy with what they see on the passenger-declaration form".

I couldn't blame them. You see, the previous night, once the bus had left Park Station, a piece of paper had been circulated for passengers to declare what they had in those big striped bags. I did not complete the form because I had only one relatively small bag and obviously had nothing to declare; but I saw that almost all passengers had declared goods to the value of R500. Now really!

So now a new piece of paper had to be filled in, and the driver warned, "Please be more truthful this time." This new requirement took a very long time as each passenger had to complete the form in front of the bus, with the driver looking on like a hawk. Once we were all standing outside, the hold of the bus was opened and, at the instruction of the customs officials, bags were randomly taken out to be inspected. If your bag was selected it was your responsibility to open it, and the customs official, who by now had a piece of paper listing what all the passengers had declared, checked the contents of the bags against what had been officially declared.

It was a ridiculously time-consuming exercise that took more than an hour. In total about twenty bags belonging to seven passengers were thoroughly searched. The rest of us were ordered to get back onto the bus.

Once we had settled back in our seats, I asked Michael what happened if the officials found that you had under-declared. He gave a succinct answer: "Customs officials never confiscate your goods or arrest you. All you have to do is pay them. Most Zimbabweans returning home have bought a lot of stuff in South Africa; if you are unlucky to have your bags chosen to be inspected, you have to pay up – mostly in cash. So the customs officials are the real beneficiaries of the collapse of the Zimbabwean economy."

I was pleasantly surprised that the road from Beitbridge to Bulawayo was generally good, with no potholes. Relaxing in my reclining seat, I noticed that at certain points the road ran parallel to the railway line for a couple of kilometres. As we got closer and closer to Gwanda the scenery, which since Beitbridge had been dominated by dry, short grass and trees, became greener and greener. We dropped three passengers next to a big (by Gwanda standards), white National Social Security Authority (NSSA) building.

En route to Bulawayo we were treated to the classic movie *There's a Zulu on my Stoep*, starring Leon Schuster and John Matshikiza, who had died of a heart attack just over two weeks earlier. John wrote a very entertaining and insightful column in the *Mail & Guardian* called "With the lid off", which I used to enjoy a lot. Although I was watching the Schuster movie for the umpteenth time, I still enjoyed it, as did my fellow passengers. I'm not sure whether or not it was because most of them had come through customs without being caught, but they were in stitches and some even had tears rolling down their cheeks. It reminded me that what I most love about Africans is their ability to rise above challenging and trying circumstances and genuinely smile and laugh out loud.

Near Bulawayo the scenery not only became greener but the bush was also getting thicker and thicker, and when we eventually arrived in Zimbabwe's second largest city – seven hours late – we were met by the beautiful sight of jacaranda trees in full purple bloom lining the streets. Another thing I immediately noticed was how broad the streets in Bulawayo were. This, Michael told me, was a leftover from the nineteenth century when a span of oxen had to be able to make a U-turn in the road.

Bulawayo

I had not visited Bulawayo for nine years, and besides wanting to see the town again, I planned to visit the nearby Solusi Mission where the late Chief Albert Luthuli, former president of the ANC and the first African to win the Nobel Peace Prize, was born. His father, John Bunyani, was an interpreter for the Seventh Day Adventist missionaries in what was then called Southern Rhodesia, where his wife, Mtonya (né Gumede) gave birth to their son.

I must confess I did not know that Luthuli was Zimbabwe-born until about ten years ago when I started reading more about his life. Something else I found out then was that Luthuli was not a hereditary chief (after all, his father was a missionary interpreter) and that he was, according to some sources, approached by the Abakholwa elders of his community at present-day Groutville outside Stanger (KwaDukuza), north of Durban, to lead them; other sources say he was voted in as chief. Whatever the case may be, the elders had to wait two years before Albert John Mvumbi Luthuli agreed to take up the chieftainship in 1936.

Since the bus was officially scheduled to arrive in Bulawayo at 9:30 – and not at 16:30 as it did – I had thought I would ask around and then take public transport to the Solusi Mission, returning to Bulawayo in time to catch the overnight train to Harare, the capital city. I had not intended to spend the night in Bulawayo, but because of the massive bus delay I now had no choice but to drop the visit to the mission and head straight to the railway station. With the time almost 17:00, I took a cab, an old white Toyota Corolla – which cost me R50 (yes, the cab driver wanted rands and not Zim dollars, and who can blame him?) – and rushed to the station.

When he heard I was from Johannesburg, Mr Ndebele, the grey-haired cab driver, told me that he had lived in Soweto for eight years, working as a backstreet mechanic. "I came back to Zim when the South Africans started killing us," he said, showing no emotion. He was referring to what were termed xenophobic attacks, which saw more than a hundred people from other African countries lose their lives about five months earlier because South Africans were accusing them of taking their jobs.

The old man's remark was a frank reminder of the dilemma I would be facing as a South African traveller: should I or should I not tell people I met on the trip that I was from South Africa?

Baba Ndebele also told me that since most Zimbabweans could only afford to travel by train, it was advisable to buy a ticket a few days in advance. That clinched it for me.

My decision not to spend the night in Bulawayo had nothing to with my liking or not liking the town – in fact, I like it a lot – but I had only thirty days to get to Nairobi, via Zambia, Tanzania, Rwanda and Uganda. Every day counted and I could not afford to deviate from the strict timeline I had drawn up – you can never have a proper itinerary when doing a trip like this. So as a principled man it was merely a case of being true to my plan of action.

As the rattling, debilitated car stopped outside the cream-white railway building, Baba Ndebele looked at me and said, "I will be very surprised if you still get a ticket." He accompanied me to the reservations office. Although there were a few people outside the building, there was no queue. A good sign, I thought.

I tried to charm the lady wearing bright red lipstick on the other side of the glass counter. "Good afternoon, my sister," I said. "Please tell me the good news that you still have a first-class ticket for the Harare train for tonight."

She smiled and said, "You must be joking. The train is full."

"Oh come on, my sister," I pleaded, forcing myself to smile. "I am sure you can make a plan."

"I told you the train is full. Most people book a week in advance to ensure that they get seats." This time she was not smiling.

On a trip like this you must be flexible and be able to make decisions on your feet. There and then I decided that since the plan was to get to Harare the following day and from there proceed to Lusaka, and since the Bulawayo–Harare train was full, an alternative would be to take an overnight train from Bulawayo to Victoria Falls, cross over to Livingstone in Zambia, and from there take one of the many buses going to Lusaka. Whether I went via Harare or via Victoria Falls and Livingstone did not matter; as long as I could spend the following night in Lusaka I would be happy.

All this flashed through my mind while the red-lipsticked railway cashier was staring at me. It was time to implement Plan B.

"So can I have a Victoria Falls first-class ticket for the train leaving tonight?"

After checking on the computer she said, "You are so lucky, there is only one ticket left in first class."

"Do you take South African rands or US dollars?" I asked. I had read in the newspapers back home that certain Zimbabwean establishments had started taking currencies other than the Zim dollar.

"No, I do not, but you can change your rands next door."

Baba Ndebele, who all this time was standing next to me, pleaded with her in Ndebele – which I understand because it is very close to Zulu, my home language – to keep the ticket for us.

"Okay. Rush," she instructed us. Greatly relieved, we went to the restaurant next door to change the money, leaving just one gentleman in the queue. For R100 I got Z$40 000. This was very confusing because I had expected to become a Zim millionaire by changing R100 into Zim dollars. What was even more confusing was that earlier on, while I was talking to the railway cashier next door, I saw a Z$5 billion (5 000 000 000) note on her desk. I was comforted though by Baba Ndebele's assurance that the train ticket cost Z$14 000, which translated to approximately R35. But just to be sure, I asked about the five-billion note.

"Now and then, because of the high inflation, our government takes out zeros from the notes so people do not have to carry loads of money when trading," Baba Ndebele explained.

Still a bit confused, I asked, "If they take out the zeros and then issue money with fewer zeros, does it not confuse people?"

"Not really. People get used to it very quickly."

I asked him all these questions as we went to fetch my backpack from the boot of his car. We shook hands and he wished me well.

I hurried back to the reservations office, one of the Z$20 000 notes ready in my hand. Thank goodness, there was no one in the queue. Without even greeting the cashier, I pushed the money underneath the glass.

She pushed it back. "The first class is now full. Somebody came in and bought the last ticket." She said it with such a serious expression that I knew she was not joking.

"But I pleaded with you, a few minutes ago, to hold the ticket for me," I reminded her as calmly as possible, trying to hide how pissed off I was.

"What if you did not come back? I cannot just hold tickets which have not been paid for. Soon after you left, somebody came and bought the ticket. What was I supposed to say to him?" she replied, closing the files in front of her.

So how much did he pay you? I was tempted to ask.

She stood up from her chair as I was still staring at her in disbelief and, pointing towards her left, said, "Go and try the economy class next door," before turning her back on me and leaving the office.

Heavily disappointed and angry, I grabbed my bag and slowly walked the more than a hundred metres alongside the main railway office to the economy-class reservations office, hidden somewhere at the back. Now I had to implement Plan C: take the economy class to Harare.

Unlike the first-class office, on the economy side there were about ten people queuing. As soon as I had joined the queue, with three people behind me already, my cellphone started vibrating in my trouser pocket. I tried ignoring it because, with about thirteen strangers around me in a back building of the station, I suspected some guy was either going to snatch it from me or calmly ask me to hand it over.

Whoever was calling persevered, so in the end I decided to take the risk of answering.

It is amazing how we sometimes prejudge others purely because we know their plight and therefore assume they are thugs, thieves and criminals. As I was talking on the cellphone to Lulu, holding it tightly and constantly sneaking a look over my shoulder to see who was behind me, it became clear that the people in the queue were minding their own business and were not in the least interested in my possessions, including my cellphone.

The people in front of me were being issued tickets and the queue was moving quickly, but when my turn came I was told by the cashier that the train to Harare was full – both the first and economy class. I took a deep breath and resorted to Plan D: economy class to Victoria Falls. To my huge relief there was an economy-class ticket available, for which I paid z$4650 (about r12).

I had not been at Bulawayo station for an hour and had already been forced to change plans three times, but now at 18:15, with the train leaving at 8 p.m., I could relax. I decided to go back to the restaurant next to the first-class reservations office where I had changed my R100 earlier on. When I got there, I noticed that all four fridges were virtually empty, except for a few 300-ml bottles of Sparletta. I bought two of them. Besides the sandwich, the 500-ml Coke and one litre of bottled water I bought in Musina, that was all I consumed that day.

By train (3rd class) to Victoria Falls

After enjoying the icy-cold Sparletta Apple, I decided to step outside and sit on the floor of the veranda of the cream-white railway building. People were starting to arrive at the station as I sat contemplating the coming night in third class.

By sheer coincidence this was going to be the third time I would be taking the Bulawayo–Vic Falls train. The first two times were in the late nineties and on both occasions I travelled first class. I had, in fact, made the Bulawayo–Vic Falls return journey twice in three months. I had come up to Zimbabwe to bungee jump, but at Victoria Falls I was told that they did not take credit cards, only cold cash, and in US dollars *nogal*. So, a bit disappointed, I went back to Durban, where I was living at the time, and returned two months later. The fact that I was now going to use third class was making me slightly uneasy, but I had no choice: Lusaka was waiting for me.

At 18:30 the railways official opened the main door which lead through the first-class reservations office to the platforms. A board at the side of the reservations office announced that the Victoria Falls-bound train was departing from platform four at 20:00. Even though there was no pre-booked seating in third class, I couldn't understand why some people were running and others walking very fast towards the train, given that there was still an hour and a half before the time of departure. So I continued sauntering at a leisurely pace as people rushed past me.

Their behaviour made sense when I eventually got to the train. The first reason was immediately obvious: there were bad coaches and there were awful ones, and it was to your advantage to get there first and pick yourself a bad one. The second reason dawned on me a bit later: people wanted to sit next to the window so they could rest their heads on the sill during the night because the seat backs were too low for you to rest your head. A third reason appeared only when it was too late: people walked up and down the aisle all night, making sleep impossible for anyone sitting on an aisle seat.

I moved through four coaches, two of which were bad and two of which were worse – dirty, grimy and smelling terrible. People had nevertheless already occupied some seats in all four coaches. The next coach looked far better than the previous four, but all the seats had been taken. I decided I was going to take a seat on the following coach, irrespective of how it looked or smelled because by now I knew I was not going to find a decent coach.

Indeed, the next coach, because it was bad, was not full, but all the window seats had been taken. I sat down next to Washington, a youngster who was also headed for Livingstone. We were right at the front (or at the back, depending on which way you look at it) of the coach, which meant I was going to be sitting right next to the toilet for the whole night. In fact, my seat was next to two toilets, one opposite the other.

The toilets smelled strongly of urine. There were whiffs of an even stronger smell – but for shit's sake, let's not go there. The good news is that my broad, round African nose adapts very quickly. Within a few minutes it had done just that and, in no time, I started detecting whiffs of lavender and citrus – which reminded me of my flight back from Namibia to Johannesburg on the company private jet, a Cessna Citation Excel, four days earlier. The Citation takes eight passengers, but on that occasion there had been only five of us. The whole experience of being flown in a private jet can be overwhelming at first: being ushered past check-in counters by the pilot (so no queues), and on board the plane enjoying the sheer luxury of ultra-comfortable swinging reclining chairs and personal service, as well as a well-stocked bar. And of course sweet-smelling loos. It is how flying should be, but then again, just like sleeping with a beautiful woman, the novelty soon wears off.

Anyway, that is how life is: one day you are literally flying high in a private jet, and the next week you are sitting right next to a shit-stained, stinking toilet.

It was not even ten minutes before my torn seat with protruding springs and bits of sponge coming out started to feel very uncomfortable. From that moment on I knew that it was going to be a very long night. I checked the time. It was 19:05. There was still almost an hour left before we were due to depart, and I was already tired of sitting on the broken seat.

The number of people walking up and down the aisle looking for desirable seats increased. As the coach filled up, I realised how close to each other the seats actually were and how cramped we were. The seat configuration was such that you had rows of three people seated facing each other on both sides of the aisle. The only exception was the two-seaters right at the end of the coach next to the toilets, one of which Washington and I had occupied. Facing us on a three-seater sat a young girl of about sixteen with an infant on her lap and an elderly couple. With the seats so close to one another, it was impossible to stretch your legs without stepping on the feet of the person sitting opposite you. The best way was to turn slightly to one side so that your legs went between the two pairs of legs opposite. It was like rubbing salt in a wound.

The train left on time and we started our trek in a north-westerly direction. I did a quick headcount. There were twenty-eight of us, although, as I had been told earlier by the cashier, the coach could "comfortably hold thirty-two people". At the first two stations more passengers came on board, and fairly soon our coach was chock-a-block.

What made the situation worse was that most (if not all) passengers wanted the windows closed. I knew that the best way to survive this stuffy, uncomfortable, unhealthy environment was to fall asleep. So, in an attempt to sleep, I closed my eyes. But sleeping was all but impossible with the constant moving of people up and down the aisle, especially drunk youngsters who were singing at the top of their voices. A permanent bright light on the ceiling of the coach was not helping either. Against all odds, however, I dozed off and had a relatively good sleep. When I woke up it felt like I had been asleep for a very long time. I checked my watch. It was 21:37. I had been in dreamland for about forty-five minutes.

Most people were sleeping as if everything looked and felt pretty normal to them. Only one elderly grey-headed man was talking non-stop to two other elderly men. He spoke in Ndebele, so I could easily follow: he had been a chef in one of the hotels at Victoria Falls until he was retrenched because "these white people from overseas stopped visiting". He was promised a year's salary but he had not yet received his money for the previous two months. Hence he was on his way to Victoria Falls to find out why.

The former chef was one of those people who are comfortable talking out loud to strangers about personal issues. He mentioned that after being retrenched he had taken to being a full-time traditional healer, a gift from his ancestors that he had ignored for a long time because of his job.

He was blessed with the ability to make barren women fall pregnant, he explained, and boasted how he himself had impregnated married women who had been struggling to conceive. After sleeping with him, they all fell pregnant. The good news, he said, was that their husbands thought the babies were theirs.

The beauty of travelling by public transport is that you meet a lot of different and sometimes very interesting people. This elderly man with grey hair, grey beard and nicely trimmed moustache also talked about the great time he had had sleeping with foreign tourists at the hotel where he used to work.

One of the two men who had been listening attentively to him all this time asked if he made tourists pregnant as well. "I do not know," he replied. "They always insisted on condoms, except when they were too drunk."

In the middle of nowhere, just after leaving Somisi station, the train suddenly stopped. After a few minutes the ticket examiner came to our coach and said in Ndebele: "There is one person who controls the traffic of trains on this line. He has left his office because he had to go and sort out something with the technician. So in order to ensure the safety of everyone we will wait until he comes back and gives us the go-ahead. It may take a few minutes, an hour or a few hours."

He left to address the people in the next coach. So the waiting began. It was now around 11 p.m. Some passengers, mostly youngsters, got off the train while others continued sleeping. A few opened their *padkos*, consisting mainly of *pap* and cabbage.

Fully awake now, I decided to buy myself a 300-ml bottle of Sprite from a young man who was selling cooldrinks and biscuits. The drink cost z$2 000, but since he did not have change he took my z$10 000 note and promised to return with the change in five minutes. The only thing I noticed about him was that he was wearing a T-shirt promoting Simba Makoni, a chemist-turned-politician who, although he had long been a senior member of Mugabe's ZANU-PF, entered the March 2008 elections as an independent candidate and received 8.3 per cent of the national vote.

Another wait began. The train had not moved for more than an hour and, having been robbed of my z$8 000 change by a youngster, I was definitely not having a good time. I remained in my seat, trying unsuccessfully to get some sleep. It was even more frustrating now that the train was standing still. I tried bending and putting my head on my knees. It did not work. But I kept my eyes shut.

I started thinking about Zimbabwe and the plight of her people and of Mbeki's failed quiet diplomacy. Our ex-president must hold the world record for a head of state visiting another country the most times within a specified period. His failed attempts at solving the impasse in Zimbabwe reminded me of a soccer player who misses a lot of goal-scoring opportunities throughout the season until his team ends up being relegated from the Premier League.

Suddenly I felt somebody tapping me on the shoulder. It was the youngster with my z$8 000 change. Again the issue of not trusting other people had come back to haunt me. I'm not sure if I'm just paranoid by nature or whether it is because I live in Johannesburg, but at the back of my mind I'm forever conscious of the possibility of becoming a victim of crime. Throughout the trip it would strike me repeatedly how much we South Africans are living in a mental prison. And how, irrespective of how often we vote in general elections, we are not free from all sorts of anxieties.

At 13:20 the train sounded its horn and after two hours we were on our way again. The blinding ceiling light was proving to be such a nuisance that I decided to get a hat from my backpack which I had stored on the overhead rack. I normally use the balaclava to keep my head warm during cold nights, but this time I was going to cover my eyes with it.

At long last it was dark and I could get some sleep. I half woke up now and then when youngsters came singing and laughing up and down the aisle. I was set to get some decent sleep after the last lout seemed to have fallen silent; but then the baby of the young girl sitting opposite us started crying and wouldn't stop. The elderly woman next to her finally suggested that she check the baby's nappy. Wow, that infant had shit a storm. However much my nose had adapted to sitting next to the toilet, the stinky poo just about gave me a headache. The nappy was changed, and because it was not one of those disposable types it was put in a small black plastic bag and stored on the overhead rack too. Peace and quiet was restored.

I attempted to doze off again, but in no time it was dawn and the train pulled into a station where quite a few people jumped off. Then several passengers started brushing their teeth and spitting through the open windows of the moving train. This looked like a normal thing to do. Quite a few people were doing it, but the ones who were not did not look surprised at all. The good thing was that fresh air now came into the coach. Even better, some of the windows were left open.

As the sun started rising in the east I could see and somehow feel that we were approaching Victoria Falls. It warmed up and soon an unpleasantly hot wind was coming in through the open windows. The train stopped more often now and people got off while others climbed aboard on their way to Vic Falls. The scenery outside was beautiful. We were travelling through the Hwange National Park. I even saw elephants strolling amongst the green trees.

For some reason we just never seemed to reach Victoria Falls. The train would stop and I would think: Well, this is it. Only to find we were not at our final destination yet.

It took fourteen and a half hours to cover the 451 kilometres between Bulawayo and Victoria Falls.

Victoria Falls

As I've mentioned, I had used the Bulawayo–Vic Falls train twice before. On both occasions it was truly an overnight journey and we got to Victoria Falls just after sunrise – and vice versa. In fact, people used to take the overnight train on Sunday evening and arrive in Bulawayo in time for work on Monday morning. Considering how late our train arrived – it was 10:30 – it did not seem an option for working people anymore. Well, if you still had a job.

Washington, the youngster who was also on his way to Livingstone, told me that the last bus for Lusaka left at noon. So I had one and a half hours to walk from the station to the immigration offices, get stamped out of Zimbabwe, walk about two kilometres to Zambian immigration, get stamped into Zambia, take a cab to cover the nine kilometres to Livingstone and purchase a bus ticket to Lusaka. I knew that it was going to be close but I was willing to give it my best shot.

It was a genuinely hot African day. For a moment I was tempted to take a cab from the station to the immigration offices, but considering that I was on a tight budget and that the offices were less than two kilometres away, I decided to take a brisk walk. I took a shortcut, using a path between the trees like some other passengers who were also on their way to the immigration offices. Past the modern Kingdom Hotel we walked, following the pathway through the trees, then past the main entrance to the park. I was tempted to make a quick detour to view the Falls but abandoned the idea; Lusaka was waiting for me.

When I got to the immigration offices, some women who had managed to walk faster than I did were already standing in the queue. There must have been twelve people ahead of me and, just as at Beitbridge, the queue was moving quickly. In no time I was stamped out of Zimbabwe and directed to yet another queue for the customs officials to check my bag.

The customs officer on duty, a short, dark woman, was perched on the table and all travellers had to open their bags while she gave instructions from above. When my turn came she asked me to take my jacket out of my bag so that she could see what was hidden underneath. I obliged, and after she had satisfied herself that I was not smuggling anything out I was told to proceed. It was another brisk walk to the legendary Victoria Falls bridge over the Zambezi River, the longest and biggest river in Africa draining into the Indian Ocean.

There was no one jumping at the time, but as I walked past the bungee platform I heard someone saying, "Hey, big man from South Africa." When I turned around, there was Rastaman, a bungee jumpmaster whom I had met ten months earlier when, together with nine friends (my wife included), I had come up to Livingstone to celebrate New Year's Eve, 2007. We had driven up through Botswana, but at the border we were informed our vehicles couldn't enter Zambia because we didn't have proof of ownership. We eventually left the cars at Kasane airport, crossed the Zambezi by ferry and took a bus to Livingstone. During the few days we spent there, two guys and three women did the 111-metre bungee jump from the bridge. That is where I met Rastaman.

"Where are you going?" he asked me. When I told him I was on my way to Rwanda by public transport, he said, "You are a crazy man."

How about you, standing on the bridge and pushing people from a platform the whole day? I was tempted to ask, but instead said, "Well, someone has to be, I guess."

We shook hands and off I went. With the bungee platform behind me, I thought that I should perhaps have told him that when I got to Jinja in Uganda I intended to bungee there as well. It was a great irony that, although it had not been planned, I was back, crossing the Victoria Falls bridge where my African adventures had begun in 1999.

When I look back on my life, my first bungee jump in Zimbabwe in August 1999 at the age of twenty-four has to be the event that opened a totally new world to me. I always encourage young people to do adventurous things because doing so instils a sense of achievement and self-confidence in you from a young age, resulting in you growing up with an I-can-do-whatever-I-put-my-mind-to attitude.

A short way beyond the bridge, which is half in Zimbabwe and half in Zambia, I put my backpack down and turned around, looking at the Zambezi as it meandered through the gorge and at the bridge – Cecil John Rhodes's brainchild, completed in 1905, three years after the death of the man who dreamed of linking Cape Town to Cairo by means of a railroad.

Thinking of the way things were in Zimbabwe, I could not help but remember the title of Alan Paton's famous book *Cry, the Beloved Country* – even though it refers not to Zimbabwe but South Africa in the 1940s. I could not help but think about:

— people who had to buy their groceries in South Africa and were forced to bribe Zimbabwean customs officials to bring them into the country;
— people who lived in a country where several zeros could be taken away from the currency overnight;
— people who were forced to leave home and then had to return because they feared death at the hands of their fellow Africans;
— people who brought door frames and beds and tables home in their luggage;
— people without papers who were deported in lorries and had to bribe the very same policemen who were deporting them to allow them back across the border in the very same lorries;
— people whose president publicly proclaimed: "Only God can remove me."

I concluded, as I picked up my backpack, that whoever thought and, heaven forbid, uttered the words "There is no crisis in Zimbabwe" was either:

— smoking a pipe;
— drinking a lot of single-malt Scotch whisky;
— living in an ivory tower;

Or:

— smoking a pipe, drinking a lot of single-malt Scotch whisky *and* living in an ivory tower.

I was reminded of Edmund Burke's timeless observation: "The only thing necessary for the triumph of evil is for good men to do nothing." Was that not exactly what had happened in Zimbabwe?

North-east with Bookers Express

I had to walk about a kilometre before getting to the Zambian immigration offices, and the Zimbabwean issue was still bugging me. I thought to myself: Isn't it amazing how people who fought for years for democracy ended up destroying the very thing they'd fought for? And how ironic that the leader of the Movement for Democratic Change (MDC) is portrayed as a British stooge by a person who himself was educated in Britain and goes around dressed like an English gentleman.

Anyway, if Zimbabweans so wished, they were entitled to have an alleged British stooge as their leader – that is democracy at work. The same went for South Africans who wanted a president without a matric certificate, a super sexy (allegedly) polygamist who – at least once – slept with an HIV-positive woman without a condom, and who was once without money for even a car wash despite his provincial minister's salary. There is no wrong or right. If da people want a singing president, let them have him. As we say in Zulu, it is *intando yeningi* – what the majority of people want. That is, after all, the definition of democracy.

My mind was so preoccupied that I did not notice how fast I was walking. By the time I got to the Zambian immigration offices, I was not only sweating, I was exhausted. Besides making love/having sex/bonking/humping (or whatever term tickles your warm parts), I had not done any type of physical exercise for months.

When my turn came after standing in the queue for a few minutes, it was exactly 11:55. Since I was no longer confident that I was going to make the midday bus to Lusaka, I said, when the immigration official asked me where I was going to stay in Zambia: "Jollyboys Backpackers here in Livingstone."

"Why Jollyboys?" he asked with a broad smile.

I was not expecting that question and had to think very quickly. "Well, it was the first place I found on the internet," I said with a straight face, not mentioning that I had stayed there ten months earlier with my nine friends.

"Is it not because of the women who book there at Jollies?"

"Oh really?" I pretended to be surprised, although I knew that single women do indeed, now and then, book at Jollies.

"So, how many days of fun and adventure do you want?" he asked with an even bigger smile.

"Seven," I said, blushing.

He stamped my passport and, after thanking him, I sprinted out of the office. As I was shooting through the gate, a soldier sitting on a rock stopped me and asked to search my bag. "I'm not harassing you. It is part of the procedure," he said as he was going through my clothes.

In no time I was running towards a few blue cabs parked on the side of the road. In passing I somehow managed to change my left-over Z$24 000 with one of the informal currency traders (incutras) for ZMK10 000. Quite honestly, I had no clue how many Zambian kwachas I was supposed to get.

I chose a cab with three passengers already seated inside. "I'm rushing for the twelve o'clock Lusaka bus," I said, trying to catch my breath.

"But my friend, it is already just after twelve," the cab driver complained, looking at his watch.

Fortunately there were no cars on the road as we sped past the Zambezi Sun Hotel towards Livingstone. The other passengers were locals with more time on their hands, so the cab headed straight to the bus rank. As we slowed down in a flurry of dust, a white bus with BOOKERS EXPRESS written on the side was warming up to leave. While winding down his window, the cab driver brought the cab to a screeching halt and shouted, "Lusaka! Lusaka!"

It turned out to be the exact bus I was looking for. I gave the cab driver a ZMK10 000 note, expecting 5 000 kwachas change because he had told me that the fare from the border to Livingstone was ZMK5 000. He handed me ZMK4 000 only, and when I brought to his attention that the change was a thousand short he said, "But if it was not for me, you would not have found the bus, my friend."

Indeed. Much as I hated being short-changed by a thousand kwachas, I agreed that he had done his best to get me onto the Lusaka bus.

All this happened in a matter of seconds. I dashed to the waiting bus, only to be told at the door by the driver's assistant that I had to buy the ticket at the bus kiosk, a stone's throw away.

The ticket cost ZMK55 000 and I had only ZMK4 000 left. "Do you take South African rands?" I asked the clean-shaven young man at the kiosk.

He thought for a while (while I kept glancing over my shoulder at the idling bus) and said, "Okay. Give me hundred and ten rand."

I gave him R120 and he handed me the ticket. By now the bus had started to move forward. "What about my ten rand change?" I asked hurriedly.

"I don't have rands."

"Give me ten rand in kwachas then!" I said with one eye on the bus and the other on him.

The bus sounded its horn and I decided to stop arguing about R10. I was back at the door of the bus with a few long strides and leapt in.

Despite not getting my ZMK1 000 and R10 change from the cab driver and the bus company's cashier respectively, I was happy that – as per my original plan – I was going to spend the Sunday night in Lusaka. I did, fleetingly, think about what the immigration official had said about single women at Jollies, but getting to Lusaka was far more important than hanging out (or is it sticking around?) with beautiful ladies.

The comfortable, blue-velvet reclining seats and three television sets on Bookers Express were a definite improvement on the previous night's ordeal in the third class of the train to Vic Falls.

As the bus was pulling out of the old, small, but very likeable town of Livingstone, a lady in a bright yellow two-piece walked up the aisle, grabbed the microphone and, after the driver's assistant helped her switch it on, said, "Let us pray."

Holding the microphone in her right hand, with her eyes closed and her left hand raised and opened as if she wanted to touch the ceiling of the bus, she started praying with a very solemn look on her face: "In the name of the living God ..." On and on she went in English before switching to a local language which I did not understand.

I must confess that I am one of those people who cannot pray. More often than not my mind starts wandering and before I know it I'm thinking about other things and cannot finish the prayer. My mother blames it on the devil.

Anyway, the woman was speaking louder and louder. In fact, she was carrying on like a person possessed. The expression on her face and the way she lifted her leg and stomped it on the floor made me realise how shallow my own belief system was. I could see that she felt what she was praying about. Eventually she switched back to English and concluded with: "In the name of the Father, the Son and the Holy Ghost, I proclaim that this will be a safe journey."

Everybody, myself included, said, "Amen."

On the outskirts of Livingstone we had to go over a weighbridge. Unlike the Johannesburg–Bulawayo Greyhound, the Bookers Express was given the green light on its first attempt, and we were on our way. I leaned back in the three-seater I was sharing with no one. The bus was not even half full.

It was a comfortable ride, but I could not help but notice how bad the road was. The potholes were so big that on a number of occasions the driver had to switch to the right side of the road to avoid them. Thank goodness, except for the odd truck, there was not much oncoming traffic.

The road turned to 100 per cent gravel after a while. It was clear from the parked earthmoving equipment that road reconstruction was about to take place. But, thanks to the comfortable seats, I did not feel any of the unevenness of the road. What made the trip even more memorable was Lucky Dube's music being played on the sound system. Listening to the late reggae star's greatest hits with the Zambian landscape as a moving backdrop filled me with great pride that a homebru talent was being enjoyed beyond South Africa's borders. It made me sad to realise that not only had such an icon been gunned down by hijackers, but that we seldom appreciate people while they are alive. It is only when they are no more that we see their true value. We will probably also only truly appreciate Joseph Shabalala of Ladysmith Black Mambazo when he is gone.

After two hours on the dirt road, we rejoined the tar road at the one-horse town of Zimba. While the bus was picking up passengers, I leaned out the window and bought myself a 500-ml bottle of ice-cold Manzivalley water from a street hawker. It was just after 14:00, and it was my first "meal" of the day.

It turned out that half of the water was frozen solid. However, I had a very simple solution to defrost the ice: I put the bottle between my thighs. I'm sure I do not have to tell you that I am, in the real sense of the word, hot. In no time at all the ice melted and I could enjoy the rest of the water.

I was getting worried about a place to sleep in Lusaka because Zambia's capital city is known to have limited budget accommodation. Let me be proactive, I thought, and phone a few places with my roaming cellphone. I had written down the telephone numbers of two backpackers in Lusaka but not the city's dialling code.

I moved over to ask the guy sitting across the aisle in the same row as I was, but when I saw what he was concentrating on so hard – *Relationship Rescue* by Dr Phil, "the white man who was made a household name by a black woman" – I hesitated. But finally I said to him, "I'm sorry, I'm looking for the dialling code for Lusaka. Can you please rescue me?"

I knew I was being cheeky by putting it this way, but he didn't seem bothered. He neither smiled nor showed any sign of irritation as he said, "They recently changed the code and I am not sure what the new one is. I'm sorry."

I asked the young lady in the seat right in front of me.

"I don't know because I only phone people on their cellphones and they've recently changed the code in any case," she replied without turning her head.

Not being able to phone a backpackers to book a bed was bad news, especially as we would be arriving at night. Three years earlier, on my Cape-to-Cairo trip, I ended up in a very dodgy place – after spending a lot of time and money being driven around Lusaka in a cab only to be told repeatedly that the decent places were fully booked.

An hour after leaving Zimba, the bus stopped at another small town called Kalomo where quite a few passengers boarded. Kalomo boasted a Pentecostal church, a Catholic church, a His Highness church and a Bread of Life church. Taking a cue from the number of churches in such a small town, the woman who had prayed earlier on and the local gospel songs that were now being played on the bus, I concluded that Zambians must be very religious people. Later, on the same road, I saw the sign: ZAMBIA ADVENTIST UNIVERSITY.

Soon after Kalomo we stopped at Choma for a leg stretch. Even though I hadn't had any solid food to eat, I was not feeling hungry and bought only a cold 500-ml Coca-Cola. After half an hour everybody was back on board and we continued eastwards. The driver changed the compact disk and started playing Rebecca Malope, South Africa's Queen of Gospel.

I wondered whether we South Africans would ever listen to music from our African brothers and sisters in our buses and taxis.

I was still pondering the question when the young lady in front of me stood up, turned around and offered me a big long sausage. I could barely hear her but I'm pretty sure she said, "Please have it. I bought two at Choma and I'm already full."

Am I not the one who is supposed to offer you a sausage? I thought to myself; the whole thing struck me as very ironic.

I took the sausage and, just to be nice, I asked what her name was.

"Charity," she said with a smile that drew my attention to her full lips. With that she turned around and slouched back in her seat.

The sun was setting behind us. We were listening to spiritually uplifting music, and although I didn't know where I was going to sleep in Lusaka, I felt that I was, once again, living my dream: travelling independently in Mother Africa and creating memories that I was going to share enthusiastically with my grandchildren one day. It struck me that we all stress about being good employees and submitting reports on time – corporate bullshit like that – while sacrificing our true selves. Yet I couldn't imagine anybody, except someone who has been totally screwed by the system, ever saying to his or her grandchildren, "I've had a great life because I submitted all my reports to Head Office on time."

When I looked out the window again, it was dark and thousands of stars were shining from the cloudless African sky. Seeing so many stars reminded me of John Gribbin's book *In Search of the Big Bang*, in which he talks of the "Principle of Terrestrial Mediocrity". We humans, he says, are living on a relatively ordinary planet (Earth), orbiting a relatively ordinary star (the Sun), in a relatively ordinary galaxy (the Milky Way), which is one of countless galaxies in an expanding universe; therefore, there is nothing special about us.

At that moment I could not agree with him more.

Lusaka

When we eventually reached Lusaka, Zambia's capital city, at 20:10, it was 29 degrees – the screen behind the bus driver showed both the time and temperature.

The bus stopped at the huge and almost empty bus terminal and I was pleasantly surprised that nobody came to harass me, as usually happens when you step out of a bus in a big town or city. There were no bus touts, no hustling taxi or cab drivers. Just a few hawkers packing up their stuff and the last remaining buses leaving the terminal.

I was also pleasantly surprised at how safe I felt walking towards the main road with my backpack. Not once did I feel I might be robbed. The honesty of my brothers in other African countries baffled me once again. Back home we are forever being told that poverty is the main reason for the high crime rate. Yet when you go to other African countries you see dire, naked poverty and very low crime levels. It poses a question which I have struggled with since my epic Cape-to-Cairo trip in 2005.

QUESTION 1: What is the real cause of crime in South Africa?

Once on the main road, I flagged down a blue-and-white-striped cab.

"I suggest we try Koumboka Backpackers first. It's central and normally travellers rush to Chachacha Backpackers," the taxi driver with long dreadlocks suggested when I told him that I didn't want to drive around looking for reasonably priced accommodation.

Two guys were already sitting in the back seat, but I didn't feel uneasy in the company of the three strangers at this late hour.

When we pulled up outside Koumboka – in less than five minutes – I happily left my backpack on the back seat between the two guys, one of whom also had dreadlocks. The driver went with me to check whether Koumboka could put me up.

"Please tell me you have a bed for me in your dormitory for tonight," I said to the tall, dark receptionist without even greeting him first.

"Well, you can stay as long as you like," he said with a smile.

I was very relieved that I had made it to Lusaka and, to boot, had found a decent place (in backpacker terms) to stay.

I had a small problem, though. I had run out of Zambian kwachas and I had to pay the taxi driver. "Do you by any chance exchange money?" I asked the man at the reception.

"Yes," he replied, adding, "but our rate is not the best in Lusaka."

I couldn't care less. I exchanged US$50. For how much I cannot even recall, except that it was enough to pay the taxi driver.

"Thank you very much, my brother," I said as I handed him the agreed ZMK20 000 for services rendered.

"Not to mention it, my brother."

His response bewildered me. I did not expect this type of smoothness from an ordinary taxi driver.

One of the guys in the back of the cab passed me my backpack, which looked very much intact.

On my way to reception I passed through a thatched bar where a few patrons were watching a live Serie A (Italian premier soccer league) game. I didn't stop to watch because I couldn't wait to take a shower. Considering that I last had a bath back in Johannesburg on Friday morning and it was now Sunday evening, I had gone for about sixty hours without bathing. The good news about being a man is that I could probably have put another sixty hours on the clock without anything smelling fishy …

After checking in I dropped my bag on one of the beds and headed for the shower. That there was no hot water didn't bother me. I was having such a good time in that shower and making such a noise that someone walking past might have suspected that an experienced masseuse was giving me a head-to-toe massage.

Only when I returned to the ten-bed wooden dormitory did I notice how cramped it was. Five double bunks were arranged in more or less a full circle in the small room, an extension of a back room of the main house. The main house also contained a few bedrooms and a huge lounge where breakfast and dinner were served. I later discovered that the back room was occupied by a woman who was driving a boldly decorated Toyota Quantum kombi with a Gauteng registration (SSP 141 GP) and "Volunteer Scientology Minister" written on both sides.

I still find it hard to understand how L Ron Hubbard, a science-fiction writer, managed to invent a religion like Scientology based on something that had been said so many times before: that people are immortal beings and essentially good, all-knowing, non-materialistic, and capable of unlimited creativity. What is different about Scientology, perhaps, is that it promotes spiritual rehabilitation as a type of counselling ("auditing").

Feeling refreshed and in high spirits because I had made it to Lusaka within forty-eight hours of leaving Johannesburg, I had to have a beer (or two). I decided on Mosi, which is marketed as Africa's finest beer. The barman, the soccer game being over, had changed the TV channel from sports to the news. They were showing a tribute to the late Zambian president Levy Mwanawasa, who had died of a heart attack about two months earlier, on 19 August 2008.

On account of Mwanawasa's death, a presidential election was scheduled for later that month. Luckily I would by then be out of the country. One thing (amongst others) I know about travelling in Africa is to avoid being in a country which has just had elections, because you can never predict whether the losers (justifiably or not) will accept the outcome.

Soon after the tribute to Mwanawasa, a recorded interview with one of the presidential candidates, Hakainde Hichilema of the United Party for National Development (UPND), was broadcast. He was eloquent, well spoken and confident about the changes his party would bring to Zambia. He promised free education and improved and efficient service delivery.

While Hichilema was still pleading with his fellow Zambians to vote for his party, a lively debate ensued at the Koumboka bar. Three local guys were arguing – in English – about whether the UPND would bring real change to Zambia. After all, with an average per-capita income of US$395 and a life expectancy of forty years, it is one of the poorest countries in the world.

The argument got heated when one man said that although Hichilema was intelligent and could serve Zambia well, he would never vote for him because he was a Tonga, and if he and the UPND should win, the Tonga would think they were the superior ethnic group in the country.

Well, if these guys are pushing the ethnic card, screw them, I thought to myself. Can't they see an ethnically based political party is unsustainable? As more and more people outgrow their ethnic differences, support for such a party naturally diminishes – whoever believes otherwise must ask the Honourable Chief Mangosuthu Buthelezi of the soon-to-be-extinct Inkatha Freedom Party.

I walked back to the dormitory past the Scientology kombi, a bit wobbly after four Mosi dumpies. Two of my roommates were already asleep so I quietly crept into bed too, all the while mulling over how all types of religion seem to spread so easily in Africa. First the Arabs introduced Islam, and then the Europeans arrived with Christianity in its various shapes and forms. And now there was Scientology. Would religion with African origins be accepted as easily in other continents? I wondered, drifting off.

I was woken by the arrival of two guys who carried on chatting as if everyone else was awake as well. I was amazed, because in a dormitory a few unwritten rules are usually observed, which are, in fact, common-sense good manners:

- speak softly when other people are sleeping;
- change the mode of your cellphone to "discreet" or "meeting";
- switch off the lights if you are the last person to enter at night.

I opened my eyes, a bit peeved, but I realised this kind of disturbance is the price you pay for forking out less for accommodation. Then one of the guys took out his cellphone and started sending – and receiving – text messages, one after the other.

- do not send text messages when other people are sleeping;
- switch off your cellphone if you expect to receive messages during the night.

The next morning I discovered who I had shared the dormitory with. Two of the guys, dressed in suits and carrying briefcases, were Zambians from the Copperbelt who were in Lusaka on business. (Backpacker places in other African countries are used as budget accommodation by locals, unlike in South Africa where they are exclusively used by foreigners.) The other two guys had typical Somalian/Ethiopian/Eritrean features (tall, thin, with a high, round forehead – almost like a cross between African and Indian).

"My name is Mohammed and I am from Johannesburg," one of them introduced himself.

"No ways! I am also from Johannesburg. Where about do you live?" I asked enthusiastically.

"Morninghill next to Eastgate."

I must confess that I had never heard of such a suburb before. It was only once I was back that I discovered the small suburb did exist – right next to Bruma and just north of the Eastgate Shopping Mall.

"So are you visiting Zambia?"

"No, I have just come down from Tanzania. I am heading down back to South Africa. Which borders did you use coming up this side?" he asked, and after a few seconds added, "How strict were the officials?"

It was a dead give-away. It was obvious that he and his pal, who didn't speak a word of English, were from the Horn of Africa and illegally making their way down south. Although I told him which border posts I'd used, I avoided him afterwards.

I set off early to do the business I had planned in Lusaka, already looking forward to another cold, refreshing shower that evening. To save water, a scarce commodity in some parts of Africa, I usually shower in the evenings only when travelling like this. Rinsing off the dust and sweat – the hot sun and crowds you encounter everywhere guarantee that you'll sweat like a pig during the day – helps to ensure a good night's sleep.

The first of the six goals I had set for myself for this trip was to take a ride on a ferry on Lake Tanganyika. To accomplish that I had to get to Mpulungu, Zambia's only port town, where the MV *Liemba* docks once a week on its return journey from Kigoma, much further north in Tanzania.

My detailed plan was to take a bus from Lusaka to Kapiri Mposhi (a four-hour trip), where I would catch a Tanzanian–Zambian Railways (TAZARA) train to Kasama, and from there take another bus to Mpulungu. But I consoled myself that, although it sounded complicated, it would just be two bus rides separated by a train journey.

My first priority was to buy a first-class train ticket. I had no intention of spending another night in third class. With directions from Koumboka's receptionist, I set off on the twenty-minute walk to TAZARA House on Independence Avenue. It being a Monday morning, and as the train to

Kasama left Kapiri Mposhi on Tuesday afternoons, I could allow myself a leisurely walk to the city centre.

I sauntered down Church Street, one of the main roads leading into town, past the pink fire station not far from the white-and-blue four-storey police station, turned left into Dedan Kimathi Road, where I came across the Auditor General (AG) regional offices. The condition of the old powder-blue buildings with their asbestos roofs convinced me that the Zambian government couldn't care less about the morale or working conditions of the AG's personnel. (No prize for guessing why.) I proceeded past the bus terminal where I was dropped off the previous night to the modernish grey TAZARA House just around the corner.

Zambians are truly nice people. When I asked the security guard where I could buy train tickets, he told me, "The office on the second floor," and then softly enquired, "Where are you from?"

"South Africa," I said hesitantly. Because of the xenophobic attacks in South Africa a few months earlier, some doomsayers amongst my friends and family had advised me never to let on that I was from South Africa if I could help it, and I, too, was in two minds about the matter.

"Oh! Welcome to Zambia," he said with a warm smile, putting his hand forward to shake mine. His gesture made me cringe with shame – for my own suspicious mind and for my countrymen's lack of generosity.

Although the whole building was named TAZARA House, the Tanzanian–Zambian Railways offices occupied only the second floor. The other five floors, according to the board on the ground floor that I now spotted for the first time, were occupied mainly by financial institutions. As I walked towards the lifts, I noticed that the left lift was permanently open (read: broken). That was not a good sign. I decided to take the stairs instead of the right lift. Huffing and puffing up the stairs reminded me that being a heavyweight must not be taken lightly.

There were two glass doors, both with TAZARA OFFICES written across them. I tried the one on my right. It opened into a long, quiet corridor with a brown carpet. All the doors along the corridor were closed. I decided to make a U-turn and try the other glass door. I was beginning to feel uncomfortable. Why were there no other people buying tickets? Although the second door also opened into a long corridor, one office door was open. After the second knock a woman's voice invited me in.

I saw that she was very busy; she hardly allowed herself to look up from the newspaper in front of her.

"Go and try next door," she instructed me when I told her I wanted to buy a train ticket.

I walked through her office into an adjoining office where two gentlemen and a lady were absorbed in their newspapers as well.

"I am so sorry to bug you on a Monday morning," I said humbly. "But can I please buy a first-class Kapiri Mposhi-to-Kasama train ticket for tomorrow?" The request came out in a rather convoluted way.

"Tickets are sold only in Kapiri Mposhi and not here," a gentleman with grey hair and thick glasses informed me.

"So I cannot book a train ticket while I am here in Lusaka?" I asked, trying to conceal my frustration.

"You can. You just have to phone our booking office in Kapiri Mposhi and they will reserve the ticket for you. Then tomorrow you must get there early to pay and collect your ticket."

But then, what are you guys doing here? I was tempted to ask.

"We can give you the telephone numbers to call," the woman offered, adding a lot of value to the discussion.

"How much will a first-class ticket to Kasama be?" I was getting agitated.

None of them knew, but after a few phone calls one of the men had the answer: "Sixty-five thousand kwachas, my friend."

He gave me the number of the Kapiri Mposhi booking office. By now, however, I was having serious reservations about reserving a seat on a TAZARA train.

After I left TAZARA House I headed for Cairo Road, the financial and economic centre of Lusaka – even the National Milling Corporation, the suppliers of cake and bread flour, has a factory there. I joined Cairo Road where a striking slogan, 400 MILLION UNITED IN ONE MARKET, indicated the headquarters of the Commission for East and Southern Africa (COMESA).

I wanted to change my US dollars into Zambian currency, and since I still had about R150, I decided to change that as well. At the first bureau de change I was told they were not buying South African rands because they were overstocked on them. At the next bureau de change I was told the same thing: "Due to being overstocked on rands, we are not buying any until further notice."

It came as a bit of a shock to my South African system. With South Africa being the economic powerhouse not only of southern Africa but also the rest of the continent, why were they not taking the mighty rand?

Like a dog with its tail between its legs, I decided to try a bank, even though it is said that banks offer worse rates than bureau de change outlets.

The first bank I came across was the Indo-Zambia Bank. I walked over to the guy in the forex payment cubicle. He too was very occupied reading a newspaper.

"My brother, we are still waiting for the official exchange rate. Take a seat," he advised me, pointing to a row of chairs along the wall, and resumed informing himself about what was happening in the world.

After about ten minutes he called me back to his cubicle. "You will get four hundred and four kwachas for a rand," he said, folding his newspaper.

At least they were accepting rands.

He took my money and my passport before instructing me to go to the forex desk a few steps from him where a pretty young lady (but not as beautiful, stunning, gorgeous and sexy as my wife – yes, it *is* called sucking up to the madam) filled out some forms which, after writing down my home address, she asked me to sign. She then suggested that I walk across to the row of chairs along the wall and wait there while she processed a seemingly complex transaction.

After a few minutes she came to me and said, "Please go to the cash payment counter. That is where you will get your money and passport." And indeed, the formally dressed black man at the cash payment counter gave me my money and my passport.

Across and up the road from Indo-Zambia Bank, I spotted the Egwit Internet Café and decided to pop in and send my wife an email. I could not phone her as the battery of my cellphone had gone flat and the different type of wall plug at the backpackers had made it impossible to charge it overnight. After sending the email I decided I might as well use the facilities at the internet café to phone the Kapiri Mposhi booking office.

The first number did not exist, the guy who was helping me said. Luckily the second one rang.

"Yes, my friend, I can book a first-class ticket to Kasama for tomorrow," the male voice on the other side of the line said, to my great relief.

"So how much is it?" I asked, wanting to confirm that the price was indeed ZMK65 000, as I had been told earlier.

"It will cost you seventy-six thousand kwachas," he said, paused, and then asked, "Where are you from?"

"South Africa."

"I'm sorry, there was a mistake. The price is eighty-five thousand kwachas and I have booked the ticket for you already. Come pay and pick up your ticket tomorrow. What is your full name?"

The constant changing of prices was very disturbing. "What time does the train get to Kasama?" I enquired, a bit on edge.

"Zero two thirty in the morning."

That was it.

I was not taking the train. There was no way I was going to jump off at some remote town at 2.30 a.m. and pay ZMK85 000 for it. I nevertheless gave the man on the other side of the line my correct full name.

Before leaving Egwit Internet Café I asked the guy who had been helping me where in Lusaka I could buy ferry tickets. He looked at me for a while before asking me in a very soft voice why, if the ferry docked in Mpulungu, would the tickets be sold in Lusaka. I could see by the way he was looking at me that he thought I was really a dumb ass. Quite honestly, I was thinking the same thing.

With the train arriving at Kasama at two-thirty in the morning and no ferry booking office in Lusaka, my stress levels were by now sky-high. I tried to keep calm by following the advice my high-school teacher used to give us before we sat for a final exam: "Constantly clear your mind." Although my Monday-morning business trip was proving to be a complete waste of time, I could not let it cloud my judgement.

I decided to go back to the bus terminal to enquire whether there were any buses going directly from Lusaka to Mpulungu. Perhaps I could even leave Lusaka in the late afternoon or early evening and get to Mpulungu the following morning.

I put the question to a street hawker just outside the terminal. In response he grabbed me by the hand and, leaving his stand unattended, accompanied me to the booking office of the "best bus company in Zambia".

It soon became clear why he was holding me by my hand: the terminal was crawling with touts representing different bus companies, all looking for potential customers. Well, I could not escape the grip of the hawker. Not that I wanted to.

The booking agent at Gemini Motorways told me, as I had hoped, that their bus did the overnight trip from Lusaka to Mpulungu for ZMK150 000. Since the ferry left Mpulungu on Friday afternoons, I thought it would be best if I got there on Thursday morning so that I could buy a ferry ticket at leisure, before the last-minute buying stampede on Friday morning.

Naturally it meant that I did not have to leave before Wednesday afternoon and thus could spend more time in one of the safest capital cities in Africa. Because I almost always seemed to choose an awful bus company, judging from previous experiences, I asked the booking agent if Gemini Motorways was indeed worth considering, especially for an overnight trip.

"My friend, Gemini Motorways has thirty-eight buses and all of them are great, comfortable buses," he assured me.

It was all settled. I was going to take a bus on Wednesday afternoon. Since I did not have ZMK150 000 on me, we agreed that I could come back that afternoon or the following day to pay and pick up my ticket.

I spent a leisurely forty-eight hours in Lusaka during which I managed to buy myself the correct wall plug to charge my cellphone. But then network problems still made it impossible to phone Lulu. We continued to exchange news and views by email. In one of her emails, she warned me about a haemorrhagic disease that had killed a Zambian paramedic who had accompanied a seriously ill patient airlifted from Zambia to Morningside Clinic in Johannesburg. Three people had already died: the paramedic, a nurse and a cleaner in the ward where the sick patient passed away. That was how infectious the disease was.

It was described as a type of deadly tick-bite fever. Reading Lulu's email made my body itch all over, and for someone who didn't even have travel insurance, it was a real cause for concern.

I could, however, do nothing about the matter.

On my second day of leisure in Lusaka I detoured from the hustle and bustle of Cairo Road to Lumumba Road to see more of the city. There, just past another bus station, I came across Soweto Market. I was astounded. I was in Soweto – in Lusaka!

As is to be expected of anything Sowetan, the market, bisected by the main road, is huge and has an informal feel to it. Hawkers sell everything from their stalls and shacks situated underneath massive power lines – from fruit, vegetables, pots and garments to rice, beans and fish.

It was encouraging to see that the Zambian government, together with the Commission of the European Union, was in the process of upgrading the market. At least, that is what the big board at the entrance said. I couldn't see many signs of actual improvement yet, but still.

I walked around Soweto Market for more than two hours and not once did anyone hassle me for business. I asked a few people why it was called Soweto Market but nobody seemed to know. My own conclusion was that it was thus named by members of the exiled ANC, which had its headquarters in Lusaka during the apartheid years when the organisation was banned in South Africa. Walking in the crowded market, I said to myself: I could be walking in the footsteps of Tambo. Surely the late Oliver Reginald Tambo, the longest-serving president of the ANC, must have walked in this very same market during his time in Lusaka.

On a trip like this you need to peruse the local newspapers from time to time. The last thing you want is to be ignorant of what is happening in your host country. So on my last afternoon in Lusaka I retreated to the Koumboka bar to browse through a few papers. One of the national newspapers reported that acting president and MMD presidential candidate, Rupiah Banda, had engaged four US-based, internationally renowned image consultants to polish his image to "have more Zambians identify themselves with him".

I have often wondered whether such things really work. Was it not, yet again, some clever American making money out of a wealthy African leader with high hopes and low self-esteem? Maybe I was just being cynical, but I have learned and seen that building a brand takes time as well as consistent and constant effort. With elections less than three weeks away, how much was going to be accomplished? (Maybe it did work after all. Rupiah Banda, amidst complaints of vote-rigging by the opposition parties, went on to win the 30 October elections. Viva, image consultants, viva!)

Another newspaper reported that the MDC in Zimbabwe had said the "unity talks were a big mistake" and that the two parties, MDC and ZANU-PF, could not reach agreement on which party was going to head which portfolio. So what was new?

The same newspaper reported growing speculation that a new political party was to be launched in South Africa (and indeed it happened – the Congress of the People (COPE) was launched late in 2008). Hmm, I said to myself, it will take a new generation of eligible voters in a "free" South Africa before another party will be able to challenge the ANC seriously. South Africans, especially the darkies, will continue to vote for the ANC in the 2009 and 2014 general elections, because the struggle against white oppression started in 1912, and were it not for these guys I would, in all probability, still be working in Baas Koekemoer's garden, where I would, together with the baas (but at different times), hump the maid, Doris Ndou from Venda. Seeing that I will be turning forty in 2015, I should perhaps launch a new career then – become an honest, efficient, trustworthy, hardworking, for-the-people-by-the-people-at-your-service authentic politician … *Woza* 2019 – Viva, All Africa Party (AAP), viva!

On the international front, the worldwide credit crisis, which had started as a housing slump in the United States, was deepening. The Royal Bank of Scotland – with whom I intended opening an offshore account one day – had seen its share price slump by more than 40 per cent within a couple of days.

What confounds me about the global financial system is how certain currencies, irrespective of what happens, never seem to be negatively affected. Everybody was warning that the US was about to enter a recession and yet the dollar was getting stronger against the rand day by day.

To my uneducated brain with its limited understanding and knowledge of the dynamics of international financial systems, it simply does not add up. Look what happened straight after 11 September 2001. The US dollar became so strong it was worth R14 at one stage. The rand may be the currency of a small developing country and therefore vulnerable, but when the US gets attacked and goes through a recession, their currency gets stronger! Sitting at the bar, I concluded that the developing world seemed, somehow, to be getting screwed all the time.

I was into my sixth beer by now and my perceptions were getting skewed. I started thinking that money does not have any value in itself. Think: US$10, R10, Z$10. Which of the three paper notes has the highest intrinsic value? My point exactly. It is us who put value into worthless pieces of paper and cause the vast majority of people in the world to have money with low value while a relatively small percentage of the world's population can travel cheaply, staying in great hotels and sipping champagne the whole day long, because of their stronger currency.

I reached for my seventh beer.

North with Gemini Motorways

I t was time to leave Lusaka. For a change I had a shower in the morning before spending five hours loitering around the backpackers. Although the bus was scheduled to depart only at 16:00, I bade my hosts at Koumboka farewell at 2 p.m.

It was a very hot day, but the thought of saving ZMK20 000 and losing weight in the process made me decide not to take a cab but rather to walk to the bus terminal. There I was again led by hand to where the bus was parked, this time by a new guy. Again quite a few bus touts physically tried to pull me into the buses they represented. I was relieved to make it to the white, not-old-but-definitely-not-new bus in one piece but was shocked to see how many people were trying to board.

There was a commotion of people not only at the door but also towards the back as passengers tried to shove their luggage into the hold of the bus. Even though I had a ticket I knew that it was going to be a battle getting inside the vehicle, especially since it was an overnight bus and I wanted to keep my backpack with me.

An assistant bus driver, sweating as if he was in a sauna, stood on the steps of the bus stopping passengers with even smaller bags than mine from boarding. After I had managed to push my way in front of him, he took one look at me and said, "No, big man, you will not come in here with such a big bag. Go this way."

He used his one hand to wipe the perspiration from his brow and the other to point towards the back of the bus.

"Oh come on, my friend, this bag is not too big," I pleaded.

Before he could respond his attention was caught by another passenger attempting to board with an even bigger bag. In the meantime the crowd behind me was growing bigger and bigger.

Out of the blue, just when I was about to give up and hand over my backpack, another assistant called, "Okay, big man, you can come in."

I entered the bus a relieved man. By then I too was dripping with sweat. A lady perched on the front seat asked for my ticket before checking for my name on the passenger list. "Seat number nine," she said, which must have been the sign for a youngster, who all along had been standing in the aisle, to take my backpack right to the back row of the bus.

As I watched him putting my bag on the back seat, he looked back at me, gave a thumbs-up and said, "You see, it's safe, big man."

I was just settling into my seat when the assistant driver who had allowed me onto the bus with my bag came to me, wiping his wet face and neck with what used to be a white T-shirt, and said, "That bag is way too big, my friend. It will cost you twenty thousand kwachas."

"No, make it ten thousand," I said, knowing the money would probably end up in his pocket.

"No, it is twenty thousand. Otherwise I will take it out to the luggage section." I could see he meant business. I reluctantly gave him ZMK20 000 (about R50), and right in front of my eyes he put it in his back pocket (no pun intended).

About twenty minutes later my heart skipped a beat when I saw another youngster carrying my bag down the aisle. I got up and confronted him. It seemed that it had to be put in the hold after all, and since I did not have a receipt for my bag I would have to pay again.

"I'm not going to pay a second time," I insisted.

By now a huge Queen Latifah look-alike sister had joined the argument. I am pretty sure she was either Gemini Motorways' senior manager or one of the owners of the bus company. She was certainly no pushover. She demanded that I point out the man who had asked me to pay him ZMK20 000. I looked around but could not see him; by then another assistant driver was standing on the steps of the bus. Queen Latifah turned on her heel and went to solve other passengers' problems.

It was turning into a nightmare of a trip and the bus had not even left the bus terminal yet. By now my bag had been wedged in behind the driver's seat.

As more passengers boarded the bus, more bags ended up being dumped behind the driver's seat. Soon a tall man with a light complexion got in and started the engine of the bus. As he straightened up to leave, he gave my bag a sharp kick to ensure that it was nicely stacked into position. Then he disembarked and started chatting to some people who were loitering next to the idling bus.

By now the luggage section was full and more and bigger bags were making their way onto the bus, as well as two double-bed mattresses and a few big boxes. These were taken to the back. I realised that if my backpack had not ended up behind the driver's seat, it would have been squashed.

Stacking heavy bags at the back of the bus looked like normal practice because no passengers had been allocated the back seat. With the seat stacked to the ceiling, more and more smallish bags were being squeezed in behind the driver's seat, slowly but surely diminishing the legroom of the three people seated immediately behind the driver. Two of the passengers did not object, but the third, a short man with unkempt beard, was complaining bitterly that he had booked the ticket two weeks in advance and chose that particular seat because he knew that it had extra legroom. He was furious and started kicking at the bags stacked in front of him.

This passenger happened to be the only white person on the bus. Typical, I thought, forever whining and complaining. To me he looked like a cross between a hobo and a farmer who had inherited a commercially unviable potato farm.

It was while looking at all this confusion, with too many people working at cross purposes for the same bus company, and having been conned out of ZMK20 000, that a second question without an obvious answer presented itself.

QUESTION 2: Does inefficiency breed corruption, or does corruption breed inefficiency?

My point about the interrelatedness of corruption and inefficiency was proved when the man from whom I had bought the ticket the previous day started checking that everybody on board had a valid ticket just as we were about to depart, even though the lady on the front seat had already checked all passengers against the list and confirmed their seat numbers. It took him almost half an hour, and no sooner had he finished than a dark man with pimples started verifying that, genuinely and indeed, everybody on board had a valid ticket.

I rest my case. The problem with such corruption-ingrained systems is that nobody is trusted. Even people who are supposed to verify certain things have other people looking over their shoulder. Only when the final verifier had finally verified that the initial verifier had verified everything efficiently was the bus allowed to leave – almost an hour after the scheduled time of departure.

And yes, at that moment the woman who was entrusted with the passenger list and who had allocated our seat numbers, made a call on her cellphone and said, "We have fifty-six passengers, sir."

The bus moved forward. As it pulled out of the main terminal exit, five more passengers hastily boarded the bus. Surely they had paid the driver directly!

We turned left into Church Street and then right into Cairo Road, which eventually turned into the Great North Road.

One of the assistant drivers started handing out 500-ml bottles of Sprite. The cool liquid put a smile back on my face, although I was still smarting from having being cheated out of ZMK20 000. The bus had no music system but the seats were comfortable.

Seated next to me was an elderly man who explained that the bus was so full because there were no big towns outside the capital and so people, especially from the small towns in the north-eastern part of the country, tended to buy everything in Lusaka. Then he closed his eyes and spent most of the journey sleeping.

We had not left Lusaka for long when very tall grass and trees appeared on both sides of the road, making it difficult to see the thatched huts dotted about. But I could not miss the sign to a lodge named Shaka's Kraal.

I was intrigued, but on second thoughts it made perfect sense to me to have establishments in Zambia named after King Shaka. When he consolidated his kingdom around 1815, Zulus were scattered throughout southern Africa. Or so I was taught during history lessons at school.

During the Mfecane, as this time is known, Zwangendaba of the Gumbi clan, commander of the Ndwandwe tribe, crossed the Zambezi River and eventually settled with his followers, the Ngonis, in the north of what is now Zambia.

Another chief, Mzilikazi Khumalo, one of King Shaka's lieutenants, settled with his Khumalo clan in 1840 at Bulawayo, in what is now southern Zimbabwe. The clashes between Mzilikazi's Ndebeles and the Shonas at the time sowed the seeds of the tension that still exists between these two major ethnic groups in Zimbabwe today. (My great-great-great-grandfather must have stayed behind with Shaka.)

The Mfecane planted Zulus everywhere. Chief Soshangane fled and settled in present-day Mozambique. He conquered the Tsongas and by adding them to his Zulu followers established a massive kingdom which he named after his grandfather, Gaza. Soshangane's subjects were called amaShangane (Shangaans) and his Gaza empire included the provinces of Gaza, Sofala and Manica in Mozambique. It stretched as far as south-eastern Zimbabwe and north-eastern South Africa.

Further south, a minor Sotho-speaking chief established his kingdom, in part to fend off the aggression of the Nguni clans, at Thaba Bosiu in the Drakensberg mountains. He was known – because of the "shwe-shwe" noise a blade makes when you shave – as "the shaver": Moshoeshoe. In time he became a strong leader, but in 1869, through a treaty between the Boers and the British which drew Lesotho's current borders, he lost half his land.

Some Zulus went even further south, to today's Eastern Cape, where they were called "mfengu" – foreigners – by the Xhosa-speaking people. Today, however, the Mfengus are considered to be Xhosas rather than Zulus.

Kids kicking plastic soccer balls on dusty soccer fields and a red sun setting on the left side of the bus were sure proof that we were heading north. The road, a normal national road with two lanes running in opposite directions, was amazingly busy, with trucks trundling in both directions. I knew the Copperbelt with its copper mines was in northern Zambia, but the number of trucks on the road took me by surprise.

Unlike my neighbour, I was too tense to sleep. With wide-open eyes I watched our poor bus driver overtake truck after truck, avoiding a collision with a big lorry hurtling past in the opposite direction by making it back into the left lane in the nick of time.

Our first stop was a very busy petrol station in a small town called Kabwe, where a visit to the (dirty, strong-smelling, pee-on-the-floor) toilet cost ZMK1000 (about R2) per person.

Our next stop, at about 21:00, four hours after leaving Lusaka, was Kapiri Mposhi, where almost all the passengers disembarked to buy food from the convenience shop. Only the broke white potato farmer and I remained on board. The last thing I wanted was to eat and drink and during the night end up needing a non-existent toilet.

While the passengers trickled back in, a youngster wearing a SATA T-shirt got into the driver's seat. I didn't have time to worry about the meaning of the letters on his chest. I was too busy worrying about the fact that he not only started the engine but was clearly going to drive the bus. It looked very strange to me that such a young boy would be allowed to drive a bus, but nobody else seemed to notice.

About five kilometres outside Kapiri Mposhi we had to go across yet another weighbridge. Lots of trucks were waiting to be weighed as well. I stopped counting when I reached thirty.

Pure confusion reigned. The trucks and buses did not queue in single file, with the result that while a long truck was taking a wide turn in order to align itself properly with the weighbridge, a bus would cut in front of it to reach the weighbridge first. So trucks refused to make gaps for the buses, while the buses at the same time were trying to squeeze themselves into tiny openings. It encouraged a lot of hooting and revving of engines.

What made our situation worse was that the youngster behind the wheel could not drive properly. Because he could not balance the clutch and accelerator, he had to restart the bus a couple of times, and each time the bus would roll back slightly and the truck behind us would start hooting hysterically. It was really hair-raising stuff.

After audaciously cutting through the line and with some more false starts here and there, we eventually made it onto the weighbridge. In no time we got the green light. We drove past a board with the words "Turn left and offload. Turn right and exit." As we turned right I saw a few trucks in the holding area, but none of them had started offloading. Suddenly, before we got back onto the main road, the bus stopped. We waited for a few minutes. My neighbour, who was now wide awake after all the stops and starts and mayhem, explained that one of the assistant drivers was probably waiting for a printout from the office, which had to be shown if we were stopped by the police along the road.

It turned out there was some discrepancy in the printout and that we had to go back to the weighbridge to be weighed again. My heart sank.

The same procedure ensued: jumping the queue, cutting through hooting trucks, restarting the bus engine, letting the bus roll back to within centimetres of bumping into the truck behind us. The second time round I noticed that the light after the weighbridge was permanently green.

Turning right meant nothing – nobody could leave until they had received their printout.

We waited and, lo and behold, after a few minutes another youngster came running with the printout, and this time there were no mistakes.

Getting through that weighbridge took us fifty-eight minutes.

Then I realised that instead of leaving we were returning to Kapiri Mposhi. When I asked my neighbour what was going on, he explained, "We are going back to pick up the other passengers."

Of course: some passengers always got off in Kapiri Mposhi for last-minute shopping while the bus went on to be weighed.

They were waiting for us with their plastic bags. While they got back onto the bus a new, older driver took over.

Soon we were back at the crossroads where you turn left for the weigh-bridge, carry on straight for Kitwe and Ndola, the second biggest city in Zambia and capital of the Copperbelt province, or turn right for Mpulungu in the north of the country. We were headed for Mpulungu.

About an hour out of Kapiri Mposhi, we stopped to offload a woman passenger. Easier said than done: her luggage was stashed underneath some big bags in the dark luggage section underneath the bus. It took quite some time – three-quarters of an hour to be exact – for the SATA T-shirt-wearing youngster to haul out the heavy bags in the feeble light of the torch the driver was holding and to locate the woman's luggage.

During this time I managed to retrieve my sleeping bag from my backpack. I wanted to take a nap and it was getting cold. I glanced through the cabin and saw that all the blue curtains were billowing in the wind – none of the bus's windows could close properly, not just the one next to me.

We reached Kasama at dawn. Had I taken the TAZARA train from Kapiri Mposhi, I would have arrived at this dusty town with its many colourful buildings at two-thirty in the morning.

Three-quarters of the passengers, including the potato farmer, dis-embarked and were immediately besieged by scores of cab drivers who harassed them by holding their car keys in front of their faces and insisting on taking them home with their luggage. Or so it looked. Despite losing ZMK20 000 to a crooked Gemini Motorways driver's assistant, I was glad to be on the bus.

As we left, now under control of the driver who had driven us from

Lusaka to Kapiri Mposhi, I spotted the perfect place to have spent the wee hours of the morning had I taken the train: Niciiss Nightclub. It was too late now.

Outside Kasama the road was lined with tall gumtrees and green and colourful shrubs. A beautiful sight. And the sun rising just then turned the scene into something extra special. With so few of the original passengers left, the bus started speeding. Eish, the road to Mbala all of a sudden deteriorated significantly. It got so bad that the bus sometimes had to sneak onto the right side of the road to escape the huge potholes. The bus driver did not consider this a reason to slow down, however.

The man proved to be a real character. He was not only whistling but using his cellphone, talking and laughing loudly with one hand on the steering wheel, the other pressing the cellphone to his ear. Then he did the unthinkable: without changing gear he raised his bum from the seat, took out another cellphone from the side pocket of his trousers and started changing batteries from one cellphone to another. At one stage he had two cellphone batteries in his mouth and a cellphone in each hand, steering the wheel lightly with the heel of his right hand only.

It started to warm up by the time we got to Mbala, where more passengers disembarked. Only about ten passengers remained on board, plus four assistants, the second driver (who was now very cosy with a woman at the back of the bus), and the first driver behind the wheel. Just after the MPULUNGU 10 sign, the bus suddenly stopped and two women jumped off, walked about ten metres from the bus and squatted.

By now I was wearing my brand new sunglasses which I had bought from a street vendor on Cairo Road. Facing straight forward, I twisted my eyes to the side until they were aching to steal a look. The peeing women were squatting with their backs towards the bus and not even an inch of their bums was showing. And then they just straightened up without pulling any garments into place.

One could come to only one conclusion.

Mpulungu

Seventeen hours after leaving Lusaka, at approximately 22:00, the bus pulled into a very hot and humid Mpulungu at the southernmost point of Lake Tanganyika. As I disembarked not a single person rushed forward to offer me a taxi, which is what I expected after witnessing what had happened in Kasama. So I asked a guy on the road for directions to Harbour Inn, a recommended budget guesthouse in the town.

"Continue along the main road towards the harbour and you'll see it on your right," he told me.

Having lived for thirteen years in Durban, which is regarded as hot and humid in South African terms, I thought I was used to humidity. Not so. After about fifty metres I was already dripping wet with sweat. After 250 metres or so I was outside Harbour Inn, a bar with rooms at the back. I went through a small open gate next to the bar and found two guys, one doing his washing, the other enjoying brown bread and black coffee.

When I asked whether I could get a room for the night I received a puzzling answer from the coffee drinker: "You see, my friend, there are people in three rooms who are not sure whether they will be staying tonight or leaving. They will only know this afternoon."

My jaw dropped. "So must I wait until they make up their minds?" I asked.

"No, try other guesthouses along the main road."

Having come to terms with the fact that I would have to find other accommodation, I enquired whether the MV *Liemba* indeed docked early Friday morning and then left around mid-morning on the same day, as advertised.

"Sometimes it docks on Friday and sometimes on Saturday. It just depends." The way he was struggling to construct sentences and the serious expression on his face told me he was not joking.

"So where can I buy a ticket in the meantime?"

He turned to his friend who was now wringing out a T-shirt and conversed in a local language. He eventually said, "There are no offices here in Mpulungu. They only sell tickets on the ferry."

I left Harbour Inn very disappointed. And worried. I did not have a room but also, if there was no *MV Liemba* ticket office, I was going to be caught in a ticket stampede with everybody trying to buy their tickets at the same time.

Since it was only Thursday, and with the ferry docking either on Friday or Saturday, I figured that I had better secure accommodation for the night. But first I would walk to the harbour to confirm when exactly the ferry was expected.

The Harbour Inn was less than 200 metres from the main entrance to Zambia's only port. A security guard interrupted his conversation with an elderly man with grey hair and thick glasses to assure me that the ferry was expected only on Saturday morning.

"But I read that she gets here on Fridays," I objected, citing the information I had found on the internet while still in South Africa.

"Well, sometimes it's Friday but then sometimes it's Saturday," he said.

Noticing that I was a bit disturbed by the news, he asked, "Where are you from?"

"South Africa."

"Well this is real Africa, not South Africa, my friend."

As I was leaving the harbour, it dawned on me that even though I'd lived on the continent all my life, I still did not understand how we do things. It had taken me until that moment to realise that it's fine for guests in guesthouses to hang around without knowing whether they will stay or not; that ferries can have erratic schedules; that a ferry company has no office in the only port in the country where it docks weekly.

I walked back to town, wondering why Lake Tanganyika, which borders four countries – Zambia, the Democratic Republic of Congo (DRC), Tanzania and Burundi – is served by only one ferry which runs only once a week. But then I figured any investor who tried to get a second ferry on the lake would have to negotiate with all four governments and, by the time that very patient entrepreneur had signed a deal with the fourth government, there would be, in at least one of the four countries, a rebel group also looking for a kickback.

Mpulungu has to be one of the most humid places on Earth. By the time I got back to the bus station I looked like I had fallen into the lake and, needless to say, was the centre of attention. Wiping the perspiration from my brow, I noticed a big sign behind our Gemini Motorways bus: Sims Guesthouse and Restaurant. I walked straight there.

After checking in a big black book, the lady behind the counter at Sims, who must have served as both waitress and guesthouse receptionist, said that they had a room for ZMK20 000. I decided to take it and paid for one night.

A man was asked to show me to my room. We walked through the restaurant, past a few people who were watching a kung-fu movie, into what looked like a big hall with low walls dividing it into different rooms. A long, dark corridor led to the room I had been given.

To say I was disappointed is an understatement. My room had massive cobwebs hanging in all four corners, a filthy mattress with dark stain marks, a really dirty mosquito net with holes all over it and, to consolidate my general impression of grubbiness, a dirty floor.

"Please accompany me to the bathrooms," the man said.

We went back into the dark corridor and exited on the other side of the building where the bathrooms were located. These, basically, were three cubicles with no roof. The man pointed to a big drum with water and explained that I'd have to use one of the small red buckets to scoop water from it. I didn't have a problem with that except that the water in the big drum looked dirty. Finally, he showed me the toilets. The less said about them the better. After seeing them I knew I could never use them.

I went to my room very down in the dumps and sat down on the floor. Dirty as it was, I was better off sitting on the floor than on the stained mattress. While sitting there I noticed a big gap between the ceiling and the external wall.

I was pondering how I was going to survive a night in such a disgusting room when there was a knock at the door. It was the same man who had given me a tour of the establishment. He had brought the bedding – two sheets that had definitely seen their best days … in the seventies. They must have been white once but now they were pale grey.

After making the bed the guy had the nerve to tell me, "Please have a bath before—"

"Yes, I will," I assured him before he could even finish his sentence.

Alone once again and still sitting on the floor, I regretted for the first time undertaking this trip. Why, I asked myself, didn't I just take my wife to some exclusive island where we could sip cocktails through bent straws, with lemon slices balancing on the edges of long, concave-shaped glasses, while watching the sun set in a spectacular, endless ocean before retiring to a white cloud of a bed? Where we could hold hands while walking barefoot on the soft sand of the beach, waves crashing in slow motion around our feet, and afterwards have a steamy hot shower together in a spotlessly clean bathroom and make love in that dream of a bed?

I must have sat on that floor scribbling notes in my exercise book for at least three hours before I pulled myself together and decided to take a walk to absorb the local atmosphere.

The humidity in Mpulungu was unbearable and life incredibly slow. Everybody seemed to walk at a tortoise's pace and take their time about whatever they were doing.

I bought a 350-ml bottle of Coke in one of the colourful shops lining the potholed main road with its dirty pavements. A few locals were sitting on the veranda. After the opened Coke was handed to me, I started drinking straight from the bottle.

It took me by surprise when a middle-aged man tapped me on the shoulder and offered me a chair to sit on. Mind you, he was not even working at the shop; he was one of the customers. I looked around. All the locals were sitting on their red plastic chairs enjoying their Coca-Colas. And then I remembered – according to African tradition, people should not eat or drink while standing.

I must confess I had always known that, but it is one of those things that we no longer think about as a result of living in the city. Taking the offered seat, I realised that to the people of Mpulungu drinking a bottle of Coke was not just quenching your thirst; it was an occasion to be savoured. So I took my time enjoying my drink. It suddenly became clear to me why the guests at Harbour Inn weren't sure whether they were leaving or not without anyone raising an eyebrow.

As I continued down the main street I noticed another guesthouse by the name of Chambuluka. I decided to check out their prices. A lady with cornrows on her head showed me around. A squeaky clean room was going to set me back ZMK30 000, a third more than what I was paying at Sims. I now regretted that I hadn't shopped around before checking into Sims and paying for a night's accommodation without viewing the room first. Okay, I thought, I'll spend the night at Sims and at the break of dawn relocate to Chambuluka.

By then I had adapted to the Mpulungu way of doing things: take your time and walk slowly. So I strolled back to my depressing room at Sims. As I was opening the door, the bus driver, who was staying next door, was exiting his.

At about nine, just as I lay down to sleep, the noise of people boarding a bus increased to an intolerable level. At one stage I thought they were fighting, but it was merely the commotion of pushing and shoving and shouting that happens whenever passengers board the long-distance buses.

For two hours I tried to fall asleep. In vain. It was hot and humid, but I had no choice other than to get under my sleeping bag to protect myself from the mosquitoes. The net the guesthouse provided was riddled with holes, and worse, it had a terrible musty smell: like someone had dragged it on a gravel road for miles before dipping it in muddy water. As an additional protective measure I decided to apply insect repellent to my already sticky skin. After clogging my pores with the stuff, I lay quietly steaming under my sleeping bag.

At about eleven the bus finally left and things quietened down. Just as I was drifting off an SMS came through on my cellphone. It was Lulu saying I must phone her urgently. When I checked the message details it turned out that she had sent the message fifteen hours earlier, at 8:10 that morning. The Zambian telecommunications system clearly worked on the same principle as the people of Mpulungu: why rush if you can do it slowly?

I tried phoning, but once again a network problem prevented me getting through.

Besides a very depressing room, which I hated with all my heart, and sweating as if I were in a steam room, I was now stressing about not being able to phone home. I tried repeatedly, but the network did not allow my calls to go through.

I was dog-tired, but I lay there counting the minutes and hours until just after one in the morning when my neighbour, the bus driver, returned to his room. At Sims the screeching of the doors against floorboards ensured that you knew when your neighbour entered and exited his room.

Barely ten minutes later noise started coming from his room. From the nature of the noise I could tell that there was some serious bumping and grinding taking place. The gap between the wall and the ceiling allowed every "mmmm" and "aaaaa" to reach my ears. Because she was moaning and groaning and repeating words in a local language, I couldn't understand what the woman was saying. I was contemplating taking a peep over the low wall – which now seemed very high (a superior room like that naturally contains neither a chair nor a table to stand on) – when the driver started shooting from the hip and a few seconds later everything was over.

Being a responsible and pragmatic individual, I started worrying whether he had used a condom. Given his extremely unsafe behaviour on the bus – changing cellphone batteries while driving a speeding bus on a bad road – I feared the worst. In the end I decided to give him the benefit of the doubt. But then, what would happen to the used condom …?

Overall, it was a very disturbing, uncomfortable and hot night. Just after six, instead of rushing to check out, I decided to go to the port once again to make doubly sure that the ferry was arriving on Saturday and not Friday. When I arrived there another old man – he didn't wear thick glasses but he did have grey hair – confirmed that the ferry was "only coming tomorrow at nine hours".

At Chambuluka I was told I could check in only after 10 a.m. Since I had learned the hard way about the advisability of shopping around and since I had some free time, I decided to investigate Mbita Guesthouse across the road from Chambuluka. At their reception a big notice announced "Sorry no cheques accepted. Not even good ones." The rate was the same as Chambuluka's. The only difference was that their rooms were not self-contained and not as clean.

Happy with my decision, I returned to Sims to check out and collect my backpack, even though it was not eight o'clock yet. I could not wait to take a shower at Chambuluka. My last bath had been fifty hours earlier in Lusaka and the high humidity in Mpulungu and sweating the whole night had made my body itchy, especially my balls. I walked very slowly back down the road and spent almost two hours sitting on the veranda at Chambuluka looking at the passing parade: people moving very slowly up and down the main road.

After checking into my clean room with its clean floor tiles, I lay on the bed with its spotless linen, luxuriating in the not-quite-cool air stirred around by the fan on the floor. After a while it was time for the shower. I looked in my backpack but the toiletries bag was nowhere to be found. After a thorough search I realised that I must have left it at Sims. It was a nerve-racking moment. I started imagining how the trip would be without ever taking a shower again. So I decided to commit a crime (according to Mpulungu's unwritten rules about doing everything slowly) and rushed back to Sims. When I entered the restaurant, I heard someone shouting, "My friend, you left something!"

It was the guy who took me on the grand tour of the guesthouse the previous day and later told me to have a bath. He went to the back of the restaurant and next to the fridge picked up my black toiletries bag. He handed it to me with the words "No problem. Safe journey" and returned to the television set to put on another kung-fu movie.

Back at Chambuluka, standing stark naked under the shower, it became clear that no water was going to come out of the showerhead. I had no choice but to put my clothes back on and go out and enquire at reception. The receptionist, who spoke some English, said, "Please sir, go back to your room and I will come help you now." I went back, not quite sure what she meant, whether I should take my clothes off or keep them on. After three minutes there was a knock at the door. When I opened, there she was with a red ten-litre bucket of water.

Having grown up in the rural areas where using a bucket or basin was the only way to have a bath, the Chambuluka "shower" brought back some wonderful memories and reminded me how far I had come since the days I stood shivering with pleasure in a bucket of warm water on my mother's kitchen floor.

Refreshed, I lay on the bed and life was great once more. With the fan blowing air at its maximum over my naked body, out of the blue a universe-changing, life-enhancing formula suddenly came to my mind:

Mpulungu – pu = Mlungu (white person in Zulu)

Like Albert Einstein's famous $E = mc^2$ formula, it was going to shake the pillars of the establishment.

I spent pretty much the whole day thinking about my newly found formula. The only thing that was troubling my otherwise great day was that, after numerous attempts, the network still did not allow my calls to South Africa through. At dusk I went for dinner at the Chambuluka in-house restaurant. For ZMK7 000 I enjoyed fried fish, spinach, baked beans and *sima*, which is what we call *pap* in South Africa – *uphuthu* in Zulu – and what is termed *fufu* in north-west Africa and *ugali* in the DRC.

Before I had finished the meal, which was rather tasty, there was a power failure. A candle was hastily brought to the table. Having a meal in a dark, candle-lit restaurant felt romantic. Well, sort of – and a candle always helps one look on the bright side of life.

Thank goodness there was an almost full moon and I didn't have to walk back to my room through the courtyard in pitch darkness. The receptionist had explained that there was a battery-driven light in my room. It soon dawned on me that power failures had to be regular occurrences in Mpulungu for a guesthouse to have such emergency lights in all rooms as a precaution. Challengers Nite Club next door even had its own generator, which is why it could blast loud music into the dark stillness for the whole night.

You just cannot win: at Sims I had to put up with people buying bus tickets at night, and at Chambuluka, it being a Friday night, I had to contend with the local duf-duf sound – with some Lucky Dube songs in-between. The Nite Club DJ obviously loved his music.

Power came back on in the morning and, it being a Saturday, I thought I would be proactive (I never learn, hey?) and be at the harbour by eight instead of "nine hours" as was suggested the previous day. I quickly checked out but, since the ferry was due to leave only in the afternoon, I left my bag behind at reception in case there was a lot of pushing and shoving during the ticket-buying process.

It was another very humid day and again everyone was walking slowly. (I'm sure even a chameleon would find the pace laid-back.) I was already covered in perspiration by the time I got to the harbour.

"Oh my friend, it is you again!" the old man at the gate called before I could even greet him. "The *Liemba* should be here at eleven hours. Come back later."

I walked back even more slowly than I had arrived. An extra three-hour wait was not such a long time when you're exploring African countries north of the Limpopo, I consoled myself.

At the bus station a number of youngsters were all selling the same product: boiled eggs.

As I had already checked out, I had no room to return to. I decided just to sit on the veranda once again, killing time by watching the locals sauntering past as if life were eternal. I could not help but think: Maybe in Mpulungu people *do* live forever. It simply did not make sense to me to lead such a laid-back life. I guess the problem with living in the big city is that you get so used to seeing people rushing that it looks abnormal when everybody goes about slowly.

Just before 11 a.m. I took another walk past the bus station to the harbour. By now the humidity was truly unbearable. I slowed down to a complete standstill: from a distance I could see quite a lot of activity next to the gate. The MV *Liemba* must have docked!

Although there was a big sign – STOP: SECURITY CHECKPOINT – people were entering the main gate. Maybe the sign was meant for vehicles, I thought to myself, and also walked past the security kiosk. With so many people around I could not see the old man with grey hair this time. Having worked for ten years in the Port of Durban, the biggest and busiest harbour on the continent, I have a good idea of the infrastructure needed in a modern port. Mpulungu had none: no quay cranes, conveyor belts or silos, as I had expected. A few small forklifts, a number of dilapidated buildings and an army truck were the sum total of what I saw.

When I lifted my head, there she was – the MV *Liemba*.

I had done my background reading. Built in Germany in 1913, she was commissioned the following year as one of three vessels operated by the Germans to control Lake Tanganyika during the early part of World War I. The *Graf von Götzen*, as she was known then, was scuttled by her captain in July 1916 as the Germans were retreating from the town of Kigoma. Subsequently, in 1924, she was salvaged by the British Navy and recommissioned three years later as the MV *Liemba*. She is currently owned by the Tanzania Railways Corporation.

But something didn't look right: there was no gangway to get on board the vessel. Loads of people were simply jumping on and off. As it was lying level with the quay it was very easy for them to leap on board in front, in the middle and at the rear end. It was an unbelievable sight. People were screaming and shouting, especially towards the bow where 50-kg bags of agricultural produce (which, although I cannot be sure, looked like sweet potatoes) were being offloaded from the hatch. After jumping on board as well, I walked towards the stern-end and ended up in the restaurant, judging by the tables, chairs and a fridge full of cooldrinks, where I bumped into the chef.

"I want to buy a first-class ticket to Kigoma," I said to the man in the white coat, white hat and with two tomatoes in his hand.

"Talk to that man," he replied, pointing to a guy approximately my age, dressed in a white vest and blue jeans which hung so low on his hips that they looked like they could drop at any moment. I pretended not to notice, even though I was expecting someone wearing some type of uniform and not oversized baggy jeans.

"Well, my friend," Watson started when I told him that I wanted a ticket to Kigoma, "the ferry is only going to Kigoma on Monday. Today we have been hired by the United Nations to pick up refugees and drop them off in Congo."

"You are joking, right?" I said in disbelief.

"We will definitely be back here on Monday morning," he assured me.

"Not even tomorrow, Sunday?"

He gave me that where-are-you-from-this-is-real-Africa look. So I changed tack. "How much is a first-class ticket to Kigoma?" I asked meekly.

In response he took a nicely folded paper from the back pocket of his jeans and in the process revealed his black underpants. He looked at the paper for a while and replied, "Sixty-two thousand Tanzanian shillings."

I found dealing with Tanzanian shillings very easy because at the time a US dollar was fixed at TZS1000. So that meant US$62, which was seven dollars more than the price I had seen quoted by travellers who had posted their experiences on the internet. Since I did not have Tanzanian shillings, I asked Watson whether he accepted Zambian kwachas.

He looked at me for some time and said, "We normally deal in shillings but I will see what I can do on Monday when you come to buy the ticket."

The offloading of bags was still going on and people were still screaming and shouting. Along with everybody who was disembarking I jumped back onto the quayside.

I left the ferry a very disappointed man. I could not believe that I had another forty-eight hours to spend in Mpulungu. And then with a shock I realised that my passport stamp would be expiring the following day. Now I was worried on top of being disappointed.

No matter what happened next I had to get an extension. From a previous experience in Sudan, I knew extensions are only issued in the capital city. If so, I would have to go back to Lusaka. But, considering it was already Saturday, I could only apply for an extension on Monday and by then the stamp would have expired. Besides, if I found myself in Lusaka on Monday, I would miss the ferry because the Lusaka–Mpulungu road trip took at least seventeen hours one way.

All these things were going through my mind while I was approaching the port's main exit very slowly. On the spur of the moment I decided to ask a woman coming towards me if there were any immigration offices in Mpulungu.

"Here," she said, indicating a nearby grey building with an asbestos roof. On my way to the ferry earlier I had seen the Zambian flag outside that very building and wondered why it was there. Only now I saw the board with the words IMMIGRATION OFFICES.

"Good morning, sir," I greeted the tall, dark immigration official before telling him the story of my life. "When I entered Zambia at Livingstone, I read that the ferry leaves Mpulungu on Fridays," I informed him, "but when I got here on Thursday I was told that, instead of Friday, it would only be leaving on Saturday. And now I have just been told that, instead of going to Kigoma, it is picking up Congolese refugees and will only be here in Mpulungu on Monday. Now my problem is that the stamp in my passport expires tomorrow, on Sunday the twelfth of October," I ended with a tremble in my voice and handed over my passport.

The worst-case scenario would have been for the official to say that they didn't issue extensions in Mpulungu. Instead he said, "No problem. Come back on Monday," without even paging through my passport.

I was confused. "But do you have an extension stamp or something that can show that my stay has been extended? What if you are not here on Monday?" I asked, my voice trembling even more. The last thing I needed was to be met by another immigration official on Monday who would accuse me of having overstayed my welcome in Zambia.

"My friend, I am telling you: no problem. I will be here on Monday. No problem." He handed me my passport and started talking to the guy behind me in the queue.

I had to accept, yet again, that although I had lived on this continent all my life, sometimes I still felt like a foreigner.

Two soldiers carrying AK-47s were chatting away at the entrance gate as I left the port. What if these guys asked for my passport on Monday morning and then discovered that I was, technically, in the country illegally? Suddenly it hit me that I had another big problem: my room could have been given to someone else as I had checked out of Chambuluka!

By Mpulungu standards I walked back to the guesthouse very fast, only to discover that my room had indeed been given to somebody else. The only available room was not self-contained.

"At least it will cost you twenty instead of thirty thousand kwachas," the lady at the reception consoled me.

The room was definitely of lesser quality than the previous one – it did not have tiles on the floor and the walls were a bit dirty – but it was still a far cut above the room at Sims.

I spent the rest of the day reading Richard Branson's *Business Stripped Bare*, which talks about how he built his Virgin empire. I must admit I admire and envy his adventurous spirit. Like Albert Einstein, he is someone who has shown that a lack of formal education doesn't mean you cannot make a success of your life. Besides being a billionaire – at US$4.4 billion net worth he is the 236th richest person in the world according to the 2008 Forbes List – he was also knighted by the British queen in 1999 for his "services to entrepreneurship", which makes him Sir Richard. Reading about his life and his passion and outlook on life was enough to make me sit up with envy.

That evening I paid a visit to Mwansa Restaurant, which advertised itself as offering "the best cuisine in town. Plus value for money". I ordered fish, spinach, beans and *sima*. I enjoyed the meal (which set me back ZMK7 000) while watching a local band playing live on stage. About twenty other people, mostly youngsters, were enjoying the music along with me.

That night there was another power failure. Instead of stressing about it I lay on my bed sweating under the mosquito net and, with the late Brenda Fassie's voice in my ears (the nightclub next door was focusing on her songs), recommitted myself to pursuing my dreams, goals and ambitions in life, however odd and stupid they might look to other people. Of late I had been sloppy in this regard, I realised.

If Mpulungu was lethargic during the week, it was dead on Sundays. I was in no rush to wake up, and when I finally did open my eyes it took only five minutes for me to be bored to death. I continued lying on the bed and, inspired by my decision to do something tangible about turning my dreams into reality, I listed the truths I had learned about life. I was thirty-three, after all, old enough to have gained a few insights. Of the forty-eight insights I identified, I list only nine:

Never ever get married to a woman who is an only child. Her mother phones ten times, and that is on a good day. And if her daughter does not answer, not only does she report the matter to the police but also engages a search party. On Sunday mornings she phones at six and asks *"Nisalele yini?"* – are you still sleeping?

Although white South Africans have always seemed to show a united front, all you have to do to prove otherwise is to feed a Boer a few dops of Klippies-and-Coke and ask him about the Anglo-Boer War.

If you want a stress-free relationship, my sister, accept that men sometimes do not aim well and will thus, now and then, wet the floor of the toilet. Just wipe it and carry on. By the same token, my brother, accept that women love shopping on credit. Just pay up and smile.

Perfect, made-in-heaven relationships, not to mention the happy-ever-after bullshit, only happen in movies. If a woman with the sur-name Balls gets married to a guy named Dick there might be some chance, however.

Money is a lousy way of keeping score of success. To take it further: there is no need to keep score because we are all different and a score can only be kept if we all did the same things. But how boring would life then be?

Life is simple, but through our unceasing striving to win what we see as a never-ending race to be successful (that is, to make money), we have complicated it. And in the end, even if you were to win this "race" – which can never happen – you will still be a rat.

Life is unfair. Live with it. Sometimes really stupid, dumb people hold very senior positions. Sometimes really nice and loving people end up not finding someone to share their love with. Then you get some people who play with love all the time and get away with it.

Do not envy families that appear to be content, have it all and are 100 per cent happy. If you could be a fly on the wall you would soon see that they have their own issues, challenges and problems (maybe even bigger than yours).

Any woman who wears an expensive pair of jeans and then covers it with a shawl/wraparound is covertly sending out the message "My bum is too big for my liking."

That afternoon I received an SMS from Lulu telling me that I had been on television on a programme called "Zooming In On Men". I had done the interview one Sunday afternoon a few weeks before I embarked on the trip. I must confess that, although I am a bit apprehensive about agreeing to TV interviews (not that I receive that many requests), it always feels good to see yourself on the screen and, even though I would not see myself on the telly this time, the news put a smile on my face.

With no music coming from the nightclub that Sunday evening, I had a decent and peaceful sleep. I woke up early enough to beat the ticket queue for the *Liemba*. As before, I left my backpack behind to collect it once I had secured a place on the ferry. But this time – it was just after seven – I decided to check out only when I came back for my luggage. I took what had become my route of disappointment to the harbour with a double purpose: to buy the ferry ticket and sort out the expired stamp in my passport.

At the main gate I was greeted by the same official, who by now was calling me Mr Kilimanjaro because I had told him a few days earlier that I was going via Kigoma to climb Mount Kilimanjaro. I felt I could not tell him that I was on my way to Rwanda by public transport in case he, like some other people I know, thought I was nuts and crazy and mentally unstable.

He shook my hand and said, "The *Liemba* is confirmed for early arrival tomorrow morning."

My heart sank. I managed to keep my composure though. I was so composed, in fact, that I remembered that I still had to go to the immigration offices.

On my way there I kept thinking: What if the official who promised that he would be in the office is not in? What if he is in but pretends he has never seen me and never promised me anything?

I entered the offices and my worst nightmare came true. The official who had given me his word that he would be in on Monday morning was nowhere to be seen. Another official who had been busy with another queue on Saturday stood behind the counter.

"Can I help you?" he asked in such a very deep voice that it made my pants tremble. As I started explaining, he stopped me and said, "Oh, I remember you. You talked to my colleague the other day, right?" And after paging through my passport, he said, "Come with me to the back office."

Being invited to the back office could mean one thing only. As long it doesn't cost more than US$20, I said to myself as I followed him down a short corridor into an office with two small wooden tables, four plastic chairs and a bench. Having considered the possibility of a bribe, I had, in fact, put a US$20 note in my back pocket that morning so that I wouldn't have to open my wallet in front of any officials.

As soon as he was seated behind one of the tables, the official asked me where exactly I was heading. I had to stick to my Kilimanjaro story. To say I was on my way to find the "remote source of the Nile" at the Nyungwe forest in Rwanda would not only raise a few eyebrows, I decided, but might even lead to my stay not being extended.

He opened a big black exercise book and started copying some details from my passport. The only other question he put to me was why I needed an extension. While he wrote some more in the black book, I touched my back pocket just to make sure that the US$20 note was still there so that when the inevitable happened, I could hand it over smoothly.

The official closed the black book, raised his head and said, "I will extend your stay for another week just in case the *Liemba* is delayed in the Congo," and stamped my passport. He continued, "In my seven years of working here in Mpulungu, I have never met a black South African who wanted to board the *Liemba*. Once in a while we do, however, get one or two white guys from your country."

I was not interested in his small talk. I knew he was just buying time before asking me to grease his palm.

"Okay, Khumalo," he said, handing back my passport. "The *Liemba* should be here at seven hours tomorrow. I will see you when you stamp out tomorrow."

"Thank you very much, sir. Much appreciated," I said and stood up, not sure whether or not he was still going to ask me for something. I walked out of the office, past the public counter, and as I was about to exit through the main door I turned around and there he was, already helping another person at the counter.

"Thank you!" I shouted and gave him a thumbs-up.

I felt really bad that, exactly like others who believe that the African continent is infested with corrupt officials, I had assumed the same. I felt so bad that I even considered going back to apologise.

It was a few minutes after eight and I was already on my way back to Chambuluka. The bad news was that I would not be leaving Mpulungu just yet; the good news was that I was now legally in Zambia. And that there were still honest officials out there.

It is ironic that when you start out on an expedition you already know that now and then you will need some diversion to help you escape the frustrating circumstances you will find yourself in. Hence I always take at least two books with me. On this trip I took the Branson book and *Conversations with God* by Neale Donald Walsch. Back at the guesthouse I took up Walsch's book to fight off the boredom that was almost killing me.

I always enjoy books that challenge the status quo, books that shake the pillars of our messed-up establishment. Maybe it is because part of me absolutely loves controversy and scandal. That got me thinking how rewarding it would be to sit for a postgraduate strategy exam one day and be confronted with a question like: "Critically analyse Qhekeka Ngxosiswano kaMhlahlandlela Xulu's theory on why circumcised executives execute strategy better than colleagues with covered heads."

Around midday an SMS came through on my cellphone: "I have just done a pregnancy test and it is positive. Please phone urgently."

I do not have to tell you that it was from my wife. All of a sudden the day was getting extremely interesting. I phoned Lulu and this time around the Zambian telecommunication system obliged and the call went through. She, too, was pleasantly shocked. Although this was unexpected, we were both very excited. We agreed that she should make an appointment with her gynaecologist so she could confirm Lulu's diagnosis. The thought that I would not be able to accompany Lulu to the doctor made me even more impatient with laid-back Mpulungu.

I was brought back to the present by the sound of an approaching helicopter. I rushed out onto the veranda to investigate and there it was: a sleek black Jet Bellranger III helicopter getting ready to land about a kilometre from the guesthouse. It turned out to be carrying the Patriotic Front's presidential candidate, Michael Sata, who had come to address his supporters. Suddenly the letters I saw on the T-shirt of the young bus driver at Kapiri Mposhi made sense.

This is exactly what I need to make my day shorter, I thought as I dressed at a somewhat accelerated speed and rushed back outside.

About 3 000 spectators had gathered in the street, which was a great turnout for Mpulungu which has, according to the 2000 census, just under 60 000 inhabitants. The two buses and three trucks parked nearby suggested that people must have come from Mbala and other neighbouring towns and surrounding villages.

Within an hour – which was rather quick for this part of the world – the man of the moment stepped up to the podium accompanied by enthusiastic ululating, cheers, whistles and clapping. Dressed casually in a party T-shirt, he delivered his complete speech in the local language, which meant I did not understand a word of what he said. The crowd, however, must have been pleased with what they heard for every now and then they interrupted his speech with wild cheering and whistling.

Michael Sata read his entire speech in a flat voice, and after about an hour sat down amidst a lot of clapping. As it happens in South Africa, a local band had been invited to entertain the crowd. Judging by the excitement of the audience, it must have been one of Zambia's favourite groups, and soon the crowd was swinging. It was difficult to gauge whether the crowd had come for the music or to listen to Sata.

After one song with a hot African beat, I strolled back to the guesthouse. I had hardly taken a seat on the veranda when a greyish 4×4 with an NP registration number drove past. Having spent part of my childhood in Pietermaritzburg, I impulsively waved at the two passengers. The woman in the passenger side waved back. Without thinking I got up so as not to lose sight of her, but the vehicle had already passed and the only thing I could see was "patrollingafrica.com" boldly written on the side. I sank back into my chair. It would have been nice to talk to people from home about familiar things.

While strolling along after lunch (*sima*, fish, spinach and beans) I heard someone shouting "Mr Khumalo! Mr Khumalo!"

I had been in Mpulungu for a couple of days, but I did not expect anyone to call my name in a crowded main street. I turned around. The gentleman had a familiar face but for the life of me I could not remember where I knew him from. A split second later it clicked. It was the immigration official who had extended my stay in Zambia earlier that morning. We chatted briefly on the side of the road while people returning from the political rally dribbled past.

I felt ashamed of myself. It was my second humbling experience in Mpulungu. First, the very poor guy at Sims Guesthouse who gave back my toiletries, and now the immigration official who not only recognised me but remembered my second name. I was really taken aback.

For a change there was no power failure that Monday night and, for a change, it was a cool night. The fact that the electric fan was working made it extra cool.

On Tuesday morning I packed everything again, but this time I was absolutely sure that I was not going to spend another night in Mpulungu. During the night I had decided that if they again gave me that "tomorrow" story at the harbour, I would implement Plan E: return to South Africa via Cape Maclear on Lake Malawi. All I would have to do is take a bus – CR Carriers, Juldan Motors, Power Tools, CV Transport, any bus except

Gemini Motorways – back to Lusaka. From there I would cross to Malawi and finally visit Cape Maclear, which I had hitherto not managed to see despite having been told it is the most beautiful place on the lake. I would then return to Johannesburg via Blantyre, and Harare in Zimbabwe. My mind was made up. I was truly *gatvol* of doing nothing in a small, hot, humid rural town.

Crossing Lake Tanganyika

I checked out of my lovely guesthouse, but as a precaution left my backpack at reception. As I walked past the bus station I looked at the parked buses, thinking: Maybe I'll be taking one of you back to Lusaka later today.

"Oh, Mr Kilimanjaro! The *Liemba* is here. She came in this morning at six hours," the old grey-headed man said with a smile.

"And she is leaving today for Kigoma?" I *had* to make sure because with the MV *Liemba* you could never tell.

"Indeed she is leaving for Kigoma this morning at ten hours." His smile became even broader.

With this good news, and with the ferry scheduled to leave in less than three hours, I decided to make a U-turn and fetch my backpack. On my way back up the main road I did not meet as many people as I'd expected. I'd heard that when the *Liemba* was in town everybody headed for the port.

Saddled with my backpack I bought myself a 1.5-litre bottle of water from the general dealer. My attempt to buy a roll of toilet paper did not yield any result due to a breakdown in communication. The middle-aged woman behind the counter didn't seem to understand what I wanted. I considered miming my request – squatting, followed up with an arse-wiping gesture – but I restrained myself.

I have to confess that wanting toilet paper was kind of wishful thinking for me. In all the time I spent in Mpulungu I had not once been to the toilet; I mean properly. This was obviously the result of my eating only once a day. It was at that moment that another exceptional formula jumped into my head:

We shit so much because we eat so much.

If you eat just enough for your body to function, it is obvious that there will be no excess matter to get rid of. I couldn't understand why it had taken me so long to discover this formula. It was as brilliant as the formula (*Mpulungu – pu = Mlungu*) I had come up with three days earlier.

At the harbour I was ushered into an office where my bag was thoroughly searched by a soldier and a harbour official. Once they realised that nothing in it could hurt a fly (only a mosquito), our conversation shifted to the FIFA World Cup to be held in South Africa in 2010.

"So have the thieves and prostitutes started preparing as well?" the soldier asked out of the blue with a silly smile.

I mumbled something like "I am pretty sure it will be a safe World Cup and people will have a great time."

"So mister, do you have a souvenir for us?" the harbour official asked as I was about to walk out of the office.

"Err ... I did not know that a souvenir would be required, but since you will be coming to South Africa in 2010 I will get you a special souvenir," I said, trying to get myself out of an unexpected tight spot.

I proceeded to the immigration office after paying Harbour Management Services ZMK1000, a fee all ferry passengers had to pay, with a receipt to prove it.

On the veranda of the immigration office an official I had not seen before was busy talking on a cellphone. With the cellphone glued to his ear, he took my passport, went inside, stamped it and gave it back to me. While still laughing loudly into his cellphone, he gave me a thumbs-up.

I was officially out of Zambia, and now I could go to the ferry ticket office. What if all the tickets were sold? I ignored the worrying question as I made my way to the ferry.

It was a real challenge getting on board, unlike the first time when we all just jumped from the quayside onto the deck. Mpulungu has only one quay alongside which all ships, tugboats and ferries have to dock. Two small ships had clearly arrived first and were moored next to the quay; the *Liemba* was in the second row. So I first had to jump onto a small ship – which was being loaded with 50-kg bags of sugar – and walk across the half-closed hatch before jumping onto the ferry which lay, thank goodness, more or less at the same level as the small ship.

As I clambered aboard I heard somebody say: "Oh friend, are you ready to go? Follow me."

It was Watson, who was wearing khaki shorts and a white vest. I followed him to his office-cum-cabin. I bought myself a first-class ticket for US$62. I had no choice but to pay in US dollars. Watson informed me that because the *Liemba* was a Tanzanian ferry they only took Tanzanian shillings and US dollars. However, he assured me, I could pay with kwachas at the bar and restaurant.

Ticket in hand, I stood outside my cabin, which was right next to Watson's, and I watched fifteen boys manually loading bags of sugar from a truck named *Chief Justice* and its long trailer onto the ship next to the ferry. The young men, each with a bag on his shoulders, would run about twenty metres and dump them onto a makeshift chute which guided them into the hold of the ship. Inside the hold a few guys were stacking the bags properly. The small ship was flying a Burundian flag.

Ten o'clock, when the ferry was scheduled to leave, came and went. More passengers, carrying massive boxes, were boarding. The boxes contained mainly brown sugar, long-life milk, half-litre bottles of cooking oil and packets of lemon-cream biscuits.

Finally, when someone started taking down the white UN Refugee Agency flag, I knew that we were about to leave Mpulungu. I could hardly believe that at long last I was poised to achieve the first objective of my trip: taking a ride on the MV *Liemba*. It had taken almost ten days to get to this point. I could but hope and pray that achieving the others would not take as long, because if they did, the trip would have to last two months instead of the scheduled thirty days – of which only twenty were left.

The *Liemba* offered three different types of accommodation: third class in the front part of the ferry, which was where many of the big-luggage-carrying passengers were booked. Third class basically consisted of two halls, one for the males and the other for the females, accommodating chickens as well as people and their luggage. As to be expected, third class was very crowded but, despite such imperfect conditions, my African brothers and sisters were chatting and laughing and having a great time.

In second class, towards the stern, a cabin was shared (in theory) by six people. This section seemed equally crowded.

I was sharing a cabin in the less crowded first class with Godfrey, a Congolese national who had "a business" in Cape Town. Our cabin contained two bunker beds, a small table, a small washbasin and a narrow wardrobe. On the same level but towards the rear end of the ferry, just past the restaurant, there was an open area with white benches where the first-class passengers could relax. The cabins of the captain and the ferry's senior crew members were one flight up on the upper level, from where the ferry was steered.

After the horn was sounded – a few minutes past midday and five days late – we were off on our two-day cruise to Kigoma in Tanzania. Being flanked by a small ship and a tugboat on its left and another small ship on its right, the *Liemba* had to reverse out of a very tight spot. I guess this happened almost every time she docked at Mpulungu, for in no time she had squeezed herself out and we were really and truly leaving Mpulungu.

Phew, what a relief!

Only a small part of Lake Tanganyika belongs to Zambia. Our first stop was going to be at Kasanga, a few kilometres north, beyond the Tanzanian border.

Lake Tanganyika is said to be very deep. With an average depth of 1470 metres it is the second deepest lake in the world, after Lake Baikal in Russia. It is approximately 673 kilometres long in a north–south direction and, on average, fifty kilometres wide. Looking out over the expanse of water, I started worrying about how often the ferry, which is forever on the move, got a thorough inspection and proper maintenance.

The fact that Lake Tanganyika is so deep was not a comfortable thought to someone (me) who, although he can swim, can only do a few strokes before he needs to stand on firm ground again.

I learned to swim at the mature age of thirty-one. It was one of those things that had been on my To-Do list for ages, but I had never got round to it until I wanted to enter the reality-TV show, *Survivor South Africa*. Then I had no choice but to learn to swim.

The supervisor of the public swimming pool on the main Durban beachfront taught me. The man used to scream, yell and shout at me as if I were a child. I just had to take it – teaching the public to swim was not part of his duties. It took me about two weeks to confidently do my few strokes. As for being a contestant on *Survivor*, I was shortlisted for the first round of auditions, but since only models made it – as anybody could see when the final contestants were announced – I stood no chance.

I can say this much about swimming: it is one of those things you have to learn to do at a very young age when fear and panic do not feature in your vocabulary.

It took about two hours to get to Kasanga. Again, there was only one quayside. Mpulungu may not have the infrastructure of a modern port, but Kasanga was even worse off. A dirt road winds down to the port, which is marked by a couple of collapsing mud buildings and only one "modern" warehouse. Just as at Mpulungu, a small Burundi-registered ship named *Rwegura* was loading 50-kg bags, this time of cement. The procedure was exactly the same: a truck was parked approximately twenty metres from the ship and young boys were running with the 50-kg bags on their shoulders, dumping them onto a chute that moved them into the hold where other boys stacked them properly. The only difference was the cement dust flying about every time a bag was dumped, either on the chute or inside the hatch. I really felt sorry for the bare-chested youngsters in their loose trousers working barefoot in a cloud of cement dust inside the hold. Not one of them was wearing a mask to protect their respiratory system. In Kasanga occupational health was clearly still a foreign concept.

While passengers were jumping onto the *Rwegura* and then the *Liemba*, I saw from the corner of my eye someone handing out forms. It was a Tanzanian immigration official. After he had finished distributing the forms he moved to one of the first-class cabins which served as his office.

You can be sure of one thing when travelling in African countries: things are often done in a very casual and informal way. Just imagine if I had been standing somewhere else and no one had told me that an immigration official had come on board. I would probably have arrived in Kigoma without a stamp. But would it have made a difference? If the ferry had left on Friday as scheduled and I hadn't needed an extension I would in all probability have left Mpulungu without being stamped out, simply because I didn't know there was an immigration office there.

The queue of people outside the cabin where the immigration official had set up his office was surprisingly short. It baffled me, because I knew both Zambians entering Tanzania and Tanzanians returning home had to be stamped in. This meant that the majority of people on board the *Liemba* could not be bothered to jump through the hoops. There were just a handful of us law-abiding stooges.

When my turn came I handed the official a completed immigration form, my passport and US$50, which I knew was expected of South African passport holders when entering Tanzania.

"Oh! Dr Khumalo. Where is the other Dr Khumalo?" He was obviously referring to the soccer player. God knows how tired I am of being asked about South Africa's retired soccer hero. I cannot wait for the day *he* hands over his passport and is asked by an immigration official, "So where is Sihle Khumalo?"

It is all sour grapes and envy, I know, but this Doctor Khumalo thing got me so worked up that I completely forgot to ask the immigration official if my Tanzanian visa would allow me into Uganda, since the two countries, along with Kenya, Rwanda and Burundi, form the East African Community.

The stamp in my passport gave me until 1 January 2009 – about eighty days, not thirty as I had expected.

Within an hour the *Liemba* was reversing out of the port of Kasanga. Remembering that Tanzania was on GMT +3, I adjusted the time on my watch accordingly, which reminded me how arbitrary and unnatural official time-keeping is.

It all started in 1675 when King Charles II (famous for his large number of illegitimate children) appointed John Flamsteed as director of the Royal Greenwich Observatory to "apply himself with the exact care and diligence to the rectifying of the tables of the motion of the heavens, and the places of the fixed stars, so as to find out so much desired longitude of places for the erecting of the art of navigation".

However, different countries continued to use their own time and point of reference until 1851, when astronomers agreed on recognising an international meridian as passing through Greenwich. At an 1884 conference in Washington DC it was accepted that world time would be introduced using the Greenwich meridian line, and thus we still use Greenwich Meridian Time (GMT). The centre of the Earth – from a longitudinal perspective – is therefore nothing else but an arbitrary line which was agreed on by a few conference goers.

As the *Liemba* moved north an incredible view unfolded: on our right was the Tanzanian coastline covered in short bush and sprinkled with villages; and on our left, far on the horizon, I could make out the undulating hills of the Democratic Republic of the Congo. Above us stretched unending blue African sky, right into infinity. Most of Lake Tanganyika belongs to these two countries – 45 per cent to the DRC and 41 per cent to

Tanzania; the remaining 14 per cent to Zambia and Burundi. The *Liemba*, however, travelled through Tanzanian waters only, so we cruised closer to the Tanzanian shore.

Having made it into Tanzania and with everything so serene, I decided to give Lulu a call. I dialled her number, it rang and she answered. We had just started talking when we were cut off. I checked the screen; the ferry had moved out of cellphone range.

I had read that there would be points where the ferry would stop "in the middle of the lake", but nothing could prepare me for our next stop – at a village about a hundred metres away on the shore. There was no harbour and passengers and goods had to be paddled to the ferry. Small boats just lined up anywhere alongside the ship and passengers leapt aboard from the boats, wildly bobbing up and down. To me it looked a very dangerous exercise, but the passengers and crews were clearly used to doing things this way. Middle-aged women, youngsters and men in formal attire jumped with equal ease. I felt like a real fuddy-duddy travelling in first class.

There was a lot of screaming and shouting as passengers wanted the one and only crane to lift their bags with agricultural produce onto the deck. After about thirty minutes the horn was sounded and the fleet of local boats started moving away. We were on our way again.

It now made sense to me why the ferry's schedule was so erratic. Stopping at different villages cannot be done according to a strict time schedule. It all depends on how busy the villages are. The ferry's captain, who had a bird's eye view of most of the activities on and alongside the ferry, simply gauged when everybody who wanted to jump on board had done so before blasting the horn to signal the ferry's departure.

With a late-afternoon sun reflecting red on the still waters of the lake, a refreshing breeze blowing on my face and the sound of the engines and of water being pierced by the keel of the ferry in my ears, it really felt great to be on the *Liemba*. Sitting on the steps leading to the captain and senior crewmen's cabins on the upper level, I started thinking about the goals I had set myself while in Mpulungu. It was one of those rare moments when you take an objective and frank look at your life and admit to yourself that, good as it has been, it could have been far better. Generally I was not all that happy about what a guy like me with huge potential had *not* achieved at the age of thirty-three, which included:

- financial freedom (not living from month to month, watching the budget like a seagull watches the sea);
- emotional stability (not being in any doubt about what I would do if Janet Jackson were to ask me to move in with her);
- spiritual fulfilment (that "thing" that keeps eluding me);
- physical fitness (being able to run the 21.1-km half-marathon again without dropping dead).

Having that "me" time on the *Liemba* made me realise once again that I hate it when life happens to me. I hate the business of busyness. I want, at all times, to happen to life. I have an obsession about shaping my own life instead of forever reacting to what life presents me with. The reason why we are constantly so busy is that we are always responding and reacting to what life throws at us rather than throwing things at life.

By the time I stopped thinking about my not-so-bad-but-could-be-far-better life, it was dark. A full moon had started to rise above the horizon. It was turning out to be a perfect night. I wandered towards the stern for a better view of the sky.

I had been standing there for a while when I was joined by a Congolese national by the name of Sampiece. He told me he was travelling from Lubumbashi – the DRC's second-largest town down in the south – to Goma in the east of the country. He had opted for the ferry in the absence of road or rail transport within the DRC. He was afraid to travel by air (the DRC has one of the worst aviation records in the world) and, anyway, air travel was too expensive.

For Sampiece the chaos in the DRC meant that to get from Lubumbashi to Goma he first had to travel south to Zambia by road through the chaotic Kasumbalesa border. From Ndola, the capital of the Copperbelt, he had to take a bus north-east to Mpulungu, and from there the ferry to Kigoma up north in Tanzania. From Kigoma he'd catch another ferry to the DRC port of Uvira, right at the top end of Lake Tanganyika, and from Uvira a bus to Bukavu. The last leg of the trip was another ferry from Bukavu, at the southern tip of Lake Kivu, to Goma on the northern shore of the lake. When I asked how long it took to do the whole Lubumbashi–Ndola–Mpulungu–Kigoma–Uvira–Bukavu–Goma trip (about 1 150 kilometres as the crow flies) his response was: "It depends."

If one looks at the history of the DRC, one cannot help but ask what its people did to deserve such a tragic fate. It is Africa's third-largest country and was run as King Leopold II of Belgium's personal fiefdom for twenty-three years (1885–1908), during which time it is estimated that vast quantities of ivory and rubber were removed and up to fifteen million people died as a result of exploitation and disease.

The country was a colony of Belgium for fifty-two years (1908–1960). Its first elected leader after independence, Patrice Lumumba, was deposed and assassinated as a result of a CIA plot supported by the Belgians. The country soon descended into full-scale civil war as the rich Katanga region in the south seceded and then other regions tried to assert their independence. This so-called Congo Crisis cost the lives of more than 100 000 people. Amidst the confusion Joseph-Désiré Mobutu (better known as Mobutu Sese Seko) gained control through a coup with the help of the Americans and renamed the country Zaire. Mobutu consolidated his power by arresting, torturing and killing his political opponents and people who did not want to toe the line. Former prime minister Evariste Kimba and three other cabinet members, for example, were hanged in front of a cheering crowd of 50 000 people in Kinshasa. Throughout his reign of terror Mobutu's relationship with the US remained cosy, President Reagan publicly calling him "a voice of good sense and goodwill".

Under Mobutu the economy of Zaire virtually collapsed, the infrastructure deteriorated and corruption skyrocketed. Mobutu himself amassed monumental wealth before he was overthrown in 1997 by Laurent-Désiré Kabila, whose son, Joseph, is now president of the country renamed the DRC (Democratic Republic of the Congo). While leader of the People's Revolutionary Party, Laurent Kabila was assisted by Yoweri Museveni (now president of Uganda) and Paul Kagame (now president of Rwanda).

There was soon a fallout between Laurent Kabila and his friends, Rwanda and Uganda. It led to the Second Congo War, sometimes called Africa's Great War, because at one stage a combined force of DRC, Angolan, Namibian and Zimbabwean troops were fighting Rwandan and Ugandan forces.

If the DRC had enjoyed effective, efficient and corruption-free leadership after independence, it would, despite the brutality of its colonial past, be Africa's economic powerhouse today – considering how rich it is in resources such as copper, gold and diamonds. But from my experiences as a member of my company's exploration team there, I know for sure this will not happen in the next hundred years. The sad reality of our continent is that most of us know what needs to be done, but politicians are busy reading speeches in conferences and extraordinary summits while lining their pockets because, when all is said and done, they do not give a shit about the man or woman living in a village somewhere in the bundu.

Needless to say, I felt deeply sympathetic towards Sampiece, although communicating with him in a language that was not the first language of either of us was a challenge. After our conversation and our dismal reflections on the future of Mama Africa (the cradle of humankind *nogal*), I could no longer say it was a perfect night. But I was very glad to have met Sampiece.

Shortly after 22:00 we stopped at the next village, and as per the usual procedure local boats appeared from nowhere after a horn blast from the *Liemba*. There were about seven small boats bringing more passengers and agricultural produce. An hour later we were heading north again.

Peeping through the window the following morning confirmed that we had another glorious day in store. As I left our cabin – with Godfrey, my cabin mate, still in dreamland – I bumped into Watson.

"How many stops does the ferry make between Mpulungu and Kigoma?" I asked.

"Seventeen," he answered matter-of-factly.

"So how do the people from all these villages know when the ferry will arrive?"

"They know the schedule," he said, again matter-of-factly.

I had to conclude that whether the ferry was three days late was not an issue with the locals at all. As long as it pitched up – even after a couple of days – and picked them up with their chickens and sweet potatoes and whatever else they carried in their bags and boxes, all was well.

I spent the day hanging around on deck while the ferry stopped at different villages along the shore. Later in the afternoon a very sick woman was brought on board and put down in the open area just outside the bar-restaurant. Godfrey, who could speak Swahili and found it easy to chat with the people on board, told me that she was on her way to the hospital in Kigoma. She was given some water, which was a good idea, I thought, because she looked very exhausted and dehydrated. But I noticed that trying to swallow even a small sip was a struggle for her. From her facial expression it was clear that she was experiencing excruciating pain.

The same helpless feeling that I experienced after my conversation with Sampieçe descended on me. To think that a sick woman had to wait for a ferry that was running a few days late in order to go to a government hospital which was probably inadequately resourced …

I decided to visit the bar to prevent me from stressing too much about all the challenges facing Africa. I wanted to taste Balimi beer because it had the highest alcohol percentage – 5.8 per cent. When the barman told me that the Balimi was not cold, I decided to try the Serengeti Premium Lager. The label did not give the alcohol content; it only said "Medium beer: store in a cool and dark place". So I settled for the Safari Lager (5.5 per cent alcohol). I had only one bottle because it was lukewarm – not cold as the barman had promised – but then there is no scientific, universally accepted definition of a cold beer.

Later that evening I made the acquaintance of Barbara and Michael from Berlin and Stuttgart respectively. Michael had been so fascinated by a German TV documentary on the history of the *Liemba* that he decided to come to Tanzania to take a ride on the world-famous ferry. It used to be called *Graf von Götzen* after the governor general of German East Africa, Gustav Adolf Graf von Götzen, he told me. Apparently the *Graf von Götzen*, which was supposed to transport people and cargo, was also used for surprise attacks on the allied forces during World War I. With the allied forces gaining ground and the Germans retreating, the commander decided, rather than letting his prize ship fall into the hands of the enemy, to sink it deliberately by allowing water into the hull. The three engineers instructed to sink the vessel, however, covered the engines with a thick layer of grease instead and filled the hull with sand before carefully sending her to the bottom of the lake off the mouth of the Malagarasi River, so that she could be salvaged later. This explains why the *Graf von Götzen* was in relatively good shape when the British found her at the bottom of the lake eight years later, in 1924. Within three years she was back in service as the *MV Liemba*.

Michael, after seeing the documentary, wrote about his dream on the internet. Barbara read the piece and got hooked as well. They made contact and booked their air tickets to Dar es Salaam before even meeting face to face. They met in Stuttgart only three weeks before embarking on their twenty-five-day Tanzanian adventure.

Now that is what I call advenspontaneity (being adventurous and spontaneous at the same time).

I went to bed after midnight, having taken in a last few draughts of fresh air while looking at the passengers sleeping next to their luggage and live chickens on top of the hold.

I had not been asleep for long when Godfrey woke me with the words: "Hey Khumalo, we're in Kigoma."

Much as I would have loved to sleep for another hour or two, I greatly welcomed the news that we'd arrived – forty-four hours after leaving hot and humid Mpulungu. I peered out of the window before stepping into the corridor. I could not believe how green it was, even in the dim early-morning light. There was a small hill on the side of the port entrance which dominated the view, but I could barely make out the houses near the port because of the lush trees and shrubs.

It was time to say goodbye to Godfrey. I promised that I would give him a call in Cape Town once I was back in South Africa. When I did I was told that the number did not exist. I'm not sure whether I made a mistake while writing down his number or whether he deliberately gave me a wrong number – which is unlikely. Anyway, I lost contact with Godfrey. It would have been nice to visit him when in the Mother City.

One thing I have learned from using public transport in African countries is never to lose your ticket. I saw how diligent the ticket examiners were on the train from Bulawayo to Victoria Falls, checking tickets throughout the night. Not to mention the Lusaka–Mpulungu bus. As we disembarked from the *Liemba* we were requested to show our tickets to a lady and gentleman. Passengers who had "lost their tickets" were asked to stand aside.

Since I had my ticket ready, getting off the ferry was a breeze. I followed the other passengers, showing my yellow-fever certificate to the port health officer before proceeding to the next kiosk where I was asked by the immigration official to take off my dark sunglasses. He checked my passport and looked me up and down and then waved me into the country that was once called Tanganyika.

I looked back at the passengers screaming and shouting while trying to remove their stuff from the *Liemba*'s hold, and scribbled on my notepad: *It was worth the five-day wait. I will probably do it again in the not-so-distant future.*

Mission number one was accomplished. Next on the list was a visit to Kigali.

Kigoma

Outside the main gate quite a few taxis were waiting for customers. I presumed they were waiting for specific people because they did not harass any of the passengers walking past.

I followed passengers who had told me they were on their way to the railway station. Along the very bad road shacks had been erected and women were cooking on open fires. I was again struck by the casual way in which most African towns seem to be run and by how green everything looked, especially the huge hill opposite the harbour entrance.

After a brisk fifteen-minute walk we came to a huge white building with a colonial feel where the guy I had asked for directions outside the port was waiting for me. "Hey, mister!" he said as I got closer and, pointing at the white building, added, "This is the station."

I felt touched. He had carefully explained the way to me before walking ahead fast with his pals to make sure I did not get lost. After gesturing goodbye to me he picked up his bag and with his two friends crossed the road to a busy taxi rank.

It is one of the things which make me love Africa more every time I encounter it: despite the poverty, disease and suffering, people still have *ubuntu*. How I wished I had this kind of time for strangers instead of chasing success as defined by our capitalist society!

The plan was to buy two Central Line train tickets – one-way tickets from Kigoma to Tabora and another one from Tabora to Mwanza. The Central Line, as the name suggests, runs from the west through central Tanzania to Dar es Salaam on the east coast, passing through Tabora, Dodoma and Morogoro on the way. I wanted to stop over in Tabora because I'd read that you could board an overnight train there to Mwanza on the shore of Lake Victoria. According to the same source the Central Line left Kigoma at 18:00 three times a week: Tuesday, Thursday and Sunday. It being a Thursday morning, my timing was perfect.

After buying the tickets I planned to visit the Livingstone Memorial in the village of Ujiji on the outskirts of Kigoma, where Stanley met the Scottish missionary in November 1871. Afterwards I would return to the train station in time to catch the train to Tabora. So after all the anxiety and inconvenience that the long wait for the *Liemba* had caused me, things were looking up. (I never seem to learn that the most elaborate plans I make come to nothing, hey?)

There were already a few passengers queuing in front of a closed window. To double-check in advance, I asked the security guard if there was indeed a train to Tabora that afternoon. He did not speak a word of English, so he led me to an office with "Assistant Station Master" written on the door. A man in a uniform, presumably the assistant station master, was about to leave the office. He told me that first-class tickets should be booked at least two weeks in advance.

Ag no! I was still trying to think what options were left, given Tanzania's reportedly bad roads, especially in the western part of the country, when he said, "You can't just rock up and expect a first-class ticket to be waiting for you. However, if you'll settle for a third-class ticket, I'm sure you can still get one."

After my Zimbabwean experience this was a rather disturbing suggestion. The man must have seen my inner consternation on my face for as he walked away he said, "You can talk to the station master next door. Maybe he can help you."

I had read somewhere that you can get first-class tickets at the last minute if you're willing "to talk nicely" to the senior officials at the station. A few dollars extra would not hurt anyone, I decided.

The cleaning lady told me that the station master had stepped out for a minute; I could wait for him in the corridor. While counting the minutes I noticed a proudly displayed plaque: BEST KEPT STATION 1965. I looked around. Grass was growing between the lines; some tracks looked rusty. The last time the place was looked after must have been as part of the preparations for the 1965 audit, I thought. Suddenly it was not such a comforting prospect that I was going to spend two nights on a train from Kigoma to Mwanza via Tabora.

I had been waiting outside the station master's office for about ten minutes when an older man in uniform walked past. The station master should be back in the office in about half an hour, he reassured me. One question led to the next, and he told me that the train scheduled to leave that Thursday would only be leaving the next afternoon.

The news was worrying but it was not the end of the world. It meant spending one night in Kigoma. When travelling by public transport, flexibility is the name of the game. Accepting things, especially things you cannot change, is part of the deal. For (re)planning purposes, I thought I should ask him a few logistical questions.

"What time does the train leave Kigoma?" I began.

"Five or eleven."

It took me a few seconds to ask my second question.

"Are there two trains?"

"No, the same train leaves at five or eleven."

Only then did it click that he was giving both the English and Swahili time, something I should have remembered from previous confusing experiences. According to Swahili time you start counting at six in the morning. So when it is 07:00 (universal time), Swahili time is one in the morning, and when it is 08:00 according to universal time, it is two Swahili time. Come to think of it, you start counting Swahili time in the early evening: 18:00 our time is midnight for the Swahilis.

The man told me that the train usually arrives at Tabora at two in the morning (Swahili time). Out of curiosity, I asked him why the train, which was scheduled to leave that afternoon, was delayed for the whole day.

"It was involved in an accident somewhere near Morogoro."

Oh. Was it possible to travel by road from Kigoma straight to Mwanza, I asked him next.

"Yes, there is a bus which travels straight to Mwanza. Go and enquire at Mwanga Centre," he said, pointing towards town. Mwanga Centre, I discovered, was an informal business area about two kilometres from the city centre.

It was then that I decided to move to Plan F: take a bus directly to Mwanza instead of a train via Tabora. I left the station knowing that, however atrocious the roads in Tanzania were supposed to be, I was still better off on a bus going straight to Mwanza than on a late, accident-prone train.

I walked up the main street of Kigoma under a scorching sun. Near Mwanga Centre the street became very steep for someone carrying more than ninety kilograms of his own weight plus a backpack.

I was slowly but surely coming to terms with the fact that I would be spending the night in Kigoma. So as I huffed and puffed up the hill I started to check the availability, suitability and cost of different lodges along the way.

The first lodge, Mapinduzi, although signposted on the street, was set back from the main road. After I was shown a room in a U-shaped building with a corrugated-iron roof, I knew that I could get something better for TZS10 000 (about US$10), which is what they would be charging me.

I soldiered on, now sweating like a pig. Next I checked the rooms at Kigoma Hotel. Their self-contained rooms with TV were TZS12 000. Maybe I could get something like this for 10 000 shillings, I thought. So the search continued.

It was a really long walk to Mwanga Centre, up what looked like an unendingly steep hill. I stopped to view a room at Zanzibar Lodge, but they said they were fully booked. The lady at reception kindly referred me to Mwanga Lodge, about a hundred metres further up the road.

For TZS12 000 I could get a self-contained room with double bed, clean white sheets, ceiling fan, not-so-clean-but-not-so-dirty-either toilet, a shower and a TV with a 37-cm screen. The receptionist told me that, a further 500 metres up the road, I would find the reservations office of Adventure Connection, the bus company that does the direct Kigoma–Mwanza route.

What luck! I checked in and dropped my bag in my room.

Experience had taught me that buying a bus ticket without seeing the actual bus could be disastrous, so when I eventually got to Adventure Connection's small kiosk I again asked the bus representative if theirs was a comfortable bus.

"Yes. Look, there it is," he said, pointing to a photo of the nineteen-*voetsek* skoroskoro, an ugly, ancient-looking bus on the wall. From the picture alone I knew that it was definitely going to be a very uncomfortable ride. The good news, however, was that approximately fourteen hours after leaving Kigoma I would be in Mwanza.

The price, TZS30 000, felt a bit steep, especially for such a dilapidated-looking bus. Since my attempts to change ZMK200 000 to Tanzanian shillings on the ferry had been unsuccessful, I would have to try selling the kwachas. I nevertheless booked a ticket for the following day and promised to pay and collect the ticket later the same afternoon.

Having booked accommodation as well as a bus to Mwanza, I walked back to town with a smile on my face, especially since it was a matter of just rolling downhill for two kilometres. The first bureau de change turned me down, telling me they didn't take Zambian kwachas. I tried a local bank, where the lady at enquiries told me that they didn't take any African currencies at all.

It was slowly dawning on me that having Zambian kwachas, especially in Kigoma, was more of a liability than an asset. Whilst looking for another bank on the main street, I spotted the sign "Bayport Financial Services" on a modern white building on the opposite side.

I asked three guys lounging outside whether Bayport Financial Services offered a foreign-exchange service. Without even answering my question, a guy with a severe skin problem (read: acne galore) said that he could take me to his friend who dealt in forex.

"Are you okay with the black market, black man?" he asked me in a tongue-in-the-cheek manner.

"Sure." Truth be told, I was starting to be desperate in my attempt to get rid of those kwachas and couldn't care less how poor the rate was as long I could lay my hands on some Tanzanian shillings.

Leaving his two companions in front of Bayport Financial Services, I followed Mr Nice-Guy-with-not-such-a-nice-skin through a maze of informal stalls just off the main street.

As we were weaving our way between the stalls I kept thinking to myself I would never have managed to penetrate such a complicated web of small alleys by myself. The different stalls sold everything from electrical appliances and DVDs to garments and spices.

Mr Acne Galore's friend ran a DVD stall. The minute it was mentioned that I had kwachas, the incutra told me straight: "I deal only in hard currency like pounds, euros and dollars; not some Mickey Mouse currency like kwachas."

So we resumed our search for guys who dealt in forex. We stopped at various stalls, but nobody wanted to take the kwachas. On the sixth attempt, when we were about to give up, we came across two guys in a DVD stall who were willing to exchange my kwachas for Tanzanian shillings.

I had calculated earlier that for ZNK200 000 I should get TZS58 000. However, seeing that nobody wanted to take kwachas, I figured that even

50 000 would be fine. So when one of the guys said, after using a calculator, that they would give me TZS56 000 I was over the moon.

As we were walking back through the maze of stalls I decided to give Mr Acne Galore TZS6 000 for his trouble. I was really grateful for his help. Back in front of Bayport Financial Services, as I was about to hand over the money to him, he, however, said that he wanted us to "do business" and asked where I was staying.

On the spot I decided he was not going to get any money from me, never mind business. I was booked at Zanzibar Hill Lodge, I told him, remembering a signpost I had seen earlier pointing to the other side of town.

"My name is Benga," he said, shaking my hand.

"I am Alfred." I had to continue lying.

"What time will you be back at Zanzibar Hill Lodge?"

"I should be there just after four this afternoon. See you then," I told him with a straight face. I genuinely wanted to thank him, but the last thing I wanted was to have a stranger come to where I was staying for some business, whatever that business was. I really have a problem with that kind of thing.

I spent an hour in an internet café just to update myself on developments in the rest of the world. My five-day stay in Mpulungu had isolated me to such an extent that I didn't have a clue what was happening elsewhere. I was shocked to see how the rand had deteriorated against the US dollar. It was now R10.19, whereas two weeks earlier it had been R8.70, and even then I had thought it was a bad rate. The turmoil in global markets, accompanied by the plunging of the equity markets worldwide, seemed to be accelerating.

After enjoying half a litre of ice-cold Coca-Cola and two cookies on the veranda of the general dealer next to the internet café, it was time to head out to Ujiji, six kilometres to the south of Kigoma.

The taxi rank was right next to the 1965-award-winning-best-kept train station. I could not miss the taxis going to Ujiji because they were boldly marked on the front with KIGOMA–UJIJI.

While loading the taxi with passengers, the assistant driver told me that it would cost me TZS300 to Livingstone Memorial Centre and that he would show me where to jump off.

The taxi left the rank about three-quarters full. I had not taken a taxi for about two years and it felt strangely empty. By the time we reached the steep part of the hill before Mwanga Centre, however, the taxi kept stopping to pick up passengers on the side of the road, and soon it was filled to capacity. All of a sudden it made sense why the taxi would leave the rank before it was full: nobody wanted to walk up that hill. It suddenly also made sense why the taxi had such an unusually high ceiling: passengers who didn't have seats simply stood.

Since I had been one of the last passengers to board at the central taxi rank, I was seated next to the door and all new passengers were squeezing in next to me, encroaching on my personal space. I didn't mind, however, because a woman with big twins (read: boobs) happened to stand behind me, hitting me hard on my head in a soft and soothing manner every time the taxi went over a bump, or, even more enjoyable, through a pothole. Naturally I found myself leaning back in order to get more severe beatings from the twins. For the first time I regretted not getting a haircut back in South Africa. If I had a clean-shaven head, nothing would have softened the nipple blows.

Just after Mwanga Centre some passengers, including the well-endowed woman behind me, got out and we continued on a good tarmac road to Ujiji. By the time we got there only a handful of us were left in the taxi.

I found Ujiji to be more laid-back than Kigoma, and more people were dressed in the Islamic fashion. At the spot where the driver made a u-turn to go back to Kigoma, the assistant driver told me to step out for the Livingstone Memorial Centre.

I started off down Livingstone Road in the direction pointed out to me. I walked for about a kilometre past dilapidated corrugated-iron-roofed buildings on both sides of the road until I saw a small grey building sign-posted: LIVINGSTONE MEMORIAL MONUMENT.

Inside the building I was greeted and welcomed by a short, thin, elderly black man, dressed in a grey safari suit. As we were walking towards the monument, which marks the place where Stanley met Livingstone under a mango tree on 10 November 1871, the old man explained to me that the flight of stairs leading up to the monument was where the shores of Lake Tanganyika used to be when Stanley and Livingstone had their historic meeting. "The lake has since retreated about six hundred metres to where it is today," he said. Soon we were standing at the spot where Stanley is supposed to have uttered the famous words: "Dr Livingstone, I presume."

In the museum next door to the monument there was a papier-mâché sculpture of the meeting between Stanley and Livingstone. The fifty-eight-year-old Livingstone was already a very ill man at the time. The old man who was taking me around the memorial told me a lot about Livingstone in a high-pitched voice which I struggled to understand. It sounded as if he was reciting a poem that he had crammed into his head and had to repeat as quickly as possible before he forgot it.

He insisted that it was Livingstone's efforts that had led to the abolition of slavery. I knew that Livingstone's biggest achievement was to bring to the attention of the rest of the world the shocking and inhuman slave trade on the eastern side of the continent. His explorations helped to open the "dark" continent to other missionaries and to British colonialism. In the course of his long and arduous journeys, covering almost 48 000 kilometres, he followed the Zambezi River to its source and was the first European to see the Victoria Falls as well as Lake Malawi.

It is interesting that Livingstone, who was not only an explorer and a geographer but an anthropologist, botanist, ethnologist, astronomer and medical missionary, died feeling that he had not accomplished much. He had, after all, failed to discover the source of the Nile and had not managed to convert all that many Africans to Christianity, which had presumably been his primary objective when he first arrived in Africa.

What I found particularly interesting was the story of Livingstone's porters, Chumi, a freed slave, and Susi, a former woodcutter. After Livingstone's death on 1 May 1873 in Chitambo village near Ilala in present-day Zambia, these two men carried his body for hundreds of kilometres over a period of nine months to Bagamoyo on the East African coast. Chumi and Susi attended Livingstone's funeral in Westminster Abbey and made headlines in the British press. They were heroes and celebrities in London, but the minute they returned to their motherland they were forgotten. Their own dates of death and places of burial are unknown.

I took a taxi back to Kigoma, paid for my Adventure Connection bus ticket, and decided to retreat to my room before my business-minded friend found me dawdling on the streets. As I walked back to Mwanga Lodge

I noticed that almost all the shops had generators on their verandas or just outside their premises.

When I got to my room there was no electricity.

"They normally switch the power off during the day. It will be back on just after sunset," the lady at reception explained.

I passed the time by lying on the bed, trying to enjoy a not-so-fresh muffin and warmish Fanta I had bought on my way back. Just after sunset the electricity did come back on, and soon thereafter there was a call to prayer from a nearby mosque.

The chanting can be very irritating, especially if you're not used to it. I have never been to a mosque and do not know how the muezzin who calls on the loudspeaker is selected, but to me those guys sound off-key.

After scribbling some notes on my notepad, I decided to call it a day; I would have to get up quite early the following morning. I phoned Lulu and we agreed she would ring me as soon as she returned from the doctor the next day. I found it difficult to sleep because of the thoughts that kept coming to my mind about the slave trade and other things. Places like Bagamoyo outside Dar es Salaam, Ujiji and Tabora were holding centres for slaves in the eighteenth and part of the nineteenth century. The slave trade on the eastern side of the continent was in the hands of Arabs long before the Europeans started colonising Africa. Which is why I find it strange that we Africans are forever going on about colonialism and how Europeans ill-treated our forefathers, while people who practised chaining, whipping, selling, dehumanising and degrading Africans are considered our "brothers in arms".

I was also thinking about the irony that I, a black African travelling to another African country, was so fascinated by white explorers of two centuries ago. This put an intriguing question in my mind.

QUESTION 3: Were there any black explorers and, if there were, who were they and where did they go and what did they do?

Would it not be nice for us, as Africans, to have been able to go to Europe, Asia, the Americas, wherever, and visit lakes, rivers, waterfalls and mountains that we could later claim were discovered by African explorers? We Africans seem to be obsessed with our own comfort zone. Pushing limits and taking a step into the unknown is one big mission and not something we seem to do willingly.

It was now clear to me – with all due respect – why King Shaka, the founder of the Zulu nation, decided to fight and conquer clans on the other side of the hill and river instead of building a raft and paddling across the open seas with his Zulu warriors to conquer whoever they came across. He was choosing the easier option.

We are still stuck in the comfort zone, which explains why we are more comfortable being employees than employers. Even when we do take the risk of owning businesses we do it by using a "special-purpose vehicle" (money lent to us by the very company in which we are buying stakes). In the process, politically well-connected individuals become instant millionaires by "owning" a stake in an established "white" company. Amen.

These thoughts proved eventually to be sleep-inducing. Apart from being very comfortable, my bed was the first four-poster bed on the trip, which meant that the mosquito net hung straight down and didn't touch me. Not that I would have minded; it was squeaky clean. With the fan going all night, I had a good sleep.

The alarm clock woke me up against my wishes. Although it was 04:30, (or ten-thirty Swahili time), my biological clock was still working according to South African time, which was 03:30 and just too early to rise. I nevertheless dragged myself from the wonderful bed, packed my bag and left my room exactly at five. As I locked the door the next call to prayer rang out from the nearby mosque. I must honestly say I found it presumptuous – why must the whole town know when you're going to pray?

The noise did not disturb the security guard at reception, however, and I had to wake him. While he stared at me in a dazed and confused way, I handed him my room key.

North-east with Adventure Connection

T he second I stepped into the poorly lit main street of Kigoma, I knew that I should have made an arrangement for a cab to pick me up. The poorly-lit streets were absolutely deserted: no cars, no pedestrians, just the dead quiet of very early morning. I took a few steps and then checked if anybody was following me. It was the first time on the trip that I felt terrified. I was so scared I could feel and hear my own heart pounding in my chest. The fifteen-minute walk to Mwanga Centre felt like an hour. When I eventually turned into the bus rank I saw a handful of people. Although there were other buses, only the Adventure Connection bus had its engine running.

The bus was pretty basic but not as shabby as I had expected from the photograph on the wall of the Adventure Connection kiosk. My backpack was loaded into the belly of the bus. I boarded and my ticket was checked. I had pre-booked an aisle seat – H3.

We left at 06:00, thirty minutes late. After joining the main road we took a left as if going to Ujiji. But after another kilometre or so, we took another left. We were cruising on such a good tar road that I could not understand why Tanzania was renowned for its bad roads.

Ten minutes later we were on gravel. The windows started rattling and I could immediately tell the bus had no shock absorbers. The whole vehicle was shaking uncontrollably, with the result that my whole body, especially my big tummy, wiggled like set jelly. The rattling got so bad that I was convinced that the windows, roof and sides would just fall off and that we passengers would find ourselves seated on the undercarriage, convertible-style. It continued like this for two hours until we got to Kasulu, where more passengers were squeezed in.

Although most buildings in Kasulu had old rusty corrugated-iron roofs, there were signs that it had once been a thriving town. We passed Nairobi Shopping Centre and the Jamaica shop. With passengers now standing in the aisle because there were not enough seats available, and with the weather starting to warm up, it got very stuffy.

Soon after the small town we came across a 4×4 lying on its side in the road. There were also two banged-up bicycles at the side of the road and a person lying next to one of them. Our bus slowed down but did not stop, even though it looked like the accident had just happened and pedestrians were still running to the accident scene.

A few kilometres later the road deteriorated even further and to make things worse, an increasing number of people were riding bicycles on the side. Neither the state of the road nor the number of cyclists made the bus driver slow down. When the road got even worse, he started zigzagging in an attempt to miss the huge potholes. Although I love adventure, the way the bus driver was carrying on was making me very uncomfortable; it was stupid and downright dangerous. It felt like an accident was waiting to happen at any moment.

More or less two hours after leaving Kasulu, and four hours after leaving Kigoma, the bus stopped in the middle of nowhere. It was time for passengers to go for a pee. The procedure, although I was now used to it, still fascinated me: males and females going in opposite directions in a synchronised fashion which, to a stranger like me, looked rehearsed. Since I did not know when the bus would stop again, I decided to join the ranks of the males.

As I disembarked I realised that two of the passengers were carrying AK-47 rifles, each with three magazines of ammunition tied together with an elastic band. It disturbed me a bit. No, it disturbed me a lot. I could hardly do the necessary.

When I got back into the bus I saw that both were sitting in front, just behind the driver. Now I was feeling doubly unsafe. Firstly, because of the speed we were travelling on the terrible road. Secondly, the fact that the bus was being protected by AK-47-wielding young men meant that Adventure Connection was aware of danger I had been oblivious to. At that moment I felt that maybe taking a train, even if it had meant paying a bribe, might not have been a bad idea after all. More so because I remembered just then reading back in South Africa that the situation in north-western Tanzania was not considered stable – because of the region's proximity to Burundi.

My body was still going through some intense vibrating when we stopped for a ten-minute break at Kibondo, another rural town with old rusted corrugated-iron roofs that had enjoyed a heyday some time ago.

There was only one modern building, Pentagon Hotel, in the collection of run-down buildings, most of which housed general dealers.

Seven hours after we'd left Kigoma (which felt more like fourteen on that indescribable road), we pulled into Biharamulo, the turn-off for Benacco and the Rusumu border post between Tanzania and Rwanda.

I prefer, whenever possible, to cross borders in a bus that will take me from a town in one country to a town in another country. I really dislike it when I have to change buses or taxis right at the border post, because amongst other things it means changing money from incutras who, if you are not careful, will give you counterfeit money. Besides, it makes ultimate sense to cross into a country like Rwanda in the company of other people. Which is why I decided to go all the way to Mwanza on the southern shore of Lake Victoria, from where I would attempt to find a bus doing the Mwanza–Kigali route. It meant, however, that I would be doing the Biharamulo–Mwanza section of the road twice, as I would have to return along the same road to get to Kigali via the Rusumu border.

In the meantime we, the passengers, were taking a well-deserved break at Biharamulo, while one of the assistants was crawling around underneath the bus trying to fix or sort out something. Just over twenty minutes later, once everybody was back on board, the bus driver attempted to restart the engine. Nothing happened. After several attempts and much shaking of the driver's head, it was quite clear that the assistant driver-cum-mechanic would have to dive back underneath. Another quarter of an hour and he re-emerged. The driver attempted to restart the engine. He tried three times with no result. It was only on the fourth attempt that the engine spluttered into life. Some passengers clapped in joy and celebration.

Just less than a kilometre from Biharamulo, we came to a T-junction and a sign that said: "Turn left for Benacco/Rwanda. Turn right for Mwanza". Naturally we turned right and, wow, we joined a tar road again. Now I could sit back and relax and, even better, get some sleep.

But a mere thirty minutes later the bus turned right in an easterly direction (continuing on the tar road would have taken us to Nzega where we didn't want to go), and it was back to the whole-body-vibrating thing. What I found strange was that the guy next to me had been sleeping pretty much all the way from Kigoma, while I was having a really hard time. And I wasn't even sitting in one the back seats right above the rear wheels – those poor passengers were taking all the strain.

Looking at the green scenery outside I could not help but wonder why Tanzania did not have a strong agricultural sector to produce and export food to other countries. Everywhere I looked it was green. Another thing I found odd was the collapsing roofs of many thatched houses, while the occupants were living right next to dense bush with tall grass which looked very much like thatching grass to me.

I expected Mwanza to be two, three hours from Biharamulo. I was wrong. We had been on the road for more than three hours – ten hours from Kigoma – and there was still no sign of the place. And the road was not getting any better. It got me thinking that even if there was a Mwanza–Kigali bus, it would perhaps not be such a good idea to back-track and travel this way again. I started considering alternatives. What compounded my indecision was that there were all of a sudden a number of heavily armed soldiers along the road who occasionally stopped the bus and, after chatting to the driver, let us continue. It felt like we were travelling in an area that could, in the true sense of the word, erupt at any time. And then I remembered reading somewhere before embarking on the trip that the use of the Rusumu border post was not advisable. That recollection was all I needed to convince me that returning on the same road was not a good idea at all.

Four hours after leaving Biharamulo, just when I thought we were entering Mwanza, we arrived in the sprawling town of Geita. Mwanza was still ninety kilometres away, it turned out. A few passengers got off but even more passengers got on. The road from Geita, although also very bad, was at least being improved, judging by all the earthmoving equipment about.

After another half an hour, we had our first glimpse of the largest body of water in Africa, Lake Victoria. A few minutes later the bus stopped and everybody started disembarking.

This must be Mwanza, I thought to myself.

However, the passengers were leaving all their luggage on the overhead luggage racks. I tried to find out what was happening but none of the people I asked spoke a word of English, so I sheepishly followed them. It turned out that we were about to board a ferry to cross over to the peninsula in the southern part of the lake on which Mwanza is built. I shuffled on behind the other passengers and ended up in a queue to buy a ticket for the ferry.

After about ten minutes, I paid my TZS500 (half a US dollar) and I was handed a ferry ticket – only to have it torn in half by another man literally one step further. What an excellent way to create jobs.

It took another half an hour before everyone had been issued ferry tickets. As I was walking towards the MV *Misungwi*, an SMS from Lulu came through: *I saw the doctor and she confirmed the pregnancy.*

Very excited, I replied immediately, saying that I would phone once I had found accommodation in Mwanza.

Boarding the MV *Misungwi* reminded me of the time when Lulu and I and eight of our friends had crossed the Zambezi River by ferry ten months before on our way to Livingstone. I could not help but notice that the Zambezi ferry was far more basic than the one I was boarding.

Unlike the ferry that operated between Botswana and Zambia, which only had one floor, the *Misungwi* had three floors: a bottom floor where all vehicles were parked with a sitting area for passengers; a first floor with wooden benches where most passengers sat, and a second floor with a restaurant and bar, where I immediately headed. While deciding what to order I spotted a "No Smoking" sign with the following warning: NO NAKED LIGHTS.

Since I still had to find accommodation in Mwanza, I decided against having a beer – except for half a litre of water, I hadn't consumed anything the whole day – and chose something alcohol-free which claimed to be "stronger than the strongest thirst": Stoney ginger beer.

The guy at the counter looked at me as if I were from another planet before exclaiming, "Stoney? Beer?"

"Stoney ginger beer," I replied, pointing at a bottle in the fridge.

After taking my TZS500 he handed me the ginger beer, but still looked unconvinced that he was doing the right thing. When I looked at the 350-ml bottle closely, after throwing most of its thirst-quenching liquid into my wide-open throat in one go, I saw it was labelled "Stoney Tangawizi". Well, it looked and tasted like Stoney ginger beer, so it must have been Stoney ginger beer.

It was already dark when the ferry left the shore and I could not see much of the lake. It took about twenty minutes to ferry the passengers from two buses, eight 4×4 cabs and five fully loaded trucks across to the peninsula. We got off the ferry and back into our bus in pitch darkness. The bus assistants came prepared; they both had torches with which they guided us from the ferry to the bus about fifty metres away.

As usual there was some pushing and shoving before we were all settled back in our over-familiar seats. (I do not understand this pushing and shoving when people use public transport in African countries. All passengers disembarking from the same bus will return to the same seats. Why then the need to push each other?)

It took another hour before we got to the bus terminus in Mwanza, Tanzania's second-biggest city after Dar es Salaam. We arrived there at exactly 21:00, fifteen hours after leaving Kigoma at six in the morning, shaken to the bone for at least eleven of those hours on the road.

For me the highlight of this very uncomfortable trip was undoubtedly a sign outside a building in a two-shop village: VATICAN LUBRICANT. It made my mind go into overdrive. Again my simple, practical way of looking at things took over. Think Vatican, Roman Catholic headquarters. Think Catholic priests do not marry; not a woman in sight in the Vatican (except a few nuns). So why Vatican lubricant?

I leave the rest, including the lubricant, to your imagination.

Mwanza

The bus station was well lit but there was not a bus in sight. I went to collect my luggage. What I received was a backpack covered not only with a thick layer of dust but also with oil. It had a thin film of black sludge all over. Thank goodness I had put the backpack into a cover because I anticipated the dust, but the oil was a bit of a surprise.

I took one of the cabs offering their services to Deluxe Hotel. We drove through a very sleazy and dodgy part of town. Think Hillbrow in Johannesburg; think Point Road in Durban (before it became Mahatma Gandhi); think Woodstock in Cape Town before the yuppies started to move in and gentrify it, and you get a picture of the neighbourhood where I was going to spend the night.

I could not believe my eyes when the cab parked outside Deluxe Hotel. Being a Friday night the bar was packed to capacity with dancing and singing patrons. I pinched myself, following the cab driver through a mass of patrons who were having a great time in the hotel's reception area. For TZS8 000 I got myself a self-contained room with continental breakfast. Despite the noise and the less than ideal neighbourhood, it sounded like a good deal. Somehow I was still not entirely convinced, so I asked the cab driver if he could wait downstairs while I hopped up to the second floor to check my room.

"No problem, as long as you will pay me the waiting fee," he responded. I offered him his TZS2 000, as agreed in the bus rank, and took the room without checking it out. Really now, what was this "waiting fee"?

After paying at reception I was joined by a security guard who, I assumed, must have been a Masai because of his bright red cotton wrap and bead regalia. A long double-edged knife hung from his hip and he smelled of alcohol, but I followed him up a series of staircases and down a dark corridor.

He offered to carry my bag but I objected, thinking he might expect compensation of some sort. So I was following him through the dark passage half dragging my backpack behind me. After unlocking the door he turned to me and asked for his tip. I promised to see him the following day at reception. He insisted because, he explained in broken English, he was going to leave very early. I reciprocated by promising him that I would also be leaving very early, so either way we were going to meet "bright and early at reception". Besides the fact that accompanying guests was clearly part of his duties, I knew that any money I would give him now was going to be deposited in the bar downstairs very soon.

After he left I had a look around my room. Deluxe Hotel was anything but deluxe: a basic double bed in a dirty room with dirty walls. However, there were two great things about the room. One, as at Mwanga Lodge in Kigoma, it contained a four-poster bed with the mosquito net hanging straight down. Two, there was a proper, fully functioning shower (although without warm water).

To put things in perspective: the last time I did not have to use a bucket to take a shower was back at Koumboka Backpackers in Lusaka, nine days earlier.

It is amazing how things change. Growing up in rural KwaZulu-Natal with no running water, I, like everybody else, used a bucket or basin to wash my body; and I felt clean and refreshed. Nowadays without running water it just does not feel like a good hygienic bath. I guess it's true that what you do not know you do not miss.

After spending a good fifteen minutes under a cold shower and feeling genuinely refreshed, it was time to talk to my wife about the imminent arrival of a new family member. However, "simcard recognition failure" appeared on the screen of my cellphone. I switched off the phone and after a minute switched it on again. It didn't do the trick. I removed the simcard and reinserted it. That didn't work either. I shook the phone and still nothing happened. Just when I was about to give up, the simcard was accepted and to my surprise it also connected to the network. I realised that all the time I was fiddling with the phone it had been flashing "low battery". So I inserted the charger in the wall plug; but the phone did not charge. With "calling" still showing on the screen, the battery died without the phone ringing even once on the other side.

That was very upsetting. I knew Lulu was going to panic if I did not call as I had promised by SMS earlier. Even worse, should she try to call me, she would get a message that the subscriber was not available. I contemplated going downstairs to enquire if they had a working plug at reception, but the thought of walking along a long, dark corridor on my own made me reconsider my options.

I then decided to sleep and to sort things out early the following morning, hoping that Lulu would remember what I had told her a couple of times before I left South Africa: If I do not SMS or email or phone, it does not mean I'm in danger or hurt. All it means is that, for some reason or other, I cannot SMS, email or call. Just stay put until you hear from me.

Just before falling asleep, I remembered that there was an urgent issue I still had to put to bed (excuse the pun). I had already decided that under no circumstances was I going to return by the same road to the Rusumu border post on my way to Kigali, even if there was a bus doing the direct route from Mwanza. I had to move to Plan G: continue in a northern direction along the eastern shore of Lake Victoria right up to Kisumu in Kenya, and from there proceed through Uganda, first in a westerly and then a southerly direction along the western side of Lake Victoria to Rwanda – a distance of approximately 1 500 kilometres, instead of the 500-kilometre direct route.

Considering that my flight back to Johannesburg was booked from Nairobi in Kenya, it meant that I would have to rush back on the same road through Uganda to Nairobi. This decision had two implications: time and cost. It was definitely going to take more time to do the trip, plus it was going to mess up my budget in a big way. However, I convinced myself that with more focus and determination Plan G was doable.

The change of plan had another implication; instead of visiting the Kigali Memorial Centre next, as I had planned, it would have to be bungee jumping at the source of the Nile at Jinja, because I would be passing through there on my way to Rwanda's capital city.

I had consumed only half a litre of water and a 350-ml bottle of Stoney Tangawizi the whole day. What was important, though, was that I had survived the terrible roads of Tanzania. Although the blaring sound system downstairs did its best to keep people up, I slept like a baby. The only slight bother at the back of my mind was that I had to find other reasonable accommodation for the following night.

When I woke up in the morning my body ached with the kind of pain that I used to experience after running a standard marathon. After taking my second morning shower of the trip (thus far I had taken showers only in the evening except when I was leaving Lusaka) I packed my bag and headed for the in-house restaurant for my continental breakfast.

I was only entitled to tea or coffee, the elderly waiter informed me. Anything else I had to pay for from my own pocket. I did not even start arguing. Instead I lifted my bag, left the restaurant in a huff, dropped the keys at reception and left Deluxe Hotel. It was just after 07:00. The Masai security guard was nowhere to be seen. He must have finished his night-shift earlier and gone home.

With the help of a map (I am a man after all), I found Karibu (the Swahili word for "welcome") Corner Internet Café. Luckily they had a proper wall plug for my cellphone charger. After checking and responding to emails, I gave Lulu a call. Naturally she had been worried sick and had phoned me five times the previous night with hour-long intervals between calls. We talked about this and that and, with excitement taking over, we started discussing what the first name of the baby would be. After a long chat we agreed that I had to find out the Swahili word for "gift". When I paid at the internet café reception a few minutes later, I asked what the Swahili for gift was. "*Zawaadi*," the gentleman said. He pronounced it "sah-waa-dee". I requested him to write it on a piece of paper and I instantly SMSed it home.

I might as well let you know that Zawaadi Solomon Lindelo Lubanzi Khumalo, weighing 3.6 kg, was born at 17:37 on 14 June 2009. Eish, if only I'd held back for five days we would've shared the same birthday – 19 June.

Now it was time to start looking for a place to stay. Having paid TZS8 000 at Deluxe Hotel, I reckoned that anything around TZS10 000 should be reasonable in terms of cost and comfort. While still thinking along these lines, I noticed the modern-looking white Mwanza Hotel opposite the internet café. So I stepped across to enquire. Their self-contained single rooms were TZS50 000, way beyond me, but the receptionist referred me to Lake Hotel, two blocks away. At Lake Hotel a self-contained room was TZS15 000, including breakfast. I checked out the room on the first floor and, although a bit more than I had hoped for, I decided to take it. (It also had a 37-cm television set.)

Now that I had found accommodation, I dropped my bags and headed back into the streets of Mwanza. It was time to start looking for a bus company that went to Kisumu in Kenya.

The problem with finding my way to the offices of the bus company was that everyone gave me directions in Swahili. Although I had promised myself on my Cape-to-Cairo trip in 2005 to learn this important language (which started as a lingua franca between Africans and Arabs), I sadly hadn't got around to doing so yet. About the fifth guy I asked in a fairly run-down part of town realised that we didn't understand each other completely and grabbed my hand. I had no choice but to follow him as he wove his way through informal stalls selling garments and fruit.

After crossing a small bridge over a very dirty stream, we turned right and zigzagged through even more stalls, eventually arriving at the Akamba Bus Services kiosk. I was waiting for this guy to ask for a tip but, after dumping me in front of the counter, he gave me a thumbs-up and vanished into the crowd.

A picture of a bright yellow Akamba bus hung on the wall. As far as I could see it was a modern, comfortable bus, and I was impressed by the professionalism of the Akamba representative who sold me the ticket. He even handed me the seating plan of the bus, asking me to choose a seat from those that were not yet allocated. The only minor problem was that he too did not speak much English. However, he somehow understood that I wanted to go to Kisumu and I understood that it would cost me TZS26 000, that the bus would leave from Nyakato at seven the next day, and that Nyakato was out of town so it would be better for me to take a cab and be there in time. It was all pretty straightforward. I thanked him and said goodbye.

A few seconds later I retraced my steps – having learned from experience to double-check if the quoted time was Swahili or English. As it turned out, the man had told me Swahili time, and the bus would be leaving at 13:00 and not at seven in the morning as I had assumed. So his arrival time at Kisumu of "six o'clock in the evening" meant midnight. Not ideal, but what could I do? Anyway, I reasoned, there would be lots of people getting off.

It was not even 11 a.m. yet and my two objectives for the day – finding accommodation and buying a bus ticket – had been achieved. Now it was time to discover Mwanza at leisure. I headed for the port, passing a tall white building on the way with a big "Passion FM" billboard.

The one thing sure to strike a first-time visitor to the Mwanza port is the massive rock formation in the lake. It sits there looking more like human handiwork than a natural phenomenon and is a beautiful sight.

Like Mpulungu's harbour, Mwanza's has been allowed to deteriorate. It had probably never been properly developed in the first place. Near the entrance I could see traces of what used to be the main railway line to the harbour, now buried under sand and overgrown with grass. The port area, especially where people and cars board the Kamanga ferry, has huge potential but is downright neglected, dirty and covered by informal structures. I guess that is the story of most towns and cities in Africa. They have so much potential that remains just that – potential – because of neglect and a lack of maintenance of the infrastructure.

The MV Victoria, which ferries people overnight to Bukoba halfway up the western side of the lake, was docked in the harbour. So it would have been possible for me to get to Kigali by taking the overnight ferry to Bukoba and from there take a twelve-hour bus ride to Kigali. The problem was, firstly, that the bus only ran on certain days (or so I was informed), and that those departure days did not coincide with the arrival of the ferry. The second problem was that even locals considered the bus from Bukoba to Kigali very uncomfortable. Well, if the locals found a bus uncomfortable it could only mean one thing: stay far away. Another minor glitch with taking the Bukoba–Kigali bus was that it went through the Rusumu border post.

As if that were not enough, the MV Bukoba, which used to do exactly what the MV Victoria was doing – ferry people between Mwanza and Bukoba – sank, with more than 800 people drowning, in May 1996. Mind you, its capacity was for 430 people only.

It so happened that one of the passengers on the vessel was Al-Qaeda's Abu Ubaidah al-Banshiri, at the time second-in-command to Osama bin Laden. (Okay, I will not let my cynical and conspiracy-theory-prone mind take over. It was indeed an accident.)

No, I was happy I had chosen not to go this much shorter route.

I decided to have something to eat and drink at a thatched restaurant about a kilometre from Mwanza's port. I walked there along a pedestrian path next to the road alongside the lake. When I saw the sign on the front of the restaurant – Yun Long Chinese Restaurant – I stopped dead in my tracks, turned and walked back to town. Supporting Chinese enterprise in Africa is contrary to my principles. Whichever way you look at it, the Chinese are the new colonisers of Africa, and what makes the deals they are signing all over the continent doubly unnerving is that the Chinese government owns the majority stake in all the companies now buying stakes in African companies. In practical terms this means that the Chinese government indirectly owns some key African companies.

You do not need a crystal ball to see that the future of the world lies in Chinese hands. If, like me, you have a dream of owning and/or running a multi-national corporation, there is one thing you have to do – learn Mandarin, which is undoubtedly the language of the future. Just imagine the competitive advantage you will have as an aspiring group chief executive by being fluent in Mandarin. Anyway, it is only a matter of time before the company you work for moves its headquarters to either Shanghai or Beijing. You have been warned!

As I was walking back to town, I could not help but think how we Africans have always been victims. First it was slavery, then colonialism, then independence marred by coups and civil wars. And now the Chinese are taking over. But of course, as long as African leaders make their annual cap-in-hand pilgrimage to the G8 summit to kneel and plead for more foreign aid because we are not self-sufficient, nobody will take us seriously. They'll just continue to see us as a burden to the world. It is because of our obsession with being comfortable with the status quo, I thought, that people on other continents will never in a thousand years exclaim: "Have you noticed how these Africans are taking over the world? Damn it!"

Back in town, now thoroughly thirsty and hungry, I settled for Sizzlers Restaurant. It was definitely not a superior tourist restaurant: it had red plastic chairs and transparent plastic tablecloths. I ordered "Half Poussin Chicken (Nairobi style)". They were out of stock. To be honest I had no clue what the dish looked or tasted like, I just loved the name. So may I please say it again: Half Poussin.

I then ordered their mixed grill (chicken, mutton, fried egg, rice, chips and tomato slices), which set me back TZS5 500. I washed it down with a very cold 350-ml Coca-Cola. The mixed grill turned out to be anything but sizzling. The mutton was off; the egg and the chips looked like they had been fried in very dark, dirty, over-used oil; the chicken was floating in a thin soup. With the exception of the mutton, I ate everything, however; the unsavoury mixed grill did fulfil its primary function, which was to fill my extremely empty stomach.

I decided to go back and spend some time in the park overlooking the lake. While sitting on the grass with plenty of time on my hands, I asked myself whether there was a good reason why Africa's largest lake and most famous falls should continue to bear the name of a British monarch. I concluded that there was a lot to be said in Queen Victoria's favour. After all, no other woman in history had ruled over approximately a quarter of the world's population at one time – roughly 400 million people. Her empire included large parts of Africa, Asia and the Caribbean, as well as Canada, New Zealand, Australia and India.

The internet research I had done produced some interesting facts on Queen Vic, the longest-reigning monarch in British history. (This means that the current British monarch, Queen Elizabeth II, will have to stay on the throne until 10 September 2015, when she will be eighty-nine, if she wants to equal the record of her great-great-grandmother.)

Among other things, Victoria:

- was a fluent speaker of German (she was of at least 75 per cent German ancestry and German was her first language);
- lost her father at an early age and was raised by her German mother;
- became queen at the age of eighteen and survived living in Buckingham Palace for over sixty years;
- married her first cousin, Prince Albert, when they were both twenty years old;
- gave birth to nine children (on an average once every twenty months over a period of sixteen years);
- had a loving and stable marriage until she was widowed at the age of forty-two, and mourned her husband by wearing black for the remaining forty years of her life.

Because of Lake Victoria and the Victoria Falls, I looked for places elsewhere in the world named after her. Of the numerous schools, streets, hospitals, buildings, parks and squares, rivers, mountains and lakes, town and states – even ships – that carry her name, the following is a tiny number I found on my search: Australia – State of Victoria, State of Queensland, Great Victoria Desert; Canada – Victoria Island, Queen's University; New Zealand – Mt Victoria in Auckland and Mt Victoria in Wellington; Nigeria – Victoria Island; Northern Ireland – Great Victoria

Railway Station in Belfast; Scotland – Royal Victoria Hospital; Seychelles – Port Victoria, the capital.

Back in South Africa she is present all over the place: in Victoria Street and Victoria Embankment (now called Margaret Mncadi) in Durban; Victoria West in the Northern Cape; in the Western Cape, Queen Victoria Street and the Victoria & Alfred (her second son and fourth child) Waterfront in Cape Town.

As far as I can see, however, Queen Victoria's biggest and most lasting legacy is the white wedding dress. Until she got married in 1840 brides wore wedding gowns of any colour, but when the Queen decided to put on a white dress for her wedding everybody followed suit. Even today girls all over the world spend sleepless nights dreaming about the day they will wear a white wedding dress and be a princess. To me it is a screaming irony that the Queen ended up wearing black for forty years. At least she was buried next to her husband wearing a white gown.

Late that afternoon, as I walking back to my hotel, I was drawn by the noise of hooting cars and what sounded like a brass band marching down Kenyatta Road, one of the main streets in Mwanza. It was indeed a brass band – five men blowing their trumpets on the back of a bakkie. The bakkie was followed by seven guys on motorbikes, who in turn were followed by a motorcade. The last car was a red two-door Cabriolet Pajero from which a bride (in white) and groom were waving at the onlookers on the side of the road.

By then young boys were running next to the Pajero and women were ululating and waving back. At the traffic circle the Pajero went round three times and brought traffic to a halt, but nobody seemed to be complaining. Passing cars were also hooting, their drivers waving and congratulating the newly-weds. It was enough to make me want to get married again (to the same woman, of course).

It was a real spectacle. One of the bikers started to show off by standing with one foot on the seat, kicking his other leg out to be parallel to the ground while keeping both hands on the handle bars.

The motorcade eventually took the road down to the port and things quietened down. But within ten minutes another wedding procession with its own brass band and motorcade came down Kenyatta Road – this time accompanied by youngsters on bicycles. Women on the side of the road started ululating again, cars hooted and everybody waved at the bride and groom in their black sedan car.

The receptionist at Lake Hotel later told me that these wedding celebrations were part of the local tradition. As he put it: "You are not married until the brass band leads you down Kenyatta Road to the lake to have photographs taken."

I'm not sure if I was the only one to pick up the coincidence of brides in white dresses going to be photographed next to Lake Victoria. No matter how you looked at it, Queen Vic, even more than a hundred years after her death, continues to reign supreme. God save the Queen!

In the early evening, I ordered a beer at the bar downstairs in my hotel. This time I opted for a Tusker, which is not a bad beer at all. There were quite a few locals chatting away over beers and other drinks. I was about to finish my second dumpie when I was joined by two women who must have been in their mid-forties. They had been sitting at another table not far from mine. Both of them had that I'm-a-widow-but-still-want-to-get-married-because-my-first-husband-died-a-poor-man look. After some light conversation I excused myself, even leaving some beer in my dumpie to create the impression that I had to go to the loo. I disappeared to my room on the first floor and never reappeared.

I was watching the news on the 37-cm television screen – not that I understood anything – when I was disturbed by a neighbour's loud praying. I turned up the volume of the television set but it did not work. So I ended up lowering it and just listened to this highly religious guy. He was basically repeating the same words over and over again: "Oh thank you, Jesus. Thank you, Lord. Oh thank you, Jesus."

I could hear him clapping his hands now and then as well. Under normal circumstances when somebody says "thank you" the words express gratitude and appreciation, but this man's voice was constantly breaking as if he was pleading "Forgive me, Jesus. Forgive me, Lord." He continued for about half an hour, repeating the words over and over. I'm not exaggerating!

I went to bed thinking I should attend a church service the following day. Earlier in the day I had noticed that there was an English service between 9 and 10.15 a.m. in one of the churches next to the lake.

Trying to sleep at Lake Hotel proved to be much more difficult than at Deluxe Hotel. I did not realise that Station Road, on which Lake Hotel is situated, is one of the main arteries in and out of Mwanza. Throughout the night heavy trucks, boda-bodas (motorbike taxis), buses and motor cars were passing not very far from my window. I really struggled to sleep. It got so bad that, while tossing and turning and turning and tossing, I even started missing Deluxe Hotel with all its sleaziness.

It was only at around three in the morning that I managed to get some decent sleep – so my intention to go to church ended up in smoke, just like a sacrifice in the Old Testament.

After taking a shower (my third morning shower of the trip), I decided to wear a clean pair of trousers, seeing that I had been wearing the same cargo pants ever since I started the trip in Johannesburg. I put on the second and last pair of trousers I had with me. I had brought five T-shirts and had already worn three. Things were not looking great from a hygiene perspective, but wearing a crisp, clean pair of pants and T-shirt made me feel marvellously fresh and beautiful.

As I was checking out I was reminded by the receptionist that I was entitled to breakfast. After the experience at Deluxe Hotel I was reluctant to go to the in-house restaurant, but I let the man convince me.

I was pleasantly surprised. They offered me mint tea (in a red flask), two slices of bread, butter, jam and a boiled egg. A real treat. After breakfast I left my backpack at reception before dashing off for my last walk in town. I sauntered past the Mahatma Gandhi Community Hall on Nyerere Road, and on my way back passed the PPF Plaza Hotel, where a new wing was being added to the existing building. My eyes were drawn to the board with the name of the main contractor: "China Railway Jian Chang Engineering". Need I say more?

Just after midday I took a cab to Nyakato, more or less six kilometres from the centre of Mwanza. The cab dropped me at the bus rank near a number of general dealer shops, a hotel with the name Nice and a restaurant called Diplomatic Foods.

I joined some passengers on the veranda of the Akamba Bus Services offices. About twenty minutes later a yellow bus stopped right in front of us and we were told that we could board. I was a bit surprised that the bus showed Kampala as its destination and regretted not having asked more questions when I booked my ticket the previous day. But sometimes, in fact, more often than not, my male ego does not allow me to ask for critical information, including directions.

In this case, before purchasing a ticket I should have asked if there was a bus going all the way to Uganda. Instead I just assumed that the bus from Mwanza would go as far as Kisumu in Kenya and that I would have to catch another bus from there to Jinja and, eventually, Kampala in Uganda.

Putting my male ego aside, I now asked the bus representative if the vehicle was headed for Kampala. Yes, he explained, after Kisumu it crossed into Uganda, passing through Jinja and ending in Kampala.

I could kick myself for not asking and buying a ticket to Kampala (which cost TZS31 000), instead of buying a ticket to Kisumu (for TZS26 000). It would have been so much more convenient to travel all the way to Uganda, and it would definitely have cost less.

North to Kisumu

Always looking on the bright side, I consoled myself with the thought that I could apply for a Ugandan visa in Kisumu, which would make crossing into Uganda at the Busia border post smooth and straightforward. And furthermore, staying over in Kisumu would give me the opportunity to visit Hippo Point, which, according to my guidebook, was a perfect spot for viewing the glorious sunsets over Lake Victoria.

I could, however, not stop worrying about the bus's anticipated time of arrival in Kisumu at midnight.

Before allowing it to be put in the hold of the bus, I again put my backpack into a bag to protect it, a necessary precaution, I felt, even though we would be travelling in a comfortable Scania F330 Intercooler (this is what was written between the headlights).

The bus had reclining seats, and after fastening my seatbelt I sat back to relax and enjoy what was left of Tanzania.

We left on a great tarred road – by Tanzanian standards – that passed through an industrial park. With nobody sitting next to me and no body vibration (and no traffic noise), I spent the first two hours of the journey catching up on some lost sleep. Now and then I opened my eyes and gazed at the bushveld scenery on my left with intermittent views of the lake.

We picked up a few passengers at a small, nondescript rural town called Lamadi. The only memorable thing about Lamadi was that there was a Cape Town Lodge (though no Capeys or Table Mountain). We continued north to Bunda, a town, like all other small towns in Tanzania, where corrugated-iron roofs were rusting on old buildings.

The scenery on the side of the road stayed pretty much the same – big bald rock formations protruding from green hills – until we crossed an enormous bridge over the Mara River from which the Masai Mara game reserve got its name. The river, which has its source in the Kenyan Highlands, winds for 395 kilometres before it flows into Lake Victoria.

Five hours after leaving Nyakato we stopped in the border town of Sirari. By now it was dusk and it had started drizzling. Judging by the number of container trucks at the border, there must have been a lot of trade between

Kenya and Tanzania. Unlike other African borders where trucks queue for kilometres on end, Sirari had a big tarred yard where trucks parked while the drivers and their assistants went through the formalities.

Who said immigration offices cannot be efficient? It took less than twenty minutes for me to be stamped out of Tanzania by an official sitting on a small chair behind a small table – not standing on the other side of a counter as was usual. I then stepped through the permanently open gate, filled in the immigration form and got stamped into Kenya by an official in a small office sitting on a small chair behind a small table. Although I did not envisage spending more than three days in Kenya before continuing to Jinja, I asked for eight days, the delays suffered in Mpulungu still fresh in my mind. The immigration official gladly obliged.

Knowing that I was going to arrive in Kisumu at midnight and that I would need a cab to take me to the nearest backpackers, it was imperative to get some Kenyan shillings. As if he could read my mind, a youngster who looked honest and decent approached me as I left the immigration offices and offered to pay KSh1 222 for my TZS22 000.

Not that I underestimate your intelligence, but considering that Zulus will read this book as well, I might as well tell you that it meant that I got one Kenyan shilling for every TZS18.

QUESTION 4: If the exchange rate was KSh75 or TZS1 000 to US$1 was I robbed if I received KSh1 222 for my TZS22 000?

While waiting for the other passengers to clear immigration I bought myself a roasted mealie cob and 150 ml of bottled water, and with the breakfast I had enjoyed at Lake Hotel in Mwanza, that was all I had for the day.

As we got back into the bus we were searched with an electronic baton by a private security guard presumably contracted by the government. After the US embassy bombing in Nairobi in which hundreds of people were killed in 1998, Kenya obviously had no choice but to implement strict border controls.

The road on the Kenyan side of the border was far better than on the Tanzanian. Not far from the border we stopped in Migori, where we had a forty-minute break because, as the bus assistant explained, "going through immigration was far quicker today than usual".

By the time we left Migori it was already dark. Coming upon and overtaking big trucks on the winding road through what seemed like an endless sugar plantation did not sit well with me, but the driver, who had been at the wheel all the way from Nyakato, seemed to have everything under control.

We stopped at Kisii, a fairly large town with a sprinkling of modern buildings, and then at Kericho. Like Gemini Motorways in Zambia, Akamba Bus Services must have been a large company. At Kericho there were six other Akamba buses going to different destinations. At the petrol station where our bus pulled in, other passengers were already crowded around one small shop and the street hawkers did a good trade in roasted mealies, potato chips, bottled water and peanuts.

We got to Kisumu at exactly 00:15. It being a Monday morning, I did not expect a buzz in the streets, but as the bus drove down different roads I was surprised at how quiet everything was. There were hardly any cars about. I was also puzzled by the fact that most passengers continued to sleep, even after the bus had stopped – until I realised they were probably on their way to Uganda.

The bus had stopped, not at a bus rank but outside the Akamba offices in a very dark, narrow street which ran parallel to Oginga Odinga Street, the city's main road, named after Kenya's first vice president. My fears were justified: I was the only one jumping off in Kisumu.

The bus driver got out, retrieved my bag from the luggage compartment and headed back to his seat. I took a deep breath and crossed the very dark street towards the offices where I had spotted two security guards sitting at the entrance of what turned out to be the passenger lounge – one sleeping and the other barely awake.

Although the area was not exactly sleazy, it was quite clear that it was not the leafy part of the town either. As I greeted the security guards, I heard the bus pulling away. There I was in a new town with two strangers just after midnight, with no place to sleep. While I was still contemplating my next move, the half-awake guard asked me, "Do you want a taxi?"

"I will organise it for you," he offered before I could respond.

I nodded, feeling a bit more optimistic. At least a cab could take me to the nearest budget accommodation.

The guard took out his cellphone (isn't technology just great?) and spoke in a local language to someone. I had no clue what they discussed. I just stood there. A few seconds later he hung up and said, "He's coming."

For an endless ten minutes I stood next to the two guards, one still in deep sleep, the other looking as if he could drop off at any moment. Although I didn't feel unsafe, it did cross my mind that I was getting too old for these African adventures of mine. I should have done these things when I was still a bachelor with no responsibilities. Now I was a family man, with a pregnant wife *nogal*. I really needed to, as Lulu always says when we have an argument, "grow up".

An ancient cream Toyota Corolla with one headlight s-l-o-w-l-y made its way towards us, coming majestically to a stop. It was the cab we were waiting for. The driver gave the security guard a few coins, surely as a gesture of appreciation for finding him a client.

The seats inside the cab were old and none of the lights on the very dark dashboard worked. I could therefore not see what speed we were doing, but if there had been any traffic officers about at that time of night we surely would have been fined for driving too slowly. And although I did not check, I suspected that the rear lights also didn't work.

The first option for accommodation was Lodgers Palace, which my guidebook described as "friendly and central". The cab driver told me that it had closed down more than a year ago. I was using the older version of *Lonely Planet – Africa on a Shoestring*, not the 50th-anniversary updated version.

The next option was New Victoria Hotel, where the driver said he would take me for KSh400. After driving a few blocks we stopped in front of it. We were told by the security guard at the main entrance that it was fully booked. Now I was starting to panic a little. I was quickly running out of options. Not a good thing, especially if it happens to be one in the morning.

The second-last option was the YMCA next to the bus station. It looked like a school: a row of white buildings with a big yard in front. We couldn't even enter the premises. The gates were locked with a chain and padlock. And there was no security guard in sight. The cab driver tried hooting but the hooter didn't work. He got out and rattled the chains against the gate but nobody emerged from the building. He walked back to the car and said, "We must not stop here for a long time. This area is very unsafe."

Now I was panicking. Not only were we in a dodgy neighbourhood but the cab driver had already dismissed my last suggestion, Monalisa Guesthouse, with the words: "It is very dirty and it's mostly used by prostitutes."

Since I had no intention of sharing anything, including a guesthouse, with a loose woman, I ruled out Monalisa, which brought me to the end of my list of possibilities. Now it was up to the driver and fate to help me find a place to stay.

We stopped in one of the big streets to discuss what options were still open. We could only think of trying a proper hotel. The cab driver, who spoke fluent English, suggested we try one last place before going to the upmarket Imperial Hotel. We drove back to Oginga Odinga Road and four blocks further he stopped in front of Central Square Guesthouse and went inside to enquire. After a few minutes, which felt much longer because I was sitting alone in the only car in a deserted street, he came back, got into the car, took a deep breath and said, "They have both single and double rooms available."

I was so excited that I didn't even ask if there would be prostitutes hanging around the place. By now even the fact that I would be charged KSh1500 – about R200 and much steeper than I had anticipated – did not matter. I thanked the driver profusely, gave him KSh1000 and US$5 because I did not have enough shillings, took my bag from the back seat and shook his hand. He drove off. As I stared after the car, my earlier suspicion was confirmed: none of the rear lights was working.

Central Square Guesthouse was on the first floor of a multi-storey building. The ground floor was occupied by various shops. I took a steep staircase to reception where, just like at Koumboka Backpackers in Lusaka, I was met by a very tall black man. I chose the only available single room. Although it was not self-contained, the shower and the toilet were close by.

I promised the receptionist that I would pay KSh700 per night for two nights and that I would do so the following day. It was two o'clock in the morning, so the man nodded his agreement and escorted me to the small room which was fitted with a single bed, a not-quite-clean mosquito net, a small table and a plastic chair. I couldn't care less; what mattered most was that I had a safe place to sleep. There was hardly any traffic noise although the guesthouse was right in the middle of town, and I slept well. I was woken by my alarm clock at 07:00.

It was my fourth morning shower but the first hot shower of the trip. For seventeen days I had had cold showers or a cold-water wash in a bucket. The water was not gushing out of the showerhead quite as strongly as I would have liked, but it still felt special to stand under a trickling hot shower. One thing about doing trips like this is that you start appreciating things that you otherwise take for granted.

Refreshed and ready to face what surely was going to be an exciting day, I went downstairs. I had the day all perfectly planned out. After changing some money I was going to apply for a visa at the Ugandan consulate and then visit the museum, which my guidebook said was a must-see in Kisumu because of the variety of both live and dead animals on display. After picking up my passport in the afternoon, hopefully with a visa, I was going to end the day at Hippo Point.

Although it was after eight, the bureau de change in the main street was still closed. No problem. I walked up the street and noticed that other shops were also still closed and concluded that it was due to the laid-back culture, just like in Mombasa on the east coast where, on my first visit, I was astounded at how late the shops opened.

I entered Meega Plaza where, with the exception of an internet café, all shops were closed. By now things did not feel right. I walked around the two-storey plaza for some time before going out into the main street again and buying a newspaper from the first vendor I saw.

It was great to be able to read an English newspaper again. Back in Mwanza I had enquired but was told by a street vendor that they did not stock English newspapers, so I stopped trying to find one.

The paper, *The Standard*, reported on its first page under a bold headline that the government was going to build new offices for Mwai Kibaki and Raila Odinga, the president and prime minister respectively, at a cost of two billion Kenyan shillings (almost US$27 million). It was great to see Kibaki and Odinga agreeing on something. As is well known, soon after the December 2007 elections in Kenya, which Odinga's Orange Democratic Movement claimed had been rigged, violence broke out and some 800 people were killed (other sources say more than 1 000) and more than half a million people were displaced. A peace agreement, which led to the current coalition government, was signed in February 2008. Interestingly, the violence started in Kisumu, Odinga's stronghold.

Sitting in a bus shelter and scanning the newspaper, I read: "Today we are celebrating the life of the father of our nation Jomo Kenyatta ..." Only then did it click that the shops were closed because it was a public holiday. "Yes," the guy from whom I had bought the newspaper confirmed, "the 20th of October is a public holiday – Jomo Kenyatta Day."

Being in Kisumu on a public holiday created a big problem for me. In fact, three problems. It meant that banks and bureaus de change were closed so I wouldn't be able to change money and, consequently, I would also not be able to pay the guesthouse. It also meant that the Ugandan consulate would be closed – and the museum probably too. It was not even ten yet and it was clear that two of the three things I wanted to do could not be done.

What a waste of valuable time, I thought as I wandered aimlessly through the empty town – until my stomach started to complain and I realised how hungry I was. I had to find something to eat, but where was I going to change money?

After enquiring about which bureaus de change might be open, I was referred to Imperial Hotel, which was right opposite the Kenyatta Sports Grounds about three blocks away from the main street and within easy walking distance.

Entering the air-conditioned reception area of the hotel with its glowingly clean walls and nicely carpeted floors made me realise how deprived I'd been of modern comforts.

"I am sorry, sir," the receptionist informed me. "We only exchange for our clients – persons sleeping in this hotel." He referred me to Riviera Casino, which meant going back to Oginga Odinga Road. The receptionist at the casino, thank goodness, agreed to change my dollars, even though I was not there to gamble. Their rate, KSh70 instead of KSh75 which was the prevailing exchange rate at the time, was not great, but I was happy to walk off with KSh3 500 in my pocket.

Thinking I would have a scrumptious brunch in one of the restaurants overlooking the lake, I walked down Oginga Odinga Road until I got to a dirt road and, after crossing two unused railway lines and walking down a very steep embankment, I arrived at the waterfront. Quite a few small restaurants lined the shore of the lake, all of them constructed of corrugated iron. They looked like a line of shacks, but all of them had a proper board with their name on it: Riziki, Tazana, Kakelo, Beach … The one right at the beginning of the row sported a very familiar name: Mandela.

Tall grass was growing between the corrugated-iron shanties, and somewhere in the back some guys were sawing up a big tree which must have fallen over. A few cars had reversed into the lake up to their rear wheels and were being washed. I was really disappointed and, although I'm pretty sure the food would have been delicious notwithstanding the informal set-up, I decided to walk back to town. Doing things so "informally" sometimes really gets to me.

On my way back up the main road I came across Lakeside Meeting Point Restaurant. It looked inviting. I had the option of sitting inside or outside on a terrace. I chose the latter and had coffee and a Spanish omelette – without bread because I was told: "They didn't deliver bread today because it is a holiday." The omelette was delicious but had no filling – so much for being Spanish – and I left the restaurant still feeling hungry.

I walked all the way back to the Kenyatta Sports Grounds opposite Imperial Hotel and sat on a low brick wall for a long time watching people walking up and down Kisumu's Central Park. One of the guys sitting next to me told me there was going to be a big celebration there later that afternoon to commemorate Jomo Kenyatta, independent Kenya's first president.

Among the people walking past I noticed that quite a few were wearing Obama T-shirts. It intrigued me until I remembered that Barack Obama's father was Kenyan. In fact, a Luo from these parts.

In the afternoon I took a tuk-tuk (a three-wheeled motorised bike with a canopy) to Hippo Point, not far from town. Why it was called Hippo Point was a mystery to me. There were no hippos in sight, only something like a park with overgrown grass, a building that was abandoned at foundation level and some tall poles which must have been lying there for years, judging by the height of the grass that had grown over them.

I don't know whether I had expected too much of Hippo Point but I thought there would at least be some kind of shelter where people could sit and watch these reportedly glorious sunsets. I don't want to sound like a complaining spoilt brat who visits different countries with preconceived ideas, but Mama Africa has such incredible natural beauty that it is a shame that she has been so neglected over the past few decades through the mediocrity of the leadership on the continent.

I must have sat on the grass for about an hour watching two youngsters washing a taxi parked right next to the lake. A few vagrants and a married couple also sitting on the grass were gazing at the lake. It was long before sunset, but some dark clouds were closing in and I decided that I'd better get back to town before it started raining. So much for the glorious sunsets at Hippo Point.

For obvious reasons taxis and tuk-tuks do not hang around Hippo Point, so it was back to town on foot. I started hitch-hiking but all the passing taxis were full. I must have walked half a kilometre or so when a boda-boda stopped and for KSh50 promised to drop me off in town. I had just mounted when I was hit by the first raindrop. And then the heavens opened.

My biggest worry was the passport in the side-pocket of my trousers. While we were speeding along the dirt road, I stood up slightly, removed my passport and managed to slip it into the small bag in which I carry my camera. By this time, with the rain getting heavier and heavier, the boda-boda was not even stopping at stop streets any more. As we entered town the taxi traffic increased. Without dropping speed we managed to zigzag past taxis, sedan cars and the odd bus here and there. It felt like we were soon going to be featured in a reality-television show called "Seconds Before Disaster". I held onto the poor biker for dear life, and every time we hit a small bump I clasped him even tighter. It is not really my thing to squeeze guys like that, but these were unusual circumstances. I couldn't even see straight.

I was greatly relieved to be dropped off at Meega Plaza in a soaking-wet state.

I walked around the Plaza trying to ignore the people staring at me in a funny way. Later I stood on the veranda of the Plaza and ate a cream doughnut while waiting for the rain to quieten down. When it had petered out to a drizzle I sprinted down the road back to the guesthouse.

No sooner was I back in my room than it started pouring again. I could hear the bands playing at the Kenyatta Sports Grounds. The heavy rain didn't seem to dampen the festivities. Judging by the screaming of the crowd, very popular bands must have been playing.

It rained continuously for about three hours before it stopped. By then it was dark and the celebrations were over too.

In Mpulungu I had a fornicating couple as neighbours; in Mwanza it was a praying man; in Kisumu my neighbour was a snorer. One of those people who snore as if they had swallowed a 50-cent coin. Just by listening to him I could tell that he was an obese man sleeping on his back, facing the ceiling with mouth wide open, dry lips and stinking breath.

The last time I heard someone snore like that was a few years back when I spent a night at a friend's flat the night before the 2004 Comrades marathon. I stayed at the flat because it was so close to the starting point. What a mistake. If the anxiety and adrenaline before a major race were not enough to keep me awake, my friend's snoring made sure that I didn't sleep a wink. The next day's race was the worst of my life.

My Kisumu neighbour must have been a gold-medal winner in the snoring stakes. It was as if he was lying on a bed right next to mine with no wall in-between. Some people complain about having not discovered their true talent. If my neighbour wasn't aware of his, I could have told him that his big talent lay in the grrrr-while-you-zzzzzzzzzz department.

Listening to him using his chainsaw on the roof rafters, I decided to leave Kisumu early the following morning even though I hadn't accomplished any of the things I wanted to do: apply for a visa, visit the museum and witness a glorious sunset at Hippo Point.

And then the snoring abruptly stopped and I fell into a deep sleep.

I woke up just after six and decided to have a hot shower; I wasn't sure when I would have the opportunity again. As I had feared the previous night, my trousers were still damp. So it was back to my dirty old cargo pants. However, I did put on the last but one clean t-shirt.

As I left my room my neighbour exited his too. I could not believe my eyes. I was 100 per cent right: he was fat and had dry lips. What I couldn't have imagined, though, was that he was sharing his bed with a woman half his age. Well, it's called love. What else could it be?

As I checked out, I was told that there was no Ugandan consular office in Kisumu. There is one in Mombasa, and the High Commission is in Nairobi. The guy at reception was very helpful. He even suggested that I take a mini-bus taxi to the border and, after crossing into Uganda, catch another taxi to Jinja. The Akamba bus, he told me, left Kisumu at one o'clock (in Kenya only universal time is quoted) and added: "It costs two hundred and fifty shillings, which is far more than what you will pay for both taxis."

Although it was not yet eight, out on the street there was a lot of activity: hooting taxis, boda-bodas, and pedestrians all moving up and down Oginga Odinga Road. At last Kisumu felt and looked like Kenya's third largest city, a busy town bristling with life.

Following the receptionist's directions to the taxi rank, I walked past the fire station and the district hospital which, looking at the peeling paint and skew gutters of both, I thought needed some serious renovation. A little further down the road the Kisumu Municipal Market, built in 1935 according to the date on the front, was bustling with hawkers selling fruit, vegetables, shoes, colourful garments – whatever. For the first time I noticed how many people in Kisumu used bicycles with a seat at the back to carry passengers. Later, I discovered that these were the original boda-bodas, and that they were originally used at border posts (get it?) to ferry passengers between the two immigration offices.

The taxi rank was a stone's throw from the market, right opposite Kisumu Boys High. After asking around I found a taxi that was going to the border town of Busia. There were only two people seated inside, which was not a good sign, but I was hopeful that it would soon fill up. After all, it was still early in the morning.

By taxi to Uganda

To pass the time before the taxi left I bought another English-language newspaper and read a long article about whether or not President Mwai Kibaki should implement the recommendations of the Waki Report. Soon after the dust had settled, a commission of enquiry was set up to investigate the cause and the instigators of the violence that erupted after the 2007 elections. According to the newspaper the Waki Report contained the names of senior people in the current government. If they were charged, it was feared, more violence and the collapse of the peace deal and coalition government might ensue. On the other hand, if the guilty parties were not charged, the government could be seen as deciding that senior officials were above the law and, just as important, it would prevent family members of the victims getting the justice they wanted.

It took almost two hours for the taxi to fill up. A quick headcount as the taxi left the taxi rank showed that we were seventeen in the fourteen-seater kombi, excluding the driver's assistant and twenty-one chickens. (The number was written on the box and I also could hear chickens chirping inside.)

As soon as we were on the open road I started thinking about my plans for the day: cross to Uganda, rush to Jinja, bungee jump there at the source of the Nile and head for Kampala. I knew it would be touch-and-go but figured it could be done.

The very tight schedule meant everything had to work like clockwork. I had already encountered the first stumbling block: the length of time before the taxi was ready to leave. Soon we stumbled upon a second stumbling block: roadblocks. There were many of them, each of which involved being stopped and a traffic officer sauntering over to the taxi for a leisurely chat with the driver before allowing him to continue in peace – despite the taxi being overloaded.

We drove past Maseno (the birthplace of Prime Minister Raila Odinga) and soon thereafter passed the equator sign. I could not believe my eyes. My assumption when I left South Africa was that I would have to stand on the equator in Uganda, not Kenya, having read that although Kisumu lies just south of the equator, there was no equator sign on the road.

The good news was that I was in the northern hemisphere now.

The taxi started speeding. I wanted to get to the border urgently, but now I started to feel uncomfortable. We went at high speed through villages where kids could have run onto the road at any time. On a few occasions the taxi driver crossed the barrier line while overtaking trucks, and once or twice he overtook on a blind rise or a corner. It was a hair-raising ride.

We made it to Luanda without mishap, however. No, not the capital of Angola but a very small town in Kenya, which has as a main feature the large number of coffin manufacturers along its main road. Coffins of different sizes and colours were all magnificently displayed on the pavement. In passing I could see guys cutting timber and building even more coffins. There must have been at least seven shops making coffins in Luanda.

To the beat of Kenyan music pumped out by the Toyota Hiace's sound system, we dropped off and picked up passengers at the central market in Ugunja (not to be confused with Unguja in Tanzania) and, with the taxi once again overloaded, proceeded to Bumala.

We were dropping off passengers at a noisy taxi rank when my cellphone rang. It was Pam, an accounts assistant from work. The cellphone company had phoned, she said. My account for the previous two weeks was R11 000. Had my phone perhaps been stolen? she wanted to know. I told her that my phone was still in my possession (she should have registered by now) but that I was travelling and that it must be the roaming costs.

After that call I was worried sick. I knew that the calls would be expensive, but I didn't expect anything like this. Once back at work, I thought, I'd tell them the truth, that while travelling in Central Africa I'd discovered that my wife was pregnant and that I had to communicate with her regularly. I'd request that my bill be settled by the company, but if they insisted that I pay from my own pocket, I'd allow a maximum of R200 to be deducted from my salary every month. And from that moment, I decided, I would communicate with Lulu mainly by SMS.

I might as well let you know that when I got back to Johannesburg the bill was almost R12 000. As it turned out, after more than a month of querying some of the things I did not understand, I received a credit of more than R7 000. (The moral of the story – do not just pay on presentation of the bill, especially when there are things you do not understand.)

On the outskirts of Busia we were stopped by a female traffic officer who, I could see from the word go, needed a head-to-toe massage. For some reason she was extremely agitated. The driver was summoned out of the taxi and had to follow her, walking behind a pair of trousers that was so tight and stretched that if she were to fart it would have torn. The driver stayed a metre or so behind her as she wiggled her way to her white Toyota Corolla parked under a tree some distance away. Two male traffic officers were leaning on it. That big-arsed traffic officer and her colleagues delayed us for thirty minutes.

Two hours after we'd left Kisumu we reached Busia. We drove past the school ("Airstrip Primary") and a teachers' training college to the taxi rank. At the entrance was a big signboard: YOU ARE 2 KM FROM UGANDA. I decided to accept a ride from one of the youngsters who were offering us their services on bicycle taxis. He grabbed my backpack and we walked across to his bicycle with a number of other youngsters following. I am not sure what exactly they were after but there must have been at least ten of them walking next to me and just staring at me.

We set off on the bicycle, my bag firmly strapped to my back. I was seated comfortably on the carrier seat, which clearly had been custom-built for passengers. The youngster pedalled to a gate about fifty metres away and stopped. Everybody was supposed be on foot beyond that gate, he told me. It seemed we had reached the Kenyan immigration offices.

While I filled in the immigration form I noticed that, instead of waiting for me on the veranda, the youngster had decided to sit with my backpack under a tree more than twenty metres from the building. I kept one eye on the form and the other on him. But then I had to stand in the queue, which meant I had to turn my back on him. I felt uneasy about the whole thing. When I turned around I couldn't see him. A big truck had stopped between the office and the tree and was blocking my view. My heart skipped a beat. Although I was near the front of the queue, I quickly ran out of the office, certain that he had disappeared with my bag. I ran alongside the truck, stopped at the rear end and looked towards the tree. And there the youngster was sitting with my bag next to him, not even looking at the immigration office. I quickly turned around, hoping that he hadn't seen that I was checking up on him.

Once again I had insulted someone by not trusting him; once again

I had been unnecessarily worried about being robbed. Sihle, when are you going to learn to relax when you travel outside South Africa? I reprimanded myself.

I had to queue all over again. Luckily there were only three people in the line by now and being stamped out of Kenya was a non-issue.

I found the young guy still sitting in the same position under the tree. As we walked towards the Ugandan immigration offices about thirty metres away, he told me that I should not change money from the guys who hang around there. "Those guys will give you fake money," he said. "If you need to change money I'll take you to a decent place where you will get a good rate."

I knew that as a South African passport holder, I needed a visa for Uganda. I also knew that visas were issued at some border posts but I was not sure exactly which. I hoped that Busia would be one, even though it is much smaller than the Malaba border post on the main road from Nairobi. My fears were allayed when, on entering the immigration office, I saw the prices of transit, single and multiple-entry visas on a notice board. Although I planned to go through Uganda twice in the next two weeks, I opted for a single visa, which cost US$50, rather than pay US$200 for a multiple-entry visa.

As the gum-chewing female immigration officer was entering my details in the large visa register, my eyes were attracted to a framed picture of a man hanging on the wall. At first I did not recognise him. I thought it was probably the Minister of Home Affairs or whatever Ugandan minister had immigration as part of his portfolio. The more I looked at the photograph, though, the more I was sure that I knew who the person was.

Concentrating hard, I realised that it was none other than the president of Uganda, Yoweri Kaguta Museveni. The photo must have been taken when he was still in his twenties (okay, maybe thirties). It didn't look like a professionally taken photograph or even as if Museveni was aware that he was being photographed. It must have been taken around 1986, when his National Resistance Army toppled Tito Okello, who had led a coup against President Obote the previous year.

It was the first time on the trip, except on the South African side of Beitbridge, that my passport was scanned. The officer asked me if it was my first visit to Uganda. It was indeed. I paid my US$50, my passport was stamped and a receipt was issued. The official handed back my passport with a broad smile and said, "Enjoy your stay."

I was officially in Idi Amin's old stomping ground.

Uganda reminded me of a tractor. You see, in Zulu a tractor is *uganda-ganda*. Which makes Museveni, black hat and all, a tractor driver. Like a good farm worker, he has been holding onto power for a very long time since toppling Okello. In the process he has restored a degree of stability to Uganda and enjoyed the perks of office, including a Gulfstream IV jet that cost US$31.5 million when it was acquired in 2000. I have read that it will be replaced by a Gulfstream 550, which will set Uganda back by almost US$60 million.

When I stepped out of the Ugandan immigration office, an incutra was waiting for me and I was immediately approached by a few others promising to give me the best rate for my Kenyan shillings. I turned them down and walked towards the taxi rank on the Ugandan side with my boda-boda man.

It struck me that almost all the guys pedalling bicycles were wearing pink shirts. Everywhere I looked there were guys in pink shirts.

"Why does everybody wear pink?" I asked.

The answer was simple: "They just love pink shirts."

We eventually got to the place where I had been promised I would get a good deal. A middle-aged man of mixed Afro-Asian appearance, sitting in a small shop selling clothes (in all probability made in China), gave me USh23 200 for my KSh1 150. Was I cheated?

QUESTION 5: – Just kidding, let's not go there again.

The youngster who was accompanying me wanted me to exchange more money. He even asked if I didn't have US dollars to exchange as well. I realised he was working for a commission. The more money I exchanged, the more money he would make.

We left the shop and took off on the bicycle. While he was pedalling me to the taxi rank, he suddenly announced that I would have to pay him KSh200 instead of the KSh20 we'd agreed on.

"No ways. Otherwise I'm jumping off," I threatened.

He kept quiet but slowed down his pedalling. My heart started to beat faster when he turned right. I was about to ask him why he had changed direction when I realised we had reached the taxi rank. I suspect I had misinterpreted the board on the Kenyan side that said Uganda was two kilometres away. It must have referred to the position of the Rand Hotel, whose signboard it was. The taxi ranks on the Kenyan and Ugandan sides of the border were definitely less than a kilometre apart, with the immigration offices between them.

If I had not employed the young cyclist I might well have got fake Ugandan money for my Kenyan shillings. I'll never know. Anyway, I gave him KSh20 which I had kept aside when I changed money earlier on. He again tried pressuring me into paying him at least KSh50 extra. Well, I had no more Kenyan shillings left and a verbal agreement is a verbal agreement. Besides, I was sure he was going to collect a commission on the exchange before he returned to the Kenyan side.

To my relief the Ugandan taxi rank had boards showing both the destination of the various taxis and the fares. It was going to cost me USh7 000 (about R35) to get to Jinja.

I had to wait more than an hour while the taxi gathered a sufficient number of passengers for the journey ahead. Being an avid reader of newspapers, I used the opportunity to buy the *Red Pepper*. I was attracted not only by the name but by a juicy headline: "Sex-mad MP names secret lovers", and the picture of the smiling "MP Mbeiza under a suspected juju spell".

I turned to page 2 of the *Red Pepper* of Tuesday, 21 October 2008. This was, in part, what I read:

Margaret Mbeiza, the sex-mad MP has totally lost it. The gorgeous legislator has gone into a trance and is reeling off a list of people she has dated all her life.

Last night, the MP shocked those around her sickbed when she named one of the biggest men in the country as her playmate. The shocking revelations emerged after the MP had been whisked to a juju man in Kaliro District as she recuperated from her trance which she fell into after divorcing her husband with whom she has four kids […]

Sources further told us last night that the MP's hysteria has escalated […]

the witchdoctor who is administering his juju on her has advised her to shaft her estranged husband five times in a day if she is to beat the spell some bad people cast on her.

"She must open her legs for the husband to enter. She must choose between insanity and opening her legs for the man she disgraced and divorced, if she is to overcome the powerful spell cast on her by powerful wizards from Congo and Tanzania," a source close to the traditional chemist told *Red Pepper* last night. However, by last evening it was not clear whether the gorgeous legislator had agreed to sleep with her former husband [...]

Gorgeous Mbeiza is suspected to have been bewitched by members from her husband's family after she slapped a sex ban on him [...]

They convened meetings and resolved to teach her a lesson.

That was the first story I read in the first newspaper I bought in Uganda. I couldn't contain my laughter, but the other passengers in the taxi did not seem to mind my squeaks and giggles. I have to confess that the more I read *Red Pepper* the more I loved it.

There was one small and serious headline on an inside page: "War looms as UPDF tanks roll into Sudan". UPDF is the abbreviation for Ugandan Peoples' Defence Forces, the country's army, which had been heavily deployed at the Uganda–Sudan border to fight the Lord's Resistance Army, a cruel and fanatical rebel group led by Joseph Kony, self-described as God's spokesman.

Some newspapers have photos of almost naked women on the back page, whilst others have them on page 3. Well, *Red Pepper* had a picture of Claire, a very dark and fit woman, on page 5. Think of tennis player Serena Williams; that is what Claire looked like. She was seated with her back to the camera in a very short black dress, strapless and teasing, her head turned towards the camera showing a very broad smile. Next to her photo appeared the following caption: "If you spend a nice, quiet evening getting to know Claire, you might just get her purring like a kitten. So, all you horny men, what are you waiting for?"

Having tasted *Red Pepper* once, I was hooked. To my excitement I discovered it was a daily paper. I knew that from that moment on I was going to read it every day for the rest of my time in Uganda. It would take me behind the scenes of a country that had been ruled for eight years by a boxing champion-turned-army general-turned-dictator – Idi Amin. Or, to give him his full title: His Excellency, President for Life, Field Marshal, Al Hadji Doctor Idi Amin Dada, VC (Victoria Cross), DSO (Distinguished Service Order), MC (Military Cross), Lord of all the Beasts of the Earth and the Fishes of the Seas, and Conqueror of the British Empire in Africa in general and Uganda in particular.

Amin is remembered, amongst other things, for giving Ugandans of Asian descent ninety days to leave the country – after God had told him to do so in a dream. Rumour has it that he was a cannibal.

Once the taxi had set off, I saw that the 115-kilometre stretch of road between Busia and Jinja was even better than the section on the Kenyan side, except in a few places where construction was taking place. One thing that pleasantly surprised me yet again was how green it was. On both sides of the road banana plantations and fields of sunflowers, sugar cane, mealies and tall green grass could be seen.

Before arriving at Jinja we passed through the towns of Bugiri and Iganga. Every third building in both towns carried a familiar brand name – MTN. South Africa, it seemed, was trying to overtake China as the continent's conqueror.

Adrift in Jinja

When we got to Jinja at 4.30 p.m., it began to drizzle. My hope to bungee and get to Kampala the same day was starting to fade. My dilemma was, should I book a room at Victoria View Hotel, right next to the taxi rank, and then head off to the bungee site a few kilometres outside town, or should I take a risk and go straight to the bungee site, rush back to town after bungeeing and find transport to Kampala? But what if I got to the bungee site and for some reason, like the time of day or the weather, I could not jump? And what if I managed to jump but by the time I got back to central Jinja there was no transport to Kampala and also no room at Victoria Lake Hotel? Decisions, decisions. In the end I decided not to book a room at Victoria Lake; I would attempt to bungee and take it from there.

I flagged down a boda-boda. I negotiated Vincent the driver down from uSh5 000 to uSh3 000. The poor guy did not want to take anything less than that, arguing: "One thousand five hundred is for the fuel and another one thousand five hundred is for this," pointing at his flat tummy. Truth be told, I had no clue how much he was supposed to charge. I simply stuck to my principle: try to negotiate a 50 per cent discount off whatever price is quoted; if I get a minimum of 33 per cent discount I'm still happy.

With my bag strapped onto my back, I leapt on the back of the boda-boda and off we went. The adrenaline was starting to pump. After all, I was on my way to bungee at the famed "source of the Nile". This was going to be my third bungee jump in ten years. My first was at Vic Falls in Zimbabwe, my second at Bloukrans in the Eastern Cape, both in 1999. So I had not felt the sensation of rushing head-first towards the ground with only the bungee cord separating me from eternity (read: death) for almost ten years.

As we got to Clive Road, one of Jinja's main streets, it started raining. Actually it started pouring heavily. I could not believe that in two consecutive days I was going to get drenched on the back of a boda-boda.

The driver didn't mind and was speeding as fast as he could, overtaking every car in his way. Because he was driving very close to the centre line, we missed the oncoming traffic, taxis in particular, by centimetres. All of this in a heavy downpour and poor visibility.

The rain was coming down so hard that I constantly had to wipe my face with my right hand, while holding on to the rail next to my seat for dear life with my left. Thank goodness I had put my passport in my backpack at the border; I was (almost) sure it would not get wet.

The strangest thing then happened: the boda-boda started losing power on an even, straight road, and within a few metres it came to a grinding halt. With the rain almost drowning out his voice Vincent shouted, "Oh, fuel!"

While cars were whizzing past non-stop, some much closer than I would have liked them to, he used his legs to push us completely off the road. Over his shoulder he gave me a hand signal to get off, which I did. Then he jumped off and lifted the seat up, exposing the fuel cap. He opened the tank, bent over and blew very hard into it. He then quickly closed it, slammed the seat back and started the engine.

Guess what? We were back in business. As we went down a hill and turned into a Shell garage near the bottom of the hill, the rain was easing off. The bowsers were out in the open, but there was a small veranda next to the petrol attendants' change rooms. Here Vincent parked, right next to another boda-boda whose driver was also seeking shelter.

I was soaking wet, but my biggest worry was my passport. I could not even start imagining what I would do if my passport had been ruined. With shaking fingers I took it out of my travel pouch and let out a long sigh of relief: it was bone dry and intact.

Together with three female petrol attendants, two boda-boda drivers and four pedestrians I stood on the veranda waiting for the rain to pass. It took another quarter of an hour for it to quieten down, with only a few droplets continuing to fall.

Then the second strange thing of the afternoon happened. Initially I could not understand what the issue was because everybody was talking in their local language. It turned out that all three ladies were flatly refusing to fill our boda-boda because it was still raining. One lady did risk it out from under the roof, but as soon as a few droplets fell on her she squealed, "Oh no!" and ran back onto the veranda.

I was speechless. I can understand it if people are not eager to work in the rain, but the rain had stopped, and I'm not just saying that because I was in a hurry to get going. There were just a few droplets falling, what in Zulu we call *amath'ezimpukane* – saliva of the flies.

"Come on. Let's go. There's another fuel station close by," Vincent said as he wiped the wet seats. At least the ladies had the decency to give him a cloth. A small problem with that cloth was that they had used it when checking the oil in vehicles. I didn't mind; my cargo pants were not so clean either.

I hopped on behind Vincent and clutched the railing behind my bum with both hands. Indeed, not much further down was a Caltex station which had a shelter over its bowsers. Vincent put in uSh1 500 worth of fuel – not even two litres. In no time we were ready to soldier on.

We took a left and rejoined Nalufenya Road (an extension of Clive Road) in the direction of the Bujagali Falls. After going up a small hill we took another left, following the "Jinja Nile Resort" sign. Passing the resort I could not help but wish I was booked there. Having roughed it for almost three weeks, I was now, more than ever before, longing for my own room with a comfortable double bed and clean bedding, clean floors and walls and a TV. I was basically longing for my own everyday reality.

The road became gravel and, because of the downpour, very muddy. The driver negotiated the slippery road extremely well and soon stopped at the bungee site. From my previous two experiences I was expecting that the jump would be from a bridge somewhere over the Nile. But as we drove into the premises I saw quite a few buildings and, out the corner of my eye, spotted the bungee platform – a steel structure towering a few metres above the ground. A staircase led up to a walkway along which you walked to the platform.

It was unbelievable. At forty-four metres high, the jump was lower than those I had done before – 111 metres at Victoria Falls and 216 metres at Bloukrans. But it was over the Nile, the longest river on planet Earth (depending on whom you ask; some people believe the Amazon is). It just does not get any better than this, I thought. Although I could not see anyone standing on or jumping from the platform, the adrenaline started pumping again.

It started raining again. Leaving the driver and my bag behind I ran across the parking lot, down some stairs, past a big yard where a few tents were pitched, following the "Reception" signs.

The reception desk was at a bar next to the bungee site. The site belonged to Adrift Camp, which also offered accommodation in the form of camping, dormitories and chalets.

The bar offered the best views in Africa, if not the world. It sat on a hill and when you look out across the low wall you see the Victoria Nile after it has flowed out of Lake Victoria a few kilometres upstream, the place generally thought of as the source of the Nile.

Before I could even greet the two guys on the other side of the counter, I read: *Dormitory – us$10; Chalet – us$50*, and heard: "Sorry, mister, due to the bad weather jumps have been halted until tomorrow morning."

I took the news on the chin. After checking the bookings register the receptionist told me that the earliest they could accommodate me was 09:30 the next day; some guys were arriving from Kampala for rafting but a few of them wanted to bungee first.

I made up my mind. It was a great place with to-die-for views and if I wanted to jump early, it made absolute sense to spend the night at Adrift Camp.

Suddenly I thought: What if Vincent, whom I had left at the parking lot, had disappeared with my bag? I ran back and found him hiding (from the rain) under the thatched shelter, holding my bag with both his arms like a mother comforting her baby. Again it was a humbling moment. There I had been thinking, just a few seconds earlier, that this very person might disappear with my bag. Maybe it's just the cynic in me who doesn't trust people, but let's blame it on South Africa's high crime rate.

Whichever way, I paid him, took my bag and we wished each other well. Although it was still raining he didn't want to wait, because, he said, "With the rain people have been stuck in town, so they will be looking for boda-bodas once the rain stops."

I went back to reception, checked into the dormitory and spent half an hour in the bar, not drinking but staring at the view. It was incredible, magnificent, unbelievably beautiful. As I was standing there in awe, a profound thought came to my mind: Capitalism has really messed things up. We all have to work so that we can have money to buy material things to keep up with people we do not know. What a waste and distortion of the simple thing called life.

I remembered reading that we work so that we can buy houses, which remain empty most of the time because we are at work; and then we buy cars which we keep parked most of the time because we are somewhere else, working. Surely it was never meant to be this way? The system, obviously with our permission, has really screwed all of us in a big way.

I waited for the rain to slow down before I went to the dormitory. It turned out to be the best place I had occupied on the trip. Not only on this trip but ever since I started backpacking. Really, the dormitory at Adrift Camp is the best place in its category that I have ever stayed at. Nothing was broken; it was clean, as in spotlessly clean; the bedding was fresh and newly laundered.

Outside the dormitory was a nicely trimmed lawn for those people who preferred to camp. Further away were showers (with hot water) and clean toilets. I returned and asked at reception whether they served dinner but was told that due to renovations the kitchen was closed. So I had two 300-ml Fanta Oranges while chatting to the Rastaman, one of the rafter guides. He tried to convince me to go rafting with him the following day. What he did not know was that my swimming really sucks big time.

Later I met a couple from Australia who were on a month-long overland East African adventure. They had just come back from southern Uganda where, they told me, they had a "great encounter" with the mountain gorillas and that it had been worth their three-hour walk in pouring rain.

When I told them I was from South Africa they were very quick to inform me that two girls in their group, who were booked into the dormitory next to ours, were also South African.

Earlier on in the bar I had seen a large group of young people chatting away and having a great time. I reasoned that the two girls from Mzansi must have been part of that group. I thought to myself: Wow, girls from South Africa, maybe I should go and introduce myself and have a decent conversation with my compatriots. On second thoughts, however, I had to face reality: a scruffy, dirty, wet, black man approaching two white girls at night might turn out to be very embarrassing for the black man who did not want his ego dented. And they had to be white. The Australian couple did not tell me that, but let's face it: with all due respect to my black sisters, how many black sisters from Soweto – or anywhere in the country for that matter – will go overlanding for a month in East Africa?

I must confess that I was sorely tempted, but I reasoned also that going up to the group of strangers and saying, "Hi everybody, I'm looking for the two girls from South Africa", might sound very cheesy and desperate. It might very well create the impression that I was looking for an easy, cheap screw. One can also never run away from the fact that, whichever way you look at it, South Africa is still a racially divided country where – I do not care who says what – the colour of your skin determines how strangers will judge and draw certain conclusions about you.

If, like me, you are a black African you are assumed to be a criminal and a thug until you prove yourself otherwise. If you are an Indian it is taken for granted that you are a scheming liar who will do whatever it takes to make it big (financially speaking). White people are assumed to be rich racists who will never rest until a white political organisation runs South Africa again. Coloureds, amongst other things, abuse alcohol and the men walk with a swagger.

Therefore to walk up to some white chicks who, although from the same country as I was, were probably not going to identify with me, made me decide against introducing (read: humiliating) myself.

I had drunk only two Fanta Oranges the whole day, but I was not hungry or even thirsty. It must have been the adrenaline that was coursing through my veins.

Despite the fact that I was scheduled to jump early the following morning, I slept like a baby (in the cleanest bedding of the trip). It felt really great to be sleeping, literally, on the edge of the Nile River, a few kilometres from its source. It was hard to imagine the difficulties the early explorers – all white guys as far as I know – experienced to get here. Compared to theirs, my trip had been a piece of cake.

When I woke up the overlanders were gone. The first thought that came to mind was that I should have introduced myself to those two South African girls after all – maybe they were great individuals.

I planned to leave Adrift Camp straight after my jump and proceed via Masaka to Mbarara instead of sleeping over in Kampala. The great thing about this plan was that, since the equator runs between Kampala and Masaka, I would be bungeeing and standing on the equator on the same day. It was promising to be the most productive twenty-four hours of the trip. Imagine: achieving two of my goals in one day!

When I stepped out of the dormitory at about 9 a.m. there were clouds in the sky, but I could still see the sun. The sound of the majestic Nile and the sight of the bungee platform made my adrenaline levels shoot up again. I went to reception and was told the jumpmaster had not arrived yet, but that he should be there before ten.

So the waiting began. Under normal circumstances I hate waiting. Not to mention waiting to do something as scary as bungee jumping. Once you have decided to do it, you must just get it over and done with. I sat there waiting, exactly like when I was parachuting in Pietermaritzburg: I'd rushed from Durban and then had to wait for hours for the weather to clear. Only now I was waiting for the bungeemaster to arrive.

Just before ten I enquired at reception and was told that the people who had booked for rafting and bungee jumping had all cancelled. "Sorry," Emmy, the guy at the bar, said, "you are the only one still booked for the bungee. Unfortunately the jumpmaster can't set up everything for just one person. Maybe later this afternoon other people will come and then you can jump."

I was bitterly disappointed. I had psyched myself up for bugger-all. Decision-making time again. One part of me said, since I was there already and other people who also wanted to jump might arrive later, I might as well stay put. Another part of me said: what if nobody turns up, or what if they do but the weather turns as bad as the previous day and messes up everything? And the worst-case scenario: what if nobody comes and it also rains in the afternoon?

Yet another part said: even if I don't jump, the ambience and the view at Adrift are worth staying for, even a few days would not be wasted time. The counter-argument in my mind, which was now in overdrive, was that I would be flying back to Johannesburg from Nairobi, so whatever I decided I'd have to pass through Jinja again on my way back from Rwanda to Kenya.

My mind was made up: I would jump on my way back the following week. I did some calculations – it was Wednesday and I would be able to go to Rwanda and be back in Uganda within seven days. So the next Thursday would be the ideal day to return to Adrift Camp.

It was time to implement Plan H: instead of jumping on my way to Rwanda, I'd jump on my way back to Kenya.

With this settled, my objective now was to stand on the equator.

The centre of the Earth

I looked at my watch – 10:25. After feasting my eyes on the majestic view of the Nile and booking a bed for the following Thursday, I hurried to the dormitory to pick up my bag. When I got to the parking lot all the boda-bodas that were there earlier had left.

"The boda-bodas come in the mornings to see if anyone is leaving and by about nine o'clock they head back to town," the security guard told me. Not to worry. He had a plan: he would phone some guy and all I had to do was buy him a cooldrink. I bought him a 340-ml tin of cold Coca-Cola for USh600 (just under R4).

It took about twenty minutes for the boda-boda to arrive. I asked him to take me first to the board that says "The source of the Nile" and then to drop me off at the taxi rank. He quoted USh10 000 but in the end settled for USh8 000. Just before we left he gave the security guard some money. I couldn't see how much; all I could see was that people were forever getting commission from different sources.

We used the main road again, which meant passing the Shell garage where the petrol attendants hadn't wanted to help us the previous day. From my back seat I now noticed that Jinja had quite a few middle-to-superior tourist hotels which a guy like me couldn't afford.

The spot signposted as the source of the Nile was not actually at the source, as I had expected. "This is the only sign that says the source of the Nile," my driver assured me. We took some pictures.

One thing about travelling alone is the schlep of having to ask other people to take your picture. As a result I do not appear in many of my travel pictures. This was, in fact, the first picture of me taken on the trip.

On our way to the taxi rank we stopped at Trend Bureau de Change, where I got USh92 500 for US$50, an exchange rate of USh1 850 for a dollar.

I could not believe my luck. The taxi heading for Kampala at the taxi rank was short of only one passenger. As soon as I was inside the assistant closed the door and we were on our way, listening to Celine Dion.

We were travelling at a moderate speed through sugar-cane plantations and scenery that reminded me of the KwaZulu-Natal coast north of Durban where there are also vast stretches of sugar cane. Only the Indian Ocean was missing. In amongst the greenery was a school named Seeta. This, I thought, would be the Kearsney College or Michaelhouse of Uganda. It looked very grand with its red three-storey buildings and big sports fields.

The first thing that struck me when we entered the capital city was the numerous A4 advertisements stuck on buildings and bus shelters promising "Penis enlargement and strength, increased breast and hip size". Whereas sexy women in the western world are supposed to have small waists, in Uganda irresistible women seem to boast big boobs and huge hips.

We drove through the suburbs of Namanve and Bweyogerere before passing the Mandela National Stadium on our right, with Mandela Sports Hotel right next to it. After the Nakana suburb and the Lugogo Mall, we hit the bumper-to-bumper traffic for which Kampala is renowned. The traffic was moving very slowly and sometimes we came to a total standstill. I could see a few hundred metres ahead and knew that we were going to be in it for a good while.

Our driver persevered through the slow-as-a-tortoise traffic for almost an hour before we got to the actual city centre. He dropped us in front of the city market (built in 1925).

The assistant driver suggested that I take a boda-boda to the new taxi rank. "That is where you will find taxis and buses going to Masaka," he said.

I caught a boda-boda just opposite the market, on Market Street, in front of the huge Tourist Hotel. The problem with traffic in Kampala is that the thousands of vehicles do not stick to their own lanes; there is a stampede of cars, bicycles, boda-bodas and buses all trying to squeeze into the narrowest of spaces. Sitting on the back of a boda-boda as it negotiated the heavy traffic was nerve-racking; I constantly wanted to shut my eyes tight. The main culprits were the buses and trucks that seemed to think they had right of way.

While swerving and weaving in and out of the traffic in his boda-boda, my driver tried to convince me to take a small bus instead of a taxi. "Taxis here are not safe," he insisted. I could not agree with him more. So when we stopped outside the very busy and chaotic Qualicell Bus Terminal, he left his boda-boda and took me by the hand to the Masaka bus. More than ten bus touts rushed and grabbed me by my other hand without even knowing where I was going. It was harassment at its worst.

As we made our way deeper into the disorganised bus terminal, the boda-boda guy would turn around and say a few words to the bus touts, which kept them at bay for a few seconds before they renewed their assault. Finally, we got to a fifty-five-seater "small" bus heading for Masaka. I paid the boda-boda his uSh1 500. He then conversed with the driver's assistant in Luganda (I think) before I was asked to pay uSh12 000 and allowed onto the bus.

Sensing I might again be overcharged, I reminded the assistant: "But I'm going to jump off at the equator. I'm not going all the way to Masaka."

"Yes, my friend, it costs twelve thousand if you are going to the equator," I was assured. Indeed, the receipt said: *Destination: Equator*.

The bus really took its time to fill up. I stepped out quite soon because it was getting hot inside. Checking out the scene, I noticed that there were a few buses going to Masaka, all loading at the same time. No wonder there were such insistent touts at the entrance to the bus terminal. It also explained why, as a passenger, you had to pay before you could board; it prevented you from leaving and changing buses.

I got back inside the very hot bus and tried to kill time with my favourite newspaper, *Red Pepper*. The headline on Wednesday 22 October was even more eye-catching (read: raunchier) than the previous one I'd seen: "I get 50 orgasms in a day". I turned to page 22 where the following story appeared:

Pretty Deborah Nakintu is a 50-a-day orgasm babe who gets wet and wild from almost any vibration. The vibration of anyone's phone, the vibration of a hairdryer, the rhythmic murmur of a photocopier are all enough to make her go oh oh oh, ahhhhh! Our reporter who had an interview with her was shocked that Deborah had three orgasms during their 40-minute interview.

It is unfortunate that at just 23, Debbie (as she prefers to be called) suffers from Permanent Sexual Arousal Syndrome (PSAS), a disease which increases the blood flow to the sex organs.

"It started off in bed where my bonking sessions would last for hours and my boyfriend would be stunned at how many times I would orgasm. Within a few weeks, I began getting more and more aroused and I just kept having endless orgasms. Then it would happen over and over again after sex. […]

"I and my boyfriend split and new lovers struggle to keep up with my sex demands.

"I have read books that say that taking antidepressants and then discontinuing has an effect on the sexual organs. That is the only thing that could explain what happens to me," she said.

Debbie has even been to a Sex Addicts Anonymous meeting in despair over her sex drive.

Debbie's friends think she is the luckiest girl ever.

On page 2 of the lovely, delicious, chilli-hot *Red Pepper* a follow-up on the sex-mad MP appeared under the headline "Juju men ask sex mad MP for her knickers".

Traditional healers in Mukono District have declared that if Margaret Mbeiza wants to recover from a spell cast on her by her enemies, she must sleep with her estranged husband and then throw her treasured knickers at a road junction. […]

The respected traditional doctor Jaja Mukasa Kiryiwa who claims to have acquired his trade in Tanzania and Lake Victoria said:

"All she needs is sleep with her husband five times in one day and then bring here the panties she will be wearing. We shall smear them with sheep blood, white flour and appeal to the sacred gods to come to the legislator's rescue. Then she will be asked to go and discard the knickers at a road junction and the next day she will go back to work and she will be fine as a dry cell." […]

Asked what they would do in case the ritual failed to succeed, one of the healers who works with Kiryiwa said it would necessitate taking Mbeiza under Lake Victoria since the juju that was in charge of her is very powerful. […]

The healer also said that to ward off future attacks, Mbeiza must end her sex ban on her husband and bonk the man regularly even if she no longer loves him. That she must shaft with him for two months before the other evil spirits are completely overcome.

It took two hours for our bus to fill up and to start moving forward. I got excited that we were finally going to leave the chaotic, boiling bus terminal. However, my hopes were dashed when even bigger buses, one of them called White Cock, also started moving forward. When he saw my jaw drop the guy sitting next to me in the back seat explained, "A lot of people do not enter any bus but instead wait for the one which is leaving because they do not want to be stuck in a bus which is still going to take hours before it leaves. That is why once one bus starts leaving, all of them pretend to be leaving as well."

What added to the confusion were the many bus touts walking between the buses, hassling passers-by.

One bus now wanted to reverse into position, but with so many other buses sitting right on its tail it couldn't. That meant a number of other buses reversing as well. With touts and travellers all over the place it was a real battlefield.

Once out of the terminal and on the main street of Kampala, another battle started – the fight with trucks, taxis, bicycles and boda-bodas. It took us just under forty-five minutes to get out of town. The following day I read in the newspaper that five people had been killed instantly when a bus plunged into cars in central Kampala the previous day. We were lucky.

As we were leaving Kampala I noticed Backpackers Hostel on our right and decided that on my way back from Rwanda I would spend a night right there. From what I could see it looked like my kind of place.

According to my guidebook the equator lay sixty kilometres to the south of Kampala. That meant I had to monitor the situation very closely. With the sun now on my right-hand side I knew that we were indeed heading south. I was sitting in the back seat with three other guys, two of whom were fast asleep. I asked the wide-awake third one to tell me when we were approaching the equator. He replied in a very soft voice that he was also going there. I could not believe my luck.

Reassured, I was sitting back still trying to get used to how green Uganda was when I saw a sign flashing by: *Equator 12 km to go*. A little later I glimpsed a spherical shape, like a globe, with bold writing across it: EQUATOR. I swung round at the speed of light. I saw curio and craft shops on both sides of the road just as in a photo I had seen months back. I knew I was at the right place.

The bus showed no sign of slowing down to stop. It was tuned to some local radio station that played local music which the passengers just loved. A few times, both men and women started to sing along with the songs. I turned to the guy who had said that he was also going to the equator. From the dazed look on his face it was clear that he had just woken up from a deep sleep. When I asked him if he was getting off at the equator, he answered with a dopey smile.

By then I was already standing, screaming and shouting at the driver's assistant, who was not the guy I'd paid at the bus rank in Kampala. Other passengers, amazed by this frantic person screaming at the top of his voice, also alerted him that there was someone who desperately wanted to get out. The assistant driver, in turn, spoke to the driver who, to his credit, did his utmost to bring the bus to a standstill. Because I was sitting right at the back, some passengers had to get up or lean over to make room for me as I made my way towards the front of the bus.

When I'd boarded the bus back in Kampala my bag was put behind the driver's seat. As I was disembarking I looked where my bag was supposed to be, but it was nowhere to be seen. My heart stopped. The first conclusion I came to was that with all that commotion in Kampala, someone must have run off with it. The passengers sitting immediately behind the driver were all requested to leave the bus so we could see whether my bag was somewhere underneath their seats. Nothing.

Those few seconds of coming to terms with the fact that my bag was lost must have taken ten years off my expected lifespan. It was stressful beyond expression. The bus was standing on the side of the road, idling, while the search continued. I was standing next to the bus, my eyes on the driver who was looking at me with an I-am-sorry-there-is-nothing-I-can-do-to-help-you-and-I-have-to-go-as-in-now look. At that moment someone touched me from behind. It was the driver's assistant, holding my bag in his other hand. Someone had apparently put it in the luggage compartment. I almost hugged the fellow.

The bus must have come to a standstill almost a kilometre from the equator, so I had to walk a few hundred metres to the line that divides the Earth into two equal hemispheres. My heart was beating faster and I started to smile, finding it difficult to believe that another of my objectives was about to be fulfilled.

I hurried past a few curio shops, not taking my eyes off the circular structure on the side of the road with bold black writing: EQUATOR.

When I reached the sign I was surprised. At school we were taught that the equator is an imaginary line, but when I got there I discovered that, at least in Uganda, it is a white line that runs right across the road.

While I was taking photographs, a thin young man came up to me and introduced himself as Hannington. He offered not only to do the water experiment (which shows water in a bowl swirling in a clockwise direction in the southern hemisphere and in an anticlockwise direction when you cross the line into the northern hemisphere) but also – for uSh10 000 – to issue me with an authentic certificate to prove that I had stood on the equator. I opted for the certificate. I didn't need any water swirling in the wrong direction to convince me that I was indeed standing on the dividing line between north and south. Really now, I had come all this way because I knew that the equator ran south of Kampala. And I was at that exact spot. No proof needed.

As I stood with one leg on either side of the white line, I looked at my watch. Date: 22/10/08. Time: 16:14. Hannington offered to take a photograph with, as he put it, "your one bum in the northern hemisphere and another in the southern hemisphere".

While he was clicking away I was thinking that applied not only to my bum but also my balls. Well, maybe not, because, although the equator cuts the Earth into two equal halves and there are two equinoxes when the sun crosses the plane of the equator – on 20/21 March and 22/23 September – it was now October (read: spring in the southern hemisphere) and the Earth was slightly tilted upwards, thus exposing more of the southern hemisphere to the sun. I decided to shift slightly to the left (downwards) in order to be right in the middle of the world. Again, I was just being practical about things.

Hannington invited me to his office – a desk inside a curio shop – where I was issued with a certificate (Number 52401509) confirming that I had stood on the equator. While I was chatting to him he took some more pictures of me to put on his website (www.ugandaequator.com). He was shocked that I had been charged uSh12 000 to get there. "Even people going all the way to Masaka pay only ten thousand!" he said. "Getting off here you should've paid eight. Taxis cost even less, just six thousand. It always happens when boda-boda guys and bus touts club together – they overcharge the tourists."

It all fell into place. But having been overcharged by some unscrupulous persons was not enough to deflate my highly uplifted spirits. After all, I had straddled the equator, putting half of me (let's not get into graphic details again) in the north and half in the south. That was far more important.

"*Angeke banothe* – they will never be rich – because of the extra shillings they robbed me of," I said.

I thanked Hannington and went and stood on the white line, waiting, on his advice, for a bus or taxi going to Masaka. From there I could get a bus or taxi to Mbarara. Not once was I hassled by the people working in the curio and crafts shops. They just sat in their shops waiting for tourists to come in. I expected to see lots of tourists, but in the thirty minutes I spent on the equator I saw only one car with four tourists. They stopped for five minutes, took pictures and left.

It was mission accomplished. Now for my next objective: visiting the Kigali Memorial Centre in Rwanda.

South to Kabale

I didn't have to wait long. A yellow bus appeared within a minute or two. I flagged it down. As it was coming to a stop the assistant driver stuck his head through the window and shouted, "Mbarara?"

I could not believe my luck; here was a very comfortable LB Coach going all the way to Mbabara.

I bought two homemade cookies and a lukewarm cooldrink from the guy selling snacks on board. It was my first meal of the day – just before five in the afternoon. Sitting there munching my not-so-delicious, not-so-filling food, I was satisfied and excited about the turn of events. Slowly the things I wanted to do on this trip were happening. No matter what the obstacles, I thought, you must never ever give up on your dreams.

I looked through the window of the not-quite-full bus at the green fields of Uganda, now dotted with large numbers of black-and-white Friesland cows – excellent milk producers, I learned in lower primary. (Who still believes Bantu education was all bad?)

The elderly man sitting next to me started chatting. He told me that the bus was going all the way to Kasese in the west of Uganda, near the border with the DRC.

Apparently the road continued on after Mbarara and then swung north to Kasese, which is the gateway to the Rwenzori Mountains and the Rwenzori Mountain National Park.

Three mountains in the park are named after three nineteenth-century British explorers – Stanley, Speke and Baker. Baker was the guy who sailed with Speke to Khartoum after Speke had found proof that Lake Victoria was indeed the source of the Nile. Baker is credited with discovering Lake Albert, which at one stage was renamed Lake Mobutu Sese Seko before reverting to its former name.

Just south of Kasese there is a small patch of water – Lake George – which connects with the bigger Lake Edward to the west and the still bigger Lake Albert to the north, which, in turn, is connected with the biggest of them all, Lake Victoria, by means of the Victoria Nile. I was still trying to figure out why the lofty peaks were given the names of explorers and the low-lying lakes received the names of royalty. George (later King George V) was, by the way, the son of King Edward VII, the first son and second child of Prince Albert and Queen Victoria. Three-quarters of Edward and half of Albert now belong to the DRC; the rest of the royal family is in Uganda.

The bus suddenly stopped in the middle of nowhere. It was time for the synchronised relieving of our bladders. This time only women, six of them, stepped out of the bus. They did not seem at all embarrassed as they squatted in the long grass, facing in the direction in which we were going.

We continued in a south-westerly direction on a tarred road across rolling green hills and plains. My neighbour and some other passengers disembarked at Masaka. It was already so dark that the driver had to switch on the cabin lights for them to identify their bags.

The road between Masaka and Mbarara was under construction and certain sections were really bad. At one stage the bus had to negotiate massive potholes in the dark, in the middle of what looked like jungle. I asked my neighbour – a responsible-looking older gentleman who had embarked at Masaka – if he would tell me when we reached Mbarara. Unlike the guy from Kampala who had sat next to me earlier, he seemed to know exactly where we were and also where to find the most reasonable accommodation in Mbarara. Right as you entered town, he said.

Seeing that I was dealing with such a knowledgeable man, I asked him if it was possible to travel from the southern town of Kisoro through the Cyanika border post to Ruhengeri in Rwanda. He was quiet for a while and then said, "Yes, it is possible. It is just that that border post is very close to Congo. And you know these Congolese, they can start their thing anytime. So I will not advise you to use that border. Instead use the main one at Katuna."

I decided there and then not to go through the Cyanika border crossing, although it meant I would have to travel straight from Kabale (about 140 kilometres south of Mbarara) to Kigali. However, I still wanted to see what has been described as "the best journey in Uganda" – the stretch between Kabale and Kisoro with an incredible view of the Virunga mountains, which consist of eight, mostly dormant, volcanoes. These mountains separate Lake Edward and Lake Kivu.

With this in mind, I decided on Plan I: take an early bus from Mbarara to Kabale and from there catch a bus or taxi to Kisoro, and then literally make a u-turn and take another bus or taxi back to Kabale, all in one day. In that way, I reasoned, I would experience the best journey in Uganda twice in one day.

Wow, what a perfect plan.

When we got to Mbarara I found a clean room with a (hot) shower and toilet at Akaanya Hotel without too much difficulty. It was not exorbitantly priced either, only uSh20 000.

When I asked the dark younger version of the pitch-black, masculine-looking Jamaican–American singer/model/actress Grace Jones at reception if the quoted amount included breakfast, she said, "No. I will not give it to you." Whatever that meant.

Instead of having a meal at the in-house restaurant I decided to go across the road and buy something to eat from a general dealer. I ended up buying a 300-ml Fanta Orange and another homemade cookie (read: old muffin).

Although it was after 9 p.m., I also bought myself the *New Vision* newspaper, which had on its front page President Museveni welcoming South Africa's (caretaker) President Kgalema Motlanthe at Entebbe International Airport for the Tripartite Summit. There was no time to do any in-depth reading, however, because I had hardly got back to my room when there was a power failure.

After a few minutes of sitting in total darkness, I heard two men talking right outside my window. I was terrified. I could feel not only my heart pounding but also my balls shrinking. I was imagining the worst. It turned out that they were starting up Akaanya Hotel's very powerful (read: noisy) generator.

With the terrific noise coming from right next to my room, I was not sure how I was going to fall asleep. The power came back on within half an hour, however, and the engine was switched off. Satisfied with the decision I had made earlier based on the old man's advice – to travel from Mbarara to Kabale from where I could head off to Kisoro and back to Kabale the same day and then carry on from Kabale to Rwanda – I fell into a deep and peaceful sleep.

The Akaanya receptionist had told me the previous evening that I'd have to leave the hotel before 8 a.m. if I wanted to find a bus bound for Kabale. I left my room at seven-thirty. Walking towards the bus station I found that Mbarara was far bigger than my first impression and that a lot of construction and upgrading of buildings was taking place. In fact, in the context of Uganda, Mbarara looked like it was going places.

After a slight hill and a left turn, I found the bus station. A few bus touts came running to me and all told me the same thing: the buses for Kabale had left at seven. "So my friend, you must take a taxi," said one of them, holding my right arm.

There were still two buses at the rank. When I enquired – from the hawkers selling bananas – I was told both buses were going to Kasese.

"I want a bus that goes to Kabale," I insisted to the youngster who was holding onto my arm. It didn't bother me much; he was not aggressive and seemed desperate to help. When I told him, for the fourth time, that I wanted a bus that was going to Kabale, he took out his cellphone, dialled a number and conversed with someone on the other side of the line for a few seconds.

"It is coming," he assured me and let go of my arm.

Within three minutes a taxi stopped right in front of us. "All buses have gone," the youngster repeated. "You must take this taxi because it is leaving now."

It was not such a bad idea considering that I wanted to get to Kabale as soon as possible.

There were five other passengers in the white fifteen-seater Toyota Hiace. The youngster went around to the driver's side and as I got into the taxi I noticed the taxi driver slipping him a few coins. Seconds later when I asked the assistant driver what the fare to Kabale was, the driver answered very quickly, "Ten thousand."

I knew immediately I was being overcharged. Why would the driver answer so quickly when my question wasn't even addressed to him? He was surely trying to get back the commission he'd paid to the tout. It's just one of those things that happen when you're travelling; you have to live with the fact that sometimes you will get screwed. Still, being overcharged twice in two consecutive days was a bit much to bear.

To add insult to injury, the taxi started careening round and round the town, hooting, reversing, stopping and hooting some more while looking for more passengers – and wasting my time. At least it gave me an opportunity to see the other parts of Mbarara.

This going and stopping and driving in circles went on for about an hour until the taxi was full. Finally we hit the road, which deteriorated as soon as we were out of town. Unlike the Kigoma–Mwanza road, which had made me decide to go all the way round Lake Victoria rather than double up on it and take the much shorter route to Kigali, this one was tarred but had deep potholes all over the surface. The driver often had to brake to prevent striking a hole. With so many buses coming from the opposite direction on their way to Kampala, he could not swerve to the right. Every time he braked, a screeching sound came from the back, which made me suspect that the brake pads were finished.

The road went from terrible to atrocious. Now the driver sometimes had no choice but to move to the extreme right-hand side of the road to go through a shallower pothole. With so much oncoming traffic, this was nerve-racking in the extreme.

At this pace my chances of going to Kisoro and back were getting slimmer and slimmer. To diminish my chances even further, the driver decided to have the brake pads checked in one of the makeshift repair centres at Ntungamo, the unofficial halfway mark between Mbarara and Kabale. Great minds think alike!

The bus was jacked up on the gravel pavement outside a small building with three cars inside, and the wheel was removed and inspected. New brake pads were indeed needed. About twenty minutes later they were delivered by a guy on a bicycle.

The process of stopping, checking and finally putting on the new brake pads took more than an hour. With this extra delay, I had to face the fact that Plan I was just not going to work.

So I changed the plan: from Kabale proceed to Kisoro, sleep over and return to Kabale the following day. From there – if transport was still available by the time I arrived – I could cross into Rwanda. This was Plan J. With so many changes of plan and so many things I still wanted to do and with so little time to do them, I was starting to panic.

We all scrambled back into the taxi and continued our journey south. Besides the never-ending, evergreen, undulating hills that looked as if they had been carved by a sculptor, I was struck by two things. Firstly, the cattle grazing on the side of the road had very long and very big horns. It was an incredible sight. The more cattle we passed, the bigger and more curved the horns seemed to become, and the bigger the bodies. The black-and-white dairy cows of the previous day had disappeared from the landscape. Just one of the beasts we were seeing now, I thought, would be enough to feed the Northern Cape's entire population (one million people).

Secondly, many young boys – who should surely have been in school – were pushing bicycles loaded with bananas. They couldn't ride their bikes because there was just not enough space left to sit on. The sight of these massive bunches of bananas being pushed along on bicycles reminded me, once again, that we in Africa just do not have the competitive edge. I saw only one rather dilapidated truck carrying a full load of bananas on the road between Ntungamo and Kabale. The rest of the banana harvest, it seemed, was being transported by bicycle.

About ten kilometres before we reached Kabale it started drizzling. A quarter of an hour later, at twelve-thirty, I was standing in Uganda's highest town, about 2 000 metres above sea level.

I decided to get more shillings before taking a taxi to Kisoro. At a Barclays Bank branch I produced the two US$20 notes which had been given to me as change in Adrift Camp back in Jinja.

"We do not take these notes because it is the 1990s series," the woman at the forex desk said. "We only take notes from 2000 onwards. However, if I do take them, you will have to forfeit ten per cent of what you're supposed to get at today's exchange rate."

"Okay, take the ten per cent off," I instructed her. I had no choice as far as I could see. So I effectively changed US$38.

QUESTION 6: Why did I effectively change US$38, and not US$36?

A bit peeved, I went back to the relatively small taxi rank to find a taxi to Kisoro. On enquiring, I was shown to a white Toyota Hiace. I stopped dead in my tracks: it was empty. I was going to be the first passenger. I knew, from the way taxis functioned, that I'd have to wait for the kombi to fill up.

I sat there looking at people going about their business, mostly going in and out of Tri-Soweto Photo Lab. Although my patience was wearing thin, I decided to stick it out. I really wanted to do the most scenic drive in Uganda.

Three hours later I had been joined by a measly five passengers. It was almost four o'clock when I decided to give up. To quit. It was time, yet again, to change the plan. Much as I wanted to see the volcanoes between Kabale and Kisoro, it was imperative that I keep my eye on the ball: I still had four goals to achieve. So Plan K was born: forget about Kisoro; proceed straight to Kigali from Kabale.

It was such a pity because now I was also going to miss seeing both Bunyonyi Lake and the Impenetrable Forest. It's amazing how things change. In my twenties nothing turned me on like penetrating impenetrable things. Then I would definitely not have passed up the opportunity to go through thick bush. Now? Well, I got out of the taxi.

The driver was not very impressed. I promised him that I would definitely go with him to Kisoro the following day. Now the challenge was to find a place to stay for the night. I checked my guidebook. Skyblue Hotel – with rooms named after different planets – looked like the perfect choice.

Three minutes later I was booked in (for USh13 000) and shown to Mars, a single, self-contained room. Skyblue Hotel was right next to Skyline Hotel, which was opposite Hideout Hotel.

Settling into Mars, I realised that this constant changing of plans had to come to an end. It was important, from that moment onwards, to have a solid, concrete plan that I would follow no matter what. I had exactly ten days before I had to fly back to Johannesburg, and here I was, still heading south – I hadn't even arrived in Rwanda yet! I was really stressing.

As I lay on the bed, I worked things backwards:

SUNDAY 02/11: fly from Nairobi;
SATURDAY 01/11: travel from Jinja to Nairobi;
FRIDAY 31/10: bungee jump at Jinja;
THURSDAY 30/10: travel from Kampala to Jinja;
WEDNESDAY 29/10: travel from Kigali to Kampala.

Today was Thursday 23 October. That meant I would be in Rwanda from Friday (the following day) until the next Wednesday. It also meant that I would have to squeeze all four of the things – three of them in Rwanda – I still wanted to do into eight days.

I had no choice. From that moment onwards everything had to work like clockwork. The first logistical matter I had to improve on was finding accommodation. I had to book in advance.

I decided to jump into action. I went to reception to ask about internet cafés. There happened to be one just around the corner. I quickly sent two emails from there: to Hostel Backpackers in Kampala, reserving a room for the following Wednesday, and to Nairobi Backpackers, booking a bed for the following Saturday. I could check their responses in Rwanda.

I also sent an email to Lulu, asking her to deposit the US$520 I had left behind so I could buy a permit to see the Rwandan mountain gorillas. I had anticipated that I would only need the money towards the end of the trip so, when I changed R15 000 to US dollars in Johannesburg, I took only US$1150 with me and left the rest behind.

My budget having been messed up by my travelling up through Kenya and Uganda on my way to Rwanda, and not the other way round as I originally planned, I decided to drop my older sister an email as well, asking her if she had some loose change for her younger brother. I wrote a long email about the procedure she should follow when depositing anything above US$70. I ended the email with a subtle bit of emotional blackmail: I said if she deposited the money I would mention her with her full name in the book I was going to write about the trip.

It was late afternoon and I decided to take a stroll along Kabale's main road. While I was absorbing the local atmosphere, I noticed a sign to Kigezi Radio Station. Being curious by nature, I decided to follow it.

It turned out to be a real radio station in a house off the main road. After introducing myself to the gentleman at reception, I asked if I could see the studio. Without questioning my purpose and using sign language, he invited me to follow him. In the studio I introduced myself to Andrew, the presenter, who told me that they broadcast to southern Uganda but that they could be heard as far as the DRC and Rwanda. He mentioned that a number of independent radio stations operated in Uganda, most of them based in Kampala, which made it tough for smaller stations to survive.

The studio looked somewhat cluttered with a mass of wires and cables criss-crossing the floor. But all Andrew's songs were pre-programmed in a computer and everything was played at the touch of a button. Not too shabby, hey?

During the ten minutes I spent with Andrew he never talked to the listeners. What a pity because I would have liked to know whether Kigezi Radio Station broadcast in English or in the local language. I should have just asked him, mind you.

I arrived back at Skyblue Hotel just after sunset. As I went past reception I asked the receptionist-cum-waiter about buses to Kigali. From his dazed appearance and slurred speech, I concluded that he was very sleepy.

"Buses leave Kampala around midnight and drive through Masaka and Mbarara and get to Kabale from seven in the morning onwards," he told me. "The biggest problem is that they are usually full because most travellers go from Kampala all the way to Kigali and thus do not pick up passengers in Kabale."

Noticing that I was looking a bit concerned, he added, "Sometimes they do pick up passengers, especially the ones that travel alone."

Back in Mars I ate a homemade cookie and polished off a litre of pure fruit juice which I had bought earlier from the well-stocked Royal Supermarket.

I went to sleep praying that at least one of the buses would be able to pick me up the next morning. The temperature had dropped and it drizzled throughout the night. My warm sleeping bag came in very handy. Although the bedding was clean, I still preferred to lie on top of the blankets provided.

Last leg to Rwanda

I woke up at five the next morning and took a hot shower using the small soap I had been given when I checked in the previous day. By quarter to six I had packed my bags and locked the door to Mars behind me. I was not taking any chances with buses not running to a strict timetable.

As soon as I stepped onto the veranda of the hotel I realised that standing on the road to wait for a bus was going to make my life very difficult. A light rain was still falling, but that was the least of my troubles. My problem was the drivers' assistants working on the minibuses bound for the border town of Katuna screaming at the top of their voices for passengers, and the taxis and cabs that were all loudly offering a special fee to prospective customers willing to pay a "premium fare for efficient transfer" to the border town. These guys, I knew, would all fall on me like a pack of hyenas.

I decided to remain on the veranda and hide my bag from the hustling mass by placing it just inside the hotel restaurant. The drawback was that once I spotted a bus coming, I would have to dash back to pick up my bag, rush out of the hotel premises and run across the road in order to be on the same side as the bus.

It still seemed a better bet than standing on the road and exposing myself to the hustlers.

By 06:00 (05:00 according to my biological clock) I was on the veranda waiting. Then it was 06:30. The number of people going to work, kids walking to school and taxis and cabs patrolling the main street of Kabale started to increase dramatically. Then it was 07:00. School kids wearing red jerseys and white shirts started to appear from all over. The boda-bodas were also now out in full force.

The drizzling had stopped but it was very chilly. Still there was not a sign of even a single bus. Then, when I least expected it and out of the blue, an MTN-branded bus approached at great speed. I flew back into the hotel, grabbed my bag and ran for dear life out into the main road. I crossed the road waving down the approaching bus like a madman. It slowed down but, instead of stopping, it started accelerating. Then it was gone. That was my worst nightmare come true: a bus going to Kigali zooming past me and leaving me exposed.

Within a few seconds half a dozen guys, all shouting at the same time what a "good deal" it would be for me if I took their specific taxi, had closed in on me. I tried telling them that I was on my way to Kigali and wanted a bus that went there.

Almost as one man they replied, "The bus that has just passed is the only one that goes all the way." They were adamant that I'd have to go to the border and, once on the Rwandan side, I'd find buses and taxis going to Kigali.

One guy thought a bit and then stated: "My friend, the next bus is only coming in at one this afternoon."

I felt confused and under pressure, but somehow I kept my wits about me. By now twenty guys were swarming around me. I tried walking back to the hotel but was blocked by most of them pushing in front of me, shoving keys in my face and shouting, "Take my taxi, my friend!"

I tried to stay calm but with so many of the guys in front of me it was easier said than done. I was still trying to cross the road to return to the safety of the hotel veranda when I spotted another bus, a white Amahoro Travel, coming. I stepped back a few paces, took a few steps to the right and raised my hand. It slowed down and stopped. The door opened and I jumped in. Whew!

I hadn't even greeted anyone on board when one of the guys who had insisted that there were no other buses going to Kigali started demanding a commission from the bus driver's assistant. "Look, I found you a passenger," he said, pointing at me. The assistant didn't respond. The door closed and the bus started moving. I didn't know which relief was the greatest: that I was on my way to Kigali or that I had escaped such torturous harassment.

As the bus gained momentum I asked the assistant if we were indeed on our way to Kigali.

He looked very confused and said, "Bujumbura, Burundi."

If there was ever a moment when I almost shat my pants, it was that one. Now I was on a bus heading for the capital city of Burundi. From all the reports I had read Burundi was the most unstable country of all and it was definitely not on my itinerary.

I started shouting loudly, "Me go to Kigali, not Bujumbura!"

The assistant driver looked at me with a twinkle in his eye and gave me a thumbs-up. At that moment a passenger nudged me from behind and explained – in very broken English – that the bus was actually going all the way to Bujumbura in Burundi, further south, but that the road passed through Kigali in Rwanda.

I was so relieved that I gave a long sigh. I turned to look for a place to sit. The bus was full of sleeping passengers; it was clear that I would have to stand in the aisle all the way to Kigali. Fortunately it was just sixty-two kilometres away and, in any case, standing up gave me an opportunity to look at and enjoy the evergreen rolling hills.

The bus was speeding even as it cut corners on the winding road. In less than thirty minutes we were at the Katuna border post. We joined the queue of passengers from the MTN bus that had passed me in Kabale. There must have been more than thirty people in front of me in the queue. Despite the efficiency of the immigration officials, it took about forty-five minutes before I was stamped out of Uganda. It was not a cheering thought that I would be going through the same border again in less than a week, and besides would have to pay another US$50 for a second Ugandan visa.

It was a walk of about 200 metres from the Ugandan to the Rwandan immigration office. All the incutras who accompanied me on the Ugandan side suddenly stopped at a small bridge between the two offices. I concluded that this must be exactly where Rwandan territory started. Interestingly the Rwandan side of the border is called Gatuna whereas the Ugandan side is called Katuna.

There was another long queue outside the Rwandan immigration office. The Rwandan official sat inside the office and we had to talk to him through a window from a small veranda. Only the seven people at the front of the queue got to stand in the shade of that small veranda; the rest had to wait in the not-so-blistering sun.

Standing in the queue, I kept hoping that the woman at the Rwandan Embassy in Pretoria/Tshwane had known what she was talking about when she told me on the telephone that South Africans did not need a visa when visiting Rwanda. I needn't have worried: she was right. After queuing for forty minutes, I was stamped into Rwanda. As the immigration official handed back my passport he said, "Have a nice time."

Before leaving Johannesburg I had read that Rwanda is the "Country of a Thousand Hills". Having grown up in KwaZulu-Natal, the name – so similar to our Valley of a Thousand Hills – stuck in my mind .

There were indeed lots of small, medium and large hills wherever I looked. Where I was standing in the aisle, midway between the back and front of the bus, I immediately noticed – when a big truck coming from the front passed us on the left – that the driver was driving on the wrong side of the road. But then I remembered it is only in former British colonies that people drive on the left. I should have expected that Rwandans, like Europeans and Americans, drive on the right.

Rwanda – together with Tanganyika and Urundi (now Tanzania and Burundi respectively) – was once part of German East Africa. In 1923, after Germany had been defeated in World War I (and the MV *Liemba* had been sunk in Lake Tanganyika), the League of Nations handed Rwanda and Burundi to Belgium to run as a mandated territory, as they both bordered on what was then called the Belgian Congo. Belgium administered the two small countries until they became independent in 1962.

Kigali Memorial Centre

I t took just more than an hour to get from the border at Gatuna to Kigali, Rwanda's capital city. Only five of us got off at the buzzing bus rank; the rest of the passengers, sleeping peacefully, continued on their way to Bujumbura, Burundi's capital city, 145 kilometres away. It was not yet midday. In fact, as Rwanda, like South Africa, is on GMT +2, it was not yet eleven in the morning.

Kigali is not known for its abundance of budget accommodation, amongst other things. It is better known for being the geographic centre (literally) and the economic, political and cultural hub of Rwanda. It is best known, in recent times, as the place where the Rwandan Genocide started in 1994.

I thought I would begin my search for a reasonably priced place to stay by checking out Gloria Hotel, one of the handful of budget hotels recommended in my guidebook. After crossing the main road from the bus rank I stopped a guy to ask for directions, hoping he could speak English. It was clear that he had no clue what I was talking about. I couldn't blame him: because of the Belgian connection French is the lingua franca. I took out my *Lonely Planet, Africa on a Shoestring*.

Within ten seconds, while I was still trying the show him the name "Gloria Hotel", ten to twelve people had gathered around us. Even guys on boda-bodas were stopping to see what was happening. Another thirty seconds and I was completely surrounded by a crowd of mostly young men. They were all talking in the same (to me incomprehensible) language, probably Kinyarwanda, Rwanda's main indigenous language. Some guys were trying to pull the book from my hands while others were just staring at me.

I started to panic.

With a backpack and asking for directions in English, it was obvious that I was a lost tourist asking to be robbed in exactly the most convenient spot: next to a big, busy bus station where thugs in any city usually hang out.

One guy, amidst the noise and confusion, told me in English that I should take a boda-boda, pointing at the five bikes which had by now stopped on the side of the road. Gloria Hotel, he explained, was not within walking distance from where we were.

I picked the boda-boda closest to me. After agreeing to pay US$2 (which at 350 Rwandan francs to a dollar, came to RWF200 more than the RWF500 he initially wanted to charge me) I hopped on the back. Before he started the bike he did something I had not come across before on my African travels: he handed me a helmet, which even had a windshield. Later I found out that all drivers in Rwanda carry an additional helmet for passengers.

We drove up a steep hill and went past what must have been Kigali's central park, a big round garden with a circular road running around it. We took a left into an exclusive, leafy, middle-to-upper-class suburb. The boda-boda took another left, and there I was in front of the Hotel des Mille Collines (Hotel of a Thousand Hills) made famous by the film *Hotel Rwanda*, starring Don Cheadle.

I was confused. I was under the impression that Gloria Hotel was near the centre of town. But I kept my mouth shut as we drove past a few embassy buildings and after a while took another left and stopped in front a massive modern hotel.

I knew we were at the wrong address, but the driver insisted that this was the place I was looking for. I went into the hotel to enquire. As I entered I was hit by the refreshing air-conditioned ambience. I looked at the cushy sofas and long reception desk and decided that if this was what budget accommodation in Kigali looked like, well, then I was all for it.

"My brother, this is Gorilla Hotel. Gloria Hotel is in town," the lady at the reception brought me back to earth.

I went back to the boda-boda accompanied by the receptionist. She spoke to the driver in Kinyarwanda, presumably giving him the correct directions. We drove back to town and voilà! – Gloria Hotel. Definitely in the city centre, with shops on the ground floor and a flight of stairs leading up to reception. I was told that a room was available for RWF 8 000.

What I saw in the room made my heart sink: a dirty, old, sagging mattress and a grubby, smelly bathroom. When I opened the exceedingly dirty curtains, a broken window was revealed.

I was not happy at all at the prospect of sleeping in such a dump, but I did not want to walk around crowded streets with a bag looking for a room. I decided I would take it for one night and then go in search of a better deal. Since I didn't have any Rwandan francs on me, I told the elderly man at reception that I was going to exchange money and return to pay for my room.

My next stop was Kigali Hotel in a suburb called Nyimarimba. For a clean, small room (so small that to stand between the window and the single bed was a tight squeeze) with a shower and an old 37-cm TV, I was quoted RWF6 500 (just less than US$20). I took it on the spot.

I found a boda-boda right outside and negotiated with the driver to take me to Gloria Hotel and afterwards bring me back via a reputable bureau de change. He agreed and off we went.

At the Gloria I decided to play it straight and told the old man: "I've found another place which is charging me less than what I'll be paying here."

No questions were asked and he gave me the key to what, a few moments ago, was my depressing room. I picked up my bag. When I dropped the keys back at reception I could see that the old man harboured no ill feelings whatsoever.

The boda-boda was waiting for me downstairs. Very close to Gloria Hotel we stopped at a bureau de change where I exchanged US$100 for Rwandan francs before heading back to Kigali Hotel. After depositing my bag in my room I walked the two kilometres back to town armed with some basic information supplied by the boda-boda driver, who had spoken English reasonably well.

For once I had accomplished so much in one day that it felt strange that it was only lunchtime. I followed the driver's directions to Corner View Restaurant, where, he said, the food was good. It was packed with working people taking their lunch breaks. I dished up everything on the buffet menu: rice, spinach, potatoes, sweet potato, beans and beef. I sat back, relaxed and enjoyed a great meal on the veranda, finishing it off with a Fanta Orange and a very loud burp.

At exactly 14:23 I left the restaurant. A few blocks down the road I came across an internet café. There was an email from Backpackers Hostel in Kampala confirming that they had booked a bed for me for the following Wednesday, but no word from Nairobi Backpackers.

There was also an email from my sister saying that she was going to deposit the money the following day; all I needed to do was to find out which banks in Kigali had MoneyGram (a facility, like Western Union, that allows for money to be transferred to a different country instantly). Once she had deposited the money (US$100) she would SMS me the reference number which would enable me to withdraw it. I was pleasantly surprised, but left a small space for disappointment. After all, my older sister had bullshitted me a couple of times before.

On my way back to Kigali Hotel later that afternoon, I popped into Bengaroitze Bar, which in South Africa we'd simply call a shebeen. It had a corrugated-iron roof, muddy walls, red plastic chairs and, most important of all, ice-cold beer. Three guys with an I-work-for-government look (white shirt, loose tie and leather jacket) were already enjoying the beer.

After two Primus beers it was time to head for my room. Just as I stepped outside into the road two ladies walked past Bengaroitze Bar in the same direction I was going. I found my eyes glued to one of the women's buttocks as they moved in a delightfully tight pair of jeans. I studied the complicated action of one buttock going up while the other one went down as one foot was pushed forward and then the other, meeting halfway for a split second as if travelling in opposite directions. I was so mesmerised by the sight that I did not notice that the two women had stopped to chat to a friend.

Only when they realised that I was not passing and turned round to look at me, did I come to my senses.

When I got to my room, a little flustered but in high spirits, I found Pussy Cat Dolls playing on the television set. I do not love their British music, but Pussy Cat Dolls have made it easier to say certain words in public. Everything was looking up so much that I decided to send my wife a couple of raunchy SMSs. She replied with a single MMS.

I woke up the next morning in a more sober frame of mind. There were two things on my schedule: to visit the Kigali Memorial Centre and to make a booking at the offices of the Rwanda Office of Tourism and National Parks (ORPTN) for a visit to the mountain gorillas. In addition, I would have to withdraw money from FINA Bank (the only bank with a MoneyGram facility in Kigali) to buy my Kigali–Kampala bus ticket. I also planned to visit Hotel des Mille Collines.

It was Saturday morning, just after eight. I was surprised at how deserted the streets were. There was hardly anybody about, no boda-bodas and, except for the odd car, nothing was moving. When I got to the centre of the city after half an hour's leisurely walking, I could not believe my eyes: all the shops were closed.

I was perplexed. I knew that the following day, 26 October, was a public holiday – Armed Forces Day. Could it be that everything was closed on a Saturday in Rwanda? Or was it actually 26 October already?

At a set of robots I decided to wait to ask a very respectable-looking man who was coming down a side street what was happening. "Is today Saturday?" I asked him.

"Yes, it is," he said, frowning.

"So shops do not open on Saturdays here in Kigali?"

"They do, but today is a very special Saturday. It's the last Saturday of the month and people do not go to work today."

Jean-Claude, the name of this Belgian-educated lawyer who had visited South Africa twice, explained: "As part of nation building and to ensure reconciliation in the country, every last Saturday of the month has been set aside for people to get to know each other better. We're encouraged to go and clean our neighbours' yards, for example."

"So it is a holiday?"

"Not really. Locally we call it *muganda*. Some shops and banks will open after one o'clock this afternoon."

As it was still before nine, I decided to visit Hotel des Mille Collines first, the location of which I knew from the previous day's ride to Gorilla instead of Gloria Hotel. The road to the hotel went past the Rwandan Tourist Office, which was closed.

I had been greatly moved by the movie *Hotel Rwanda*, which shows how the manager of the Mille Collines, Paul Rusesabagina, saved his family and more than a thousand people by bribing militia groups and the military during the attacks on Tutsis in 1994. The hotel used in the movie is actually in South Africa. It was important for me to see the real thing.

When I went to the main gate, one of the two security guards told me the hotel was closed for renovations. They allowed me to go through the gate towards the parking area, but I could not get close to the building itself because of all the scaffolding. So after asking one of the guards to take my picture with the hotel in the background, I said goodbye and left.

Since it was still long before the shops and banks were due to open,

I decided to look around the neighbourhood. I came upon the Rwandan offices of the World Bank and the United Nations Development Programme (UNDP), and then found St Michel's Cathedral and the building that housed Radio Maria right next to it. I was about to take a picture of the cathedral when I spotted the Military Prosecution offices opposite. I put my camera away. Whatever those offices are used for, the people who sit in them sound like guys you do not want to mess with.

Before walking back to town, I spent two hours in my room watching a 37-cm flickering TV screen that could not decide whether it wanted to show colour or black-and-white images. When I went out again there were more cars and boda-bodas on the road than earlier, but still not as many as the previous day. When I got to the tourism offices they were still closed. The guard at the gate spoke French and Kinyarwanda; I speak English and Zulu. A good combination for poor communication.

The guard directed me with hand signals to FINA Bank. When I got to the building on Boulevard de la Révolution, I was told by another guard that the bank was closed until Monday. So much for three out of the four things I had wanted to do. I was relieved when he assured me that the Memorial Centre was open. I signalled a boda-boda to stop and we struck a deal. For RWF1 000 he would take me to the Jaguar Bus offices to buy a bus ticket, and then drop me off at the Memorial Centre.

At the Jaguar offices I was told that indeed I could reserve a seat on the bus to Kampala for Wednesday morning, but that I could not get the ticket itself because Wednesday was still four days away. I chose the "executive" bus, leaving at 06:00, rather than the "standard" bus, departing at 05:00. My name was put on the list and I was assured that I had a place reserved.

The white two-storey building that houses the Kigali Memorial Centre was about three kilometres away. When I entered the premises, a minibus with French-speaking tourists had just arrived. There were a few locals sitting in the courtyard. I joined other visitors in the foyer where they were being addressed by one of the Centre's officials. He told us that entry was free of charge but that they were totally dependent on donations. Later I read that the Centre is subsidised by the Aegis Trust, a British NGO.

From reception I went down a flight of stairs to where the display begins. The Centre is constructed in a circular way. You start at "Before Genocide", move through "The Genocide" and finish with "After Genocide". There is no one to show you around, but the captions to the exhibits are in three languages: English, Swahili and French. There are also touch screens which play film snippets of Rwanda's history, the genocide attacks, and interviews with survivors.

I spent ninety minutes inside the building trying to piece together the conundrum by looking and listening and reading. One of the key things I wanted to understand was how and why people who had lived together for so long could commit such atrocities against their own neighbours and fellow countrymen.

Although the Rwandan genocide officially started on 6 April 1994 after a plane, carrying both Rwanda's and Burundi's presidents, was shot down as it prepared to land at Kigali International Airport, the seeds of conflict had been sown long before. Among the many things I learned was that the Belgians, as part of their official classification of Tutsis and Hutus (which had always been hazy and ill-defined categories before the colonial era), had decided that anyone who owned more than ten cows would be classified Tutsi and anyone with fewer than ten cows Hutu. Divisions between Tutsis and Hutus were fostered in a number of other ways as well, as a kind of divide-and-rule strategy designed to use the minority Tutsis to control the majority.

Over the three decades following Rwanda's independence in 1962, under a majority Hutu government, there were many massacres of Tutsis, who in turn organised active resistance from their quasi-military bases outside the country. Although a ceasefire agreement was signed in August 1993, the Hutu-dominated government secretly entered into an arms deal with a French company with a loan of US$12 million secured by the French government.

During the first three months of the genocide in 1994, more than a million people were killed, mostly Tutsis but also moderate Hutus (those who were married to or were friends with Tutsis). There was an inscription in the Memorial Centre that stated the facts:

The genocide resulted in the deaths of more than a million people. But death was not the only outcome. Tens of thousands of people were tortured, mutilated and raped, and thousands more suffered machete cuts, bullet wounds, infection and starvation. The genocide left more than 300 000 orphans and thousands of widows. Many had been victims of rape and sexual abuse or had seen their family members – including children – being murdered.

Over and above the victims who lost their lives, there were at least 500 000 women raped, many by men who were HIV-positive.

I made my way through the Memorial Centre, reading captions and descriptions, looking at the gruesome photographs and footage. Initially I was moved and emotional, especially after seeing footage of children with awful gashes and cuts where they were hit on the head with machetes. The more I saw, the more numb I became. A caption under a photograph of five smiling young people stated that, a few months after the picture was taken, two of them were chained and tied together before being buried alive. When their decomposed bodies were dug up, they were still tied together. The chain was displayed in a Perspex box below the photo.

As I moved from photo to photo, display to display, I went from one set of emotions to another – from hurting to not feeling anything. The shock and the horror I saw eventually turned me into a kind of zombie.

When I had gone around the entire ground floor, I came to the room where they showed interviews with survivors on a big screen. In one of the film snippets a young woman told how boys from next door came to her house and killed her father in front of her eyes. These were the boys she grew up with, she said, and who used to come play and eat at her house.

In the same room there were photographs of some of the victims of the genocide. More than a thousand images, mostly postcards. I found it very hard to get my mind to comprehend that all those faces hanging on the wall were of people who had been killed by their neighbours and countrymen.

I spent about ten minutes in that room before going back through the reception area and upstairs to the first floor. There I was confronted by yet more pictures of victims, but this time it was different. They were pictures of children – innocent faces, smiling faces, vulnerable faces. All those hanging on the wall were killed simply because their parents were Tutsi or perceived to be "reformed Hutus".

The room filled me with sorrow, anguish and pain. I walked out onto the veranda fighting back the tears. I found my way to the back of the building where, after going down a flight of stairs and through the memorial garden, I reached the mass grave.

As in the room with more than a thousand pictures of victims, my mind found it impossible to grasp the dimensions of what I was seeing: underneath the slab in front of me a quarter of a million bodies were buried. How do you start grasping the fact that 250 000 people are lying dead in one place right in front of you?

I remember thinking then that Joseph Stalin, the late leader of the Soviet Union, was correct when he said something like: One death is a tragedy, but a million deaths is a statistic.

Alongside the grave there was a row of trees, each trimmed in the shape of an upside-down U, a cobblestone pathway and a variety of shrubs and plants. So as you walk next to the grave, you are mostly walking beneath trees.

After walking the length of the site I retraced my footsteps and went to sit in one of the chairs in the memorial garden, less than fifteen metres away. Looking at the fountain spouting water into the air and listening to the sound of a small waterfall on my left, I sat and tried to make sense of such a senseless series of events.

I sat there thinking how intertwined the history of some African countries is. Rwanda's president, Paul Kagame, grew up in Uganda, having escaped death at the age of two at the hands of the Hutu government. He joined Museveni's National Resistance Army, which was waging a bush war against Ugandan president Milton Obote's regime between 1981 and 1986. Kagame eventually became the leader of the Ugandan-based Rwandese Patriotic Front (RFP), which was fighting the Hutu-dominated Rwandan government at the time. When Museveni became president, Kagame was officially appointed head of Uganda's military intelligence.

When the RFP eventually took over the government in Kigali after the genocide in 1994, the Hutu militias fled to then Zaire. As part of hunting down the Hutu perpetrators, the new Kigali government teamed up with Kabila (the father, not the son), and with the help of Ugandan forces marched into Kinshasa, deposing the dictator Mobutu. A year later, in 1998, it no longer suited Kabila to have the Rwandese around, but his former allies did not want to leave the DRC (as Zaire had been renamed), fearing the Hutu militias hadn't finished their evil work. As I said earlier, it sparked Africa's most destructive war, with Rwanda and Uganda on one side and the DRC, Zimbabwe, Namibia and Angola on the other.

The book *A People Betrayed – the Role of the West* by British investigative journalist Linda Melvern, which I bought two days later at the Rwandan Tourism Office, substantiated what I had read at the Memorial Centre. It revealed that when Romeo Dallaire, head of the United Nations Assistance Mission for Rwanda (UNAMIR), passed on information he had received through an informant that Hutu militia groups were arming themselves for a total onslaught against the Tutsis, a senior official at the UN issued the following statement: "No reconnaissance or other action including response to request for protection should be taken by UNAMIR until clear guidance from HQ." The official was none other than Kofi Annan, then head of UN Peacekeeping Operations.

Although Dallaire informed the UN that as few as 5 000 troops with authority to enforce peace could stop the genocide, the UN, after issuing a statement condemning the deaths of thousands of people, decided to close its mission in Rwanda completely on the very same day. Eventually, on 17 May 1994, the Security Council agreed to establish UNAMIR II with 5 500 men mandated to use force. The US agreed to provide the armoured vehicle carriers, but it took more than a month for them to arrive in Uganda.

I must confess that even before coming to Rwanda I had not been a fan of the United Nations, which I saw as a talk shop without power to act. I found it strange that two African men at the helm of the organisation – Boutros Boutros-Ghali and Kofi Annan – could have failed the African people so dismally. Despite what happened in Rwanda, Kofi Annan was promoted to Secretary General of the UN and, to crown it all, was co-recipient of the Nobel Peace Prize in 2001.

According to *A People Betrayed*, Boutros Boutros-Ghali authorised a secret US$26 million arms sale to the Rwandan government in 1990 while he was Egypt's foreign minister. These weapons were part of the long-term preparation for the extermination of the Tutsis. The genocide happened four years later, when Boutros Boutros-Ghali was Secretary General of the UN.

The Memorial Centre left me emotionally drained and physically tired. During the two hours or so I spent there, three Rwandese women had to be taken out of the building at different times because they were crying hysterically and uncontrollably. It struck me how wounded some Rwandese still were more than a decade after the genocide.

I took a boda-boda to the city centre. It dropped me outside the Nakumatt 24-Hour Shopping Centre, where I bought myself some food and tried to make plans for the rest of my stay.

If, like me, you are one of those people who dream at night about things they have seen or thought about during the day, I would not recommend that you visit the Kigali Memorial Centre. That Saturday night, the night of my visit to the Centre, was awful: it was one nightmare after another, being chased by people with machetes, being caught in the middle of a terrible battle with guns blazing and people running around screaming, with blood everywhere.

It was, by far, the worst night of the trip.

Stumped

It was not practical for me to leave Kigali the next day (Sunday). For starters, I had not bought the gorilla-watching permit at the ORPTN offices yet, so that objective had to be delayed. Secondly, the bank wasn't due to open until Monday. This meant that my trip south to Cyangugu in search of the remote source of the Nile would have to wait too. And on Wednesday I still had to leave Kigali come hell or high water and head back to Uganda.

Even if I hadn't changed my plan and decided not to travel anywhere that Sunday, the rain would have discouraged me from waking up early and being at the bus station by 06:00. It was pouring unceasingly, which suited me fine actually, because all I wanted to do was empty my head.

I eventually woke up shortly before midday, just in time for a shower. If I wanted to I could have had a warm bath because at Kigali Hotel they heated water in a central wood-burning geyser in the courtyard. The snag was that you had to fetch the hot water in a bucket from there. Since I did not mind cold water I opted for a shower.

Before looking for a place to eat I popped into an internet café not far from the hotel. More than anything else I wanted to check the headlines of the different Sunday newspapers in South Africa to get an idea of what was happening back home. One headline read: "Police might team up with private security companies to combat crime". It was so strange to read about crime because, quite honestly, it was the furthest thing from my mind right then. Despite the poverty I had seen on my journey there was very little criminal activity, and certainly no violent crime. Surfing the net I realised that in exactly a week's time I would be flying back to Johannesburg, where I would constantly have to watch my back and be on high alert. It was not a comforting thought.

Le Palmier Café with its white plastic chairs and tables was just a few metres away and I decided to give it a try. It was buzzing with local guys taking their girlfriends out for lunch. The atmosphere was great but I really struggled to communicate with the waitress who spoke no English. In the end I ordered by pointing to the fish and chips on the plate of a guy at the next table.

The service was swift. In no time the waitress brought my fish, chips and rice. It seemed standard practice to serve chips as well as rice. Unlike the fish served in Mpulungu in Zambia, the fish in Kigali were huge. They were so big that you were served the head only with a few centimetres of the body floating in a rich, dark gravy. I looked around and saw that everybody was eating fish heads. It was a very unusual sight: a restaurant full of people eating fish heads. I could not but wonder what happened to the rest of the fish, but dared not ask. Anyway, that was the best meal of the trip. The rice and gravy were delicious, the fish was tender and the chips were crisp. The waitress also gave me a small bowl of vegetables in a piquant sauce, what in South Africa we call *chakalaka*.

After the meal I watched an English Premiership match on the TV in my room. Had I known that just opposite Kigali Hotel was the Ciné Elmay – a local cinema which screened English Premiership matches on weekend afternoons that locals could watch free of charge – I would probably have sneaked in there. As the middle-aged receptionist at the hotel told me: "It's a great way of building the community."

His remark reminded me of the early 1980s when we used to go and watch TV at our neighbours' place because we didn't own a TV ourselves. It was such an occasion, especially if a great soccer game was on. It struck me how much things have changed – now people have television in their own bedrooms and do not even sit together as a family, because everyone wants to watch his or her favourite programme.

I was at the ORPTN offices in the city centre just after eight on Monday morning after a dreamless, peaceful sleep. I hadn't checked out from my two-star hotel; I told the receptionist I'd be back "now, now". At the offices there were two sections, one for administration and the other for permit reservations. The permit reservations section was on the far side of the building. I spent a few minutes looking at the brochures, postcards and T-shirts on display and the massive flat-screen LCD TV set which continuously ran "Rwanda Land of a Thousand Hills" promos.

When my turn came I stepped up to the counter eagerly.

"Are you joking that you want a permit for tomorrow?" one of the assistants asked me. "We only issue fifty-six permits for a given day. There are almost always more people looking for permits than we can issue.

You should've booked long in advance, like other people. We already have bookings for people who will be coming in twelve months' time."

"Those are white people! Right?" I joked.

The young woman with kissable lips did not get it. She continued giving me the nitty-gritty about booking in advance. "The best thing to do is to send us an email from your country and enquire if we still have permits for a specific day or days. And then if we do, you can book the permit. Remember, we do not reserve permits until you have paid the full five hundred US dollars. Plus you must ensure that you use a bank that does not charge high fees, because that will mean that we will receive less by the time the money comes through."

The booking procedure was sounding a bit complicated. So to be absolutely sure I asked, "So you don't have permits for the next day or two?"

"Definitely not, except if someone cancels – which rarely happens."

After that unambiguous reply I had to concede that seeing Rwanda's famous mountain gorillas was out of the question. Before leaving Johannesburg I had already known about the high demand and limited supply of permits and the importance of booking in advance. However, the problem was that backpacking and travelling by public transport made it impossible for me to predict where I would be on a specific date. Imagine paying US$500 and then arriving a day late, or not arriving at all for one reason or another. The obvious point is: if you want to see the gorillas in Rwanda you must be able to commit to a date in advance.

Not one to mope, I immediately shifted my focus to my next objective: a visit to the remote source of the Nile at Nyungwe Forest. Since the young woman was still looking at me I asked, "Can I get to Nyungwe forest from here using public transport?"

"Yes, you have to take a taxi or bus to Cyangugu," she replied in a more helpful way. "The road runs through the forest and there are two places where you can disembark, depending on what you want to see. However, accommodation is very limited. That is why most people tend to camp. Because even if you do find accommodation and you want to do certain trails, you'd need your own transport as trails do not start from were you will be sleeping. Also, it being such a huge forest, you need to be accompanied by a guide, and most guided hikes start very early in the morning."

I know they say you should not shoot the messenger, but the more the woman spoke and the more my dreams were being shattered the more I felt like tipping her over before lying on top of her with my heavyweight body.

Of course I didn't. Instead, to show some persistence, I asked her: "Which one of the trails must I take if I want to see the remote source of the Nile?"

She kept quiet for a while fiddling with her ballpoint pen before she looked up. I could see that she was thinking deeply. Then she said, "Everybody keeps claiming that they have the source of the Nile. Uganda is claiming that, even Burundi says they have the source of the Nile. Maybe you should go to Nyungwe and then tell us if that is indeed where the source of the Nile is."

She gave me a very cheeky smile.

Sekwanele – enough is enough, I thought to myself. I left the ORPTN offices feeling sad and slightly angry. It was not even nine in the morning yet and two of my dreams had been shattered: no permits for gorilla-watching and I could not go to Nyungwe forest because I had neither my own transport nor camping equipment.

The truth is that the mystery of the source of the Nile has not – until today – been settled. Obviously Lake Victoria could not be the ultimate source because water pours into it from several rivers. The longest river emptying into the lake will, logically speaking, have to be the true source.

If that sounds easy, it isn't really. The longest river that flows into Lake Victoria is the Kagera (sometimes called Akagera), which originates in Burundi. It is the river that separates Rwanda and Tanzania at the border town of Rusumo where I would have crossed had I used the direct route from Mwanza on the southern shore of Lake Victoria to Kigali. The Akagera, thus, should be recognised as the source if the Nile.

However, somewhere in Burundi the Ruvyironza River (sometimes called the Luvironza) flows into the Akagera. Considering that both these rivers originate in Burundi, Burundians should have the bragging rights for "Source of the Nile". Not a chance. One of the tributaries to the Akagera is the Rukarara River, which originates in the heart of the Nyungwe Forest in Rwanda.

In 2006 a three-man team, after an eighty-day exploration that started at the Nile's mouth in the Mediterranean Sea and ended where water springs from a muddy hole, said they had found the source of the Rukarara River, the Nile's furthest tributary. The same trio also calculated that the Nile was, in fact, 6 718 kilometres long – a hundred kilometres longer than originally thought.

In short, there is the remote source (Akagera), the "most remote" source (Ruvyironza) and then the origin of the Rukarara River which is surely the true source. Or is it?

I waved down a boda-boda. No, it was not yet time to go to FINA Bank and neither was I heading to the bus station to pay for my Kampala ticket. It was time to pop into the South African embassy. The previous day while relaxing and lying on the bed I had scribbled on a piece of paper something along the lines of: *This serves to confirm that Sihle Khumalo – passport number .... – came to our offices after travelling by public transport from Johannesburg, through Zimbabwe, Zambia, Tanzania, Kenya and Uganda to Kigali. We would like to congratulate him on achieving this feat.*

My idea was that this commendation could be used as a postscript to the book I intended to write.

The boda-boda guy told me that the South African embassy was out of town and he would therefore have to charge me RWF700.

We went down a very steep road, through a very scruffy neighbourhood full of shacks, up another hill. At the traffic circle right at the top stood the US embassy, a huge modern building made partially of glass and decorated with a few gigantic satellite dishes. We continued along the main road where I spotted the offices of different government ministries until we finally stopped outside Ebenezer House, a tall building that houses the UNICEF offices. Right next door I saw the South African flag flying on an enormous house. I was directed to the consular section by the security guards at the gate.

It seemed that Rwandese were not interested in coming to South Africa, for there were only three people filling in the visa application forms. When my turn came I explained the purpose of my visit to the embassy to the Rwandan girl behind the counter.

"You travelled by road from South Africa? How can we be sure of that?" she asked – a valid question that I had anticipated.

"Check the stamps in my passport. You'll see that there're no international airport stamps at all," I replied.

"What are you going to do with the letter?"

"I'll put it at the back of the book I am writing once I'm back in Johannesburg."

"Wait a minute," she said and disappeared for about two minutes. She returned with another young lady.

"Hi," the second young lady greeted me. It was a bit of a surprise because I thought a black South African would greet me with "*Sawubona*" – or another traditional greeting in any of the other eight official South African indigenous languages.

"So is the letter going to be for your own personal use?"

"Yes. I would like to ..."

"Unfortunately this is an embassy and we do not write personal letters," she interrupted, shoving my passport and scribbled page back.

Like a dog with its tail between its legs, I left the embassy. I can't tell if the second young lady was Rwandese or South African, but whatever the case, I felt I had been treated like shit. I know an embassy's mandate probably does not include writing "personal letters", but there was no justification for their treating me like a desperate and destitute asylum seeker – and no justification for treating desperate and destitute asylum seekers in that manner either.

Back in town I went to FINA Bank to withdraw the money sent through by MoneyGram. At least my older sister hadn't let me down. At the entrance of the vast banking hall there was a touch screen where you obtained your number, depending on what service you wanted. While waiting for my number to come up on the screen, I decided to change the plan once again and to move on to Plan L: go to Kibuye on the shores of Lake Kivu directly to the west of Kigali and come back in one day. By now, with Lulu and my sister having deposited the agreed amounts, I had more money than I needed and could splash out a bit.

After leaving the bank with just over US$700 in crisp notes in my wallet, it was time to head to Corner View Restaurant. No matter how hard I tried to remain calm, the embassy thing had really pissed me off. I hate being treated like a nobody. I thought about doing it properly and making an appointment with some senior official, but then, besides hating to beg for favours, my pride got in the way. I was so incensed I was not even in a mood to go to the bus rank and pay for my Kampala ticket. I thought I'd do it the next day on my way to catching a bus or taxi to Kibuye.

Walking back to Kigali Hotel I popped into a local travel agency office. I was curious to find out if Rwandair Express had started its flights to Johannesburg. The answer was a resounding yes.

"What sort of prices are we looking at?" I asked.

"A return ticket will cost you around seven hundred and twenty-five US dollars," I was informed. That meant, at the then prevailing exchange rate of R9.50 to the dollar, the Rwandair Express ticket cost more than the SAA flight (for which I had paid about R6 000).

I had another good sleep.

Before my alarm clock went off I was already up thanks to the muezzin chanting his call to prayer from the mosque next door. I'm glad it is only in Islam that the whole town has to be notified of prayer time. Imagine if all other religions also used loudspeakers to publicly broadcast their daily rituals.

I took a boda-boda down to Nyabugogo, the main bus and taxi rank. There I paid my RWF7 000 at the Jaguar Executive Coaches office, which had opened at 06:05. I was again given the bus layout to confirm my seat. Looking at the marked seats I saw that only four seats in the entire bus had been booked. Well, maybe people like doing things at the last minute, I thought.

With my next day's bus ticket sorted, I started looking for a minibus to Kibuye. There were quite a few bus touts looking for people going to Bujumbura. Clearly people were still travelling there every day despite all the reports about the dangerous instability in Burundi.

The most scenic route in Rwanda

F inding a taxi to Kibuye was not easy. I would ask one person and he'd tell me to go to one side of the spread-out rank, and when I got there someone else would tell me to go back to where I'd just come from. Some of the people I asked had no clue where the Kibuye taxis were waiting and just shook their heads. Maybe it had to do with poor communication; I struggled to make myself understood. The Rwandese in Kigali speak Kinyarwanda, and some of them a bit of Swahili and French as well. And where did that leave me?

While wandering around for a taxi I spotted a vehicle with a Gauteng registration number, DZG 872 GP. I found myself smiling broadly at the pitch-dark man behind the wheel of the black Land Rover. Alas, he didn't even see me because he was too busy talking on his cellphone.

After asking more people where to get a Kibuye taxi, none of whom had a clue, I came across a young man who must have been sent from Above. He was not only fluent in English but he knew exactly where to find taxis going to Kibuye.

I happily followed him as he led me to the entrance of the bus rank near the building that housed the Jaguar bus company. The office where I had to buy my ticket was on the opposite side.

To my surprise the Rwandese were doing what the South African government has tried and failed to do – in fact, failed dismally at doing: that is, provide an orderly system of regulating the activities of minibus taxis. I had to buy my ticket from the offices of the particular taxi association, where my name was added to the passenger list. The ticket I was issued gave 7:25 as the time of departure and indicated that the taxi would leave from next to the offices. I was impressed.

Just before saying goodbye to the young man I asked him where he'd learned English. "In South Africa," he said, and when I looked at him questioningly, he continued, "After what happened here in Rwanda in 1994, I spent three years in South Africa, but I had to come back because the South Africans did not treat me well. So now I'm back."

Before I could say anything he left. I could see that he didn't really want to talk about any of that. It made me feel really terrible, and I hadn't even told him that I was South African.

At 07:30 sharp a white Toyota Hiace arrived and fourteen passengers boarded. Our tickets were checked and at 07:40 we were on our way to Kibuye on the shores of Lake Kivu.

Because of Rwanda's thousands of hills, there were lots of twists, turns, sharp corners and zigzags in the road. Our taxi driver, as is to be expected of taxi drivers anywhere in Africa (maybe the world), overtook repeatedly over the barrier line. He really didn't care. Now and then we came up against trucks heading for Kigali, but that possibility did not cross his mind when he was overtaking buses on blind rises. It was high-tension stuff.

En route to Kibuye we passed the small villages of Gihinga, Rugobagoba, Buhoro and Musambira. We dropped our first passenger at a rural town called Muhanga. The scenery all along was beautiful and green. Everywhere I looked there were banana trees, which made it almost impossible to see the mud houses against the mountains.

It was a soul-enriching drive, except for one thing: a lady at the back was throwing up continuously. Actually, she was throwing down (into a plastic bag). What amazed me was that nobody seemed to care. Seated in the second row from the back, I was the only one who kept looking over my shoulder. The puking lady reminded me that when I was a young boy it was common for people in rural KwaZulu-Natal to throw up on buses. They were suffering from, in today's terms, motion sickness. So they would arrive well prepared, carrying a plastic bag in their luggage. It was believed in those days that you could cure motion sickness by licking the tyre of the taxi or bus which you were about to board – not that I ever saw anybody do it.

Suddenly, after a sharp bend, the taxi driver applied the brakes so hard that all of us shot forward with the momentum. No, he was not trying to avert a head-on collision nor were there cows crossing the road. Two youngsters, aged nine or ten, were engaged in some serious fist fighting right in the middle of the road. You know the kind of fight where both people are throwing punches at the same time and neither seems to stop any of the punches coming his way.

These two boys were so into the fighting that they were oblivious of where they were. The taxi started hooting but they paid no attention. It was only when the taxi had come to a standstill and one of the passengers got out to intervene that they stopped and ran away in different directions. Most passengers saw the funny side and were giggling and laughing when the driver accelerated away again.

Somewhere along the road I had noticed a board with an arrow indicating "Nyange Memorial Site". I remembered being told at the Memorial Centre in Kigali that there were other memorial sites scattered around the country, as the genocide had happened throughout Rwanda.

Sixteen kilometres before Kibuye, in a small town called Mabanza, I saw another notice board across the road from where the taxi was dropping off more passengers. It was written in the local language and I could not understand what it said except for the last word: "genocide". A few metres from the board was a mass grave – a fenced-in concrete slab with four bouquets of fresh flowers on top.

It took us about two hours to cover the 126 kilometres between Kigali and our destination. Kibuye has a perfect location right on the shore of Lake Kivu – roughly halfway between the southern and northern ends of the lake. (The DRC–Rwanda border runs north–south down the lake, closer to the Rwandan side.) Near the entrance to the town I saw a board saying CYANGUGU 130. I could not believe it; back in Kigali I had been told that Cyangugu was very far. But then again I suppose it's all relative. Rwanda is such a small country – smaller than Lesotho but bigger than Swaziland – and Cyangugu is right at the bottom of the country, on the southern shore of Lake Kivu. From Kigali it must seem far.

The last stretch of winding road into Kibuye alongside the lake was simply breathtaking. On the right-hand side lay a vast lake with a sprinkling of small fishing boats drifting on the surface, and on the left were waves of rolling green hills. What made this scene so appealing to the eye was the calmness, the almost completely still, blue water of the lake. I could understand why the route from Cyangugu to Kibuye is considered the most scenic in Rwanda.

If I'd known the previous morning what I knew now, I would've taken a bus or taxi to Butare in the south, on the main road to Bujumbura, and from there travelled west through the Nyungwe Forest to Cyangugu, where I could have spent the night. And then on Tuesday, today, I could have done the 130-kilometre scenic drive to Kibuye from the southern tip of

Lake Kivu in a northerly direction, all along the shore, before returning to Kigali. And it would still have been possible to leave Kigali for Kampala on Wednesday. But that was water under the bridge.

I walked around the very small town of Kibuye before having lunch in Restaurant Nouveauté. While I was eating my rice and beans I thought of Sampiece, the guy from DRC I met on the *Liemba* who was going to take a ferry to Uvira and then a bus to Bukavu, which is on the DRC side of Lake Kivu, right opposite Cyangugu, before going north by ferry to his final destination, Goma, on the northern shore of the lake. Come to think of it, I could have travelled with him. That would have been a real short route!

While taking a walk down Kibuye's main street I came upon a wall with a plaque: *Cemetery. More than 10 000 people were inhumated here. Official ceremony was presided by Bizumungu, President of the Republic of Rwanda, on 26 February 1995.*

It's unbelievable that so many people could have been killed in such a small town.

I returned to Kigali on a minibus from the same Atracco Express company. In Kibuye, too, the times at which taxis left were displayed. In the morning: every hour on the hour; from midday to 15:00: every 90 minutes; 15:00 to 17:00: every hour on the hour again. As in Kigali you pay beforehand, get a ticket and your name gets added to the passenger list. I took the 15:00 taxi. When it stopped in towns on the way, all the boarding passengers already had their tickets. I was impressed all over again.

As South Africans we tend to look down (very ironic, considering that we are in the very south) on other African countries. But I'll bet my last rand that I will turn forty (in 2015) before order of this kind has been established in our mafia-like taxi industry.

Our new driver did not overtake on blind rises and over the barrier line, and as a result it took longer to get back to Rwanda's capital city. We made it before sunset though, and I decided to check the news from South Africa at the internet café en route to my hotel.

I was shocked to learn of the passing away of E'skia Mphahlele, one of our grand old men of letters, a prolific writer and retired academic who spent many years in exile. I had hoped – through my publisher – to ask him to endorse my book. I had never met him but his writing struck me as insightful, mature, thought-provoking and deep. I regret never having met him, even though we both contributed pieces to a book entitled *Cheesecutters and Gymslips – South Africans at Boarding School.* His piece was taken from his highly acclaimed autobiography *Down Second Avenue.*

Rest in Peace, Old Man, I said silently, I – and surely other young black writers too – will keep the fires burning. That is a promise.

North to Jinja

Even before my alarm went off at 05:00 I was up. Not because I was scared I might not hear it and that the bus might leave me behind, but because the call to prayer was ringing out from next door. And then an absurd thought struck me: what if somebody from the mosque checked the sound system just before making a call. You know, the normal stuff they do when they're testing whether the sound system is working properly, like blowing into the microphone or tapping it with a finger. Just imagine hearing from the mosque one day: "Sound check. One two! Sound check, one two. Microphone check. One two one two one two." That will be the day!

It was drizzling outside. The previous day had been all blue skies and perfect weather. But there was no turning back. I had to get to the bus station and head north.

It was still dark when I checked out. Walking to the nearest street corner I did not see a single boda-boda on the road. It was very quiet although neither spooky like the public-holiday morning in Kisumu nor scary like the long walk to the bus station in Kigoma. There were one or two people walking on the road and a few cars drove by. After a few minutes a couple of boda-bodas passed by carrying passengers to town.

It then made sense why people who travel early book a boda-boda beforehand – I never learn, hey? I was very angry at myself for not thinking ahead. The time was ticking away. Ten minutes (and counting) had already passed and I was now, because of the rain coming down harder, standing on the veranda of a general dealer's shop. Even if it weren't raining, making my own way to the bus station was not going to get me there on time; it would require at least forty minutes of brisk walking.

Five minutes later a boda-boda appeared, coming from town and going in the direction of the suburbs. I tried flagging it down. Although he must have seen me the guy continued driving – probably to pick up someone who had pre-booked him. I was getting very edgy. Missing the bus would be a logistical disaster. I didn't even want to think about it, but the implications were starting to creep into my mind.

I was still fighting hard to keep all sorts of silly thoughts at bay when another boda-boda appeared from the direction of town. I waved half-heartedly and, to my surprise, it stopped. I told the driver I was rushing to catch the 06:00 bus. While he was still turning around to wipe the wet seat, my bum was already firmly in occupation, drying it at once. Catching a bus with a wet bum is far better than missing a bus with dry pants.

Instead of making a u-turn as I had expected, the boda-boda continued driving deeper into Nyamirambo. I shouted at him through my helmet, "Hey, I'm going to Nyabugogo bus station!"

Obviously I yelled loud enough for him to hear me in spite of the roar of the boda-boda's engine and the helmet on his head, for he gave me a thumbs-up – but continued driving further into the suburb. Then suddenly he turned onto some backstreets, most of which were dirt roads and, due to the rain, now very muddy. We drove right in front of people's houses; at one stage we even drove next to a small stream of very dirty water on a narrow path between the stream and the back of a mud-splattered house. After an eternity we went up a very steep, muddy slope. I literally held my breath as we slowly crept up the incline. I had no clue where this guy was taking me. In fact, at one stage I thought of leaping off the back.

While I was still exercising my mind about what to do, we joined a tar road. I looked around. Although I had been in Kigali for five days and thought I knew my way around, I had no clue where we were. The boda-boda continued confidently over a few humps, roared down a gently descending road and took a sharp turn to the right. And there we were, at the bus station. We had come from the opposite side of town to the one I was used to.

By this time I could not even look at my watch. I pushed US$2 (RWF700) in his hand and rushed towards the Jaguar office past a few guys who were shouting, "Bujumbura! Bujumbura!" Before I could get to the office, I saw a Jaguar bus with passengers inside starting to move. I ran in its direction waving my arms. The assistant driver standing at the door saw me and ordered the driver to stop.

I ran even faster and gave the assistant my ticket. He looked at it and, in a very upset voice, said something I couldn't understand. He handed my ticket to a youngster next to him and instructed him to do something. I was utterly confused. What had I done?

The youngster leapt out and ran towards the touts, clutching my ticket in his hand. The bus started moving forward again.

"What now?" I shouted at the bus driver's assistant. I did not know whether to jump onto the bus without a ticket or run after the youngster who had my ticket and risk being left behind by the bus, which was already nearing the exit of the bus terminal.

"Where's my ticket? What's happening?" I shouted, desperate.

By now the bus had gone through the main exit and had stopped at the stop sign on the main road. The assistant was not responding to my frantic questions, merely looking at me with a blank expression on his face. The driver was revving the engine and seemed about to take off down the main road any minute once other vehicles had passed by. My heart was in my throat. At no time during the trip had I felt so utterly confused.

Then everything happened at the same time: I felt a tap on my right shoulder and when I turned around, there stood a familiar-looking guy. I knew that I had seen him before. He gave me a piece of paper. It turned out to be a ticket. He took my backpack from me and put it in the luggage compartment underneath the bus. As I boarded the bus the assistant driver said to me: "You speak only English?"

"Yes," I said, very relieved that at least I was on a bus. As he accompanied me to my seat he tried to explain in broken English that this was, in fact, the 05:00 bus and that they had been waiting for me. There were not enough people for the 06:00 bus so it had been cancelled. Because the 05:00 bus – on which I was now seated – was a standard bus, (unlike the 06:00 one, which was an executive bus), I had paid a higher "executive" fare for a lower-grade bus. The fact that I had a ticket for a bus that had been cancelled was what had caused all the running around – and I was not even reimbursed for having been downgraded.

As I was settling in my window seat, exhausted by the events of the past few minutes, I tried to think who the guy was who had tapped me on my shoulder and given me a new ticket. Ah, it suddenly dawned on me, it was the guy from whom I had bought my ticket the previous day.

As the bus reached the outskirts of Kigali a middle-aged gentleman in a blue Jaguar Bus Coaches shirt started checking tickets and passports.

For the first time I took a proper look at my ticket. There were three things written on it – Date: 29/10; Seat no: 30A; and Fare: 20 000. The latter got me very worried because I had paid only RWF7 000 for my ticket which I'd been told was the full fare, and now I was sitting with a ticket with 20 000 written on it.

As the inspector made his way towards the back of the bus, I was becoming more and more concerned. I had spent all my francs and I was certain this was going to be one of those daylight robbery things. When the man held out his hand I gave him my passport first, which he used to fill in the particulars on the passenger list. He handed it back to me before I gave him my ticket. He took it and had a long look at it before scratching on it – just as he had done on all the others – and handing it back without saying a word, merely holding his hand out for the passport and ticket of the passenger sitting next to me.

QUESTION 7: Where did the 20 000 instead of 7 000 come from? (Clue: We were being followed by a luxurious red Kampala Coaches bus.)

The woman next to me had a small, very thin toddler on her lap, about three years old, I guessed. Although it was cold and drizzling the little girl was wearing a short dress. She was shivering despite her mother (or grandmother) doing her best to cover her with a jersey.

Seeing small children having a hard time is one of those things that get to me. My thoughts turned to my own daughter, who has a very strong, domineering personality but is also very loving; so much so that out of the blue she dishes out hugs and tells her parents that she loves them. (Of course, like her father, she is fun-loving, adventurous and extremely intelligent.) It occurred to me that the little girl next to me must have a stronger immune system than someone like Nala, who is always protected from rain and cold weather. But I wouldn't bet on it.

We were at the Katuna border post almost too soon for my liking.

As soon as the door opened everybody tried to get outside first. Initially I did not understand why, but as soon as I stepped outside it all made sense: it was raining and there was only the small veranda to shelter under. It was not comfortable on the small veranda either – nobody wanted to stand in the rain, so too many of us squeezed up into a tight zigzag in the covered area.

Soon passengers from another Kampala-bound bus joined the queue, making the squeeze even tighter. From top to toe I was pushed right up against a woman of my age with a nice rounded backside. I could hardly breathe. In the end I stuck out my tongue – not to lick her ear but for a bit of relief.

For a change the queue moved quickly and in less than fifteen minutes I had been stamped out of the land of a thousand hills. I rushed over the small bridge to the immigration office on the other side. I ran past a few (wet) incutras before entering the Ugandan immigration office. Luckily I still had about uSh25 000 left over from the previous week, so there was no need to change any money. Besides, I had spent my last franc.

At the Ugandan offices there was no queue, just three people in front of me. (The lady behind whom I stood on the Rwandan side of the border could not run as fast as I could, unfortunately.) I soon realised why the queue went quickly on the Ugandan side – it consisted mostly of Ugandans returning home.

When my turn came I handed over my passport. The officer stamped it without asking for us$50. My lucky day, I thought. As he was about to hand it back to me he looked at my passport again and double-checked with one of his colleagues. They chatted for a few seconds and then he turned to me and said, "Hey, Khumalo, you have to pay fifty dollars for your visa."

He asked me how many days I wanted and why I was visiting Uganda. I told him six days because I wanted to go river-rafting up in Jinja.

"To make it worth your while I'll give you two weeks," he said.

Thanks, I wanted to say, but nine of those days will be wasted because in five days' time I'm flying back to South Africa. Of course I did not say that. After he'd handed back my passport I simply thanked him and walked away. He did not give me a receipt.

As a result of this remarkable efficiency (in total it took about half an hour to be stamped out of Rwanda and stamped into Uganda), I decided to change my plans. It was time to move to Plan M: notwithstanding the fact that Uganda is on GMT +3, which meant I had "lost" an hour, I decided not to spend the night in Kampala. Instead I would proceed directly to Jinja. I would then have Wednesday afternoon and the whole of Thursday and Friday to wait for my bungee jump.

All the while during the trip northwards from Kigali I was still trying to work out how such quiet, friendly, warm people as the Rwandese had managed to commit such atrocities against their own people. All I could think of was that governments and leaders and politicians are able to manipulate groups of people to feel, think and act in ways contrary to civilised norms, depending on what the government and leaders and politicians want at the time.

Back in Uganda I had to get used to a few things again. For instance, cars drive on the right side, which is on the left. And I could speak English and be understood, and even buy an English-language daily newspaper. I was bitterly disappointed when I could not find my favourite paper in the whole world, *Red Pepper*.

I ended up buying the *Daily Monitor*. It catered more for middle-class readers. The main headline made that clear: "Investors lose 24 billion in Kampala in one day".

I was more interested in the headline on page 3 – "Modern vs Traditional Justice". The story that followed was of a man who, as head of a traditional court, had sentenced his two sons, who had been accused of raping their sister, to death. One of the accused was beaten to death and the other sustained severe injuries. The father was himself arrested by the police and prosecuted. This had occurred in the Karamoja region in the north-eastern part of the country, which "lived by its own rules, nearly all of them traditional".

The story contained an interesting quote from a community development officer who said that under the traditional justice system a person who kills is supposed to be killed. "You are told to dig two graves, one for the person you killed and the other for yourself. Then you are forced to bury the dead before being stoned to death and buried in the other grave next to your victim," he said. He added, "Once found guilty of incest, homosexuality and bestiality, one is killed by passing a sharp long stick through the renal area to the mouth and just thrown in the bushes."

The bus left Katuna border post exactly on the hour and headed for Kabale. I took a last look at Skyblue Hotel where I had stayed in Mars for one night. Then it was back to dodging the giant potholes on the road to Mbarara. Every now and then the front wheels would hit a deep hole and the bus would fall into it with a shudder and hop out again. Its shock absorbers must have taken severe strain.

I tried to communicate with my neighbour, but she didn't speak English. However, from time to time she would instruct me, using hand signals, to close the window. I would oblige, but when it got too warm and stuffy for my liking I would open the window again. She would not have any of it, and so we repeated the process several times.

At Mbarara the bus stopped at the Shell garage right next to Akaanya Hotel where I had spent a night the previous week. By now the "Pearl of Africa" was beginning to feel like a home away from home.

I bought myself a 300-ml fruit juice and a muffin at a convenience store and enquired if they had a copy of *Red Pepper*. They had sold out, I was told. Half an hour later we were back on the road, continuing our journey north.

I spent most of the time reading the *Daily Monitor*, but now and then I glanced through the window at the astonishing greenness. The only thing that amazed me more was the massive horns on the cattle. I concluded that in Uganda both the humans and animals were well endowed.

We passed the town of Masaka without stopping, but a few kilometres beyond the town the bus pulled off the road. It was time once again for squatting in the grass. Twelve people disembarked, all of them male. Rather disappointing; no squatting this time round. Those twelve guys did not go far from the bus, which is why I could count them so accurately.

If there is one regret that I have about this trip it is that I was too damned scared to take a photograph of that scene. It would have been a real classic: a dozen men facing away from the camera, legs slightly apart and a stream of pee falling equidistant between their feet.

We were still in the southern hemisphere. We hadn't yet crossed that white line separating us from the north.

It took about nine hours to get from Kigali to Kampala. As we entered the city we drove past Backpackers Hostel where I had reserved a room. I was feeling bad – it had been decent of them to reply to my email – but I was on my way to Jinja and there was no chance that I was going to look for an internet café to cancel the reservation.

From the bus rank on the outskirts of the city I had to take a boda-boda to the central taxi rank. My strategy to deal with drivers was still the same:

ask how much the fare would be and negotiate a 50-per-cent discount, hoping to get at least 33 per cent off. So when I was quoted uSh3 000, I insisted on paying uSh1 500. The driver said, "Okay, two thousand."

I said: "We have a deal."

Then the fun began. I was back in the Wild West, or rather the Wild North. Welcome to the real world of African boda-boda drivers: no helmets, no obeying of road signs, just go-go-go. The traffic congestion in downtown Kampala made it particularly hair-raising. There were more vehicles than the roads could handle. The biggest problem was pure lawlessness. We came across a truck holding up the traffic while trying to reverse into a construction site; nobody thought to stop the traffic behind it, with the result that the truck could not reverse and the cars behind it could not go forward – or backwards. Total chaos.

And another thing. There is a risk of being run over by a car while you are on a boda-boda, but the risk of two bikes colliding while trying to out-manoeuvre each other between the cars and trucks is even greater. Why it didn't happen all the time was a mystery to me.

Still, we made it in one piece through backstreets and thick traffic to the taxi rank. Since boda-bodas are not allowed into the taxi rank, I was unceremoniously dropped just outside and had to make my way through a maze of minibus taxis and their touts shouting different destinations. I spotted a board proclaiming: JINJA. Luck was definitely on my side: the fourteen-passenger taxi was short of two passengers only.

Having travelled on my own without coming near the fairer sex (in a manner of speaking) for a month was affecting my ability to process a normal statement without reading a sexual connotation into it. So when, on boarding the taxi, the woman sitting next to the door said, "Oh, you are so big, how are you going to enter?" I felt my ears go warm and my mind went back to happier times ...

Within a few minutes the last passenger turned up and we were off. Well, sort of. Our taxi could not move because two other taxis were parked right where we were supposed to drive out. It was such a tight squeeze that the driver of one of the other taxis had to be found and asked to move his vehicle to make way for us. Once we, along with other long-distance taxis, were outside and ready to leave, we were held up by local taxis circling the taxi rank at a snail's pace, trying to find more passengers.

We finally got onto the chaotic main road to Jinja – only to find ourselves stuck once again in the peak-hour afternoon traffic.

At least I'm on my way to Jinja, I consoled myself as we sat breathing in the exhaust fumes in the seemingly never-ending traffic jam. I was none too comfortable because the boot of the taxi was already full when I boarded, so the only place left for my backpack was my lap. The taxi somehow felt very cramped even though it was not overloaded. This made me suspect that the owner had rearranged the seats, as taxi owners sometimes do, in order to accommodate more passengers. I was squeezed in right behind the driver. I tried to lift my heels and move my ankles to get some blood circulation going. Not very successfully.

At the source of the Nile

The eighty-one-kilometre journey from Kampala to Jinja took one and a half hours. We arrived in Jinja at 6 p.m. (The time difference between Rwanda and Uganda accounts for the additional hour in what was an eleven-hour trip from Kigali, which we left at six that morning – Rwandan time.)

I was very proud of myself because, although the taxi was still on the outskirts of Jinja, I recognised exactly where we were and figured out the best spot for me to jump off. I asked to be dropped right opposite the Caltex petrol station where my boda-boda driver had filled up a week earlier when we ran out of fuel in the pouring rain. Yes, that one.

I was the first passenger to disembark. All the others were no doubt going to the taxi rank to catch local taxis to their villages.

I was no sooner on firm ground than a boda-boda stopped, and after a 33-per cent reduction on the quoted fare we were on our way. My destination was my favourite place: Adrift Camp.

Before I had left Adrift the previous week, I had made a booking for Thursday. Because of my decision not to stay over in Kampala I was now a day early for the booking.

Well, as long as I can jump today, I thought to myself as I looked at the sun about to set in the west, it will still be okay, even if I can't spend the night here. I was encouraged by the memory of the receptionist mentioning during my first visit that they did night jumps if there were enough takers.

Unlike the previous time it was not raining, although there were some dark clouds in the sky.

I did not pay the boda-boda driver until I had made sure there was place for me at the camp; I wanted to go back to town with the boda-boda if they could not accommodate me. To my delight they not only had a bed for me, but I was going to be all alone in a sixteen-bed dormitory named Overtime (don't ask me why). And Emmy, the receptionist, recognised me straight away. "So you still want to jump?" he asked.

Indeed! Adrift Camp may be a beautiful place, but the real reason I was there was because I wanted to bungee. Emmy told me that a few people had jumped that morning. To find out what bookings there were for that evening, he pulled out his cellphone and phoned the jumpmaster.

"No one is booked for tonight and the jumpmaster is going to Kampala tomorrow," Emmy told me, the phone still held to his ear. "He will only be back at five. Will you be able to jump, say just after five tomorrow afternoon? Will you still be here and would you be interested?"

"Yes, indeed."

There and then it was arranged. I was going to jump the following afternoon.

Besides having a whole dormitory to myself, I had the bar too. Since I had not had a decent meal the whole day, I ordered fish, chips and salad. The fish was tilapia from the lake and it was delicious. As a special treat I washed it down with a Nile Special Beer (5.6 per cent alcohol). Just one 500-ml bottle had me a bit tipsy and loving the sound of Tracy Chapman, four-time Grammy Award-winning artist, singing "Baby can I hold you tonight?" and "Talking about revolution" and "Fast car" and "Bang, bang, bang".

Emmy told me that Akamba Bus Company had two buses going to Nairobi every day: one left Jinja in the morning, the other, an overnighter, left in the afternoon. Better informed, I felt I had to change plan yet again, and so Plan N was devised.

My thinking was simple: bungee the next afternoon (Thursday) as part of celebrating the end of my trip, get very pissed in the evening, take the Friday-afternoon bus which arrived in Nairobi on Saturday morning, spend one night in the Kenyan capital and fly back to Johannesburg on Sunday morning. Taking a day bus on Saturday morning and arriving in Nairobi in the early evening in order to catch the plane the next morning would be cutting it too fine, I reasoned.

Things were now looking very organised.

One thing amongst many others I love about being in the countryside is that it gives me the opportunity to look at the stars at night. I spent a long time that evening standing against the low wall overlooking the Victoria Nile and studying the heavens, my mind drifting like the clouds that were becoming heavier and heavier.

Again I thought about John Gribbin's "Principle of Terrestrial Mediocrity".

Considering that there are billions of other stars (like our sun) out there, there is definitely nothing special about our planet, which is orbiting an ordinary star in an ordinary galaxy. The last few drops of Nile Special Beer had attacked my thought processes, but I still came to the conclusion that whoever thinks we humans are alone in this vast and expanding universe needs his/her head examined by an alien.

I went to bed pleased that I had made it back to Jinja and even more pleased that I would finally bungee jump over the Nile River the next day. I had a good sleep. I was not scared of sleeping in a sixteen-bed dormitory alone, but I must admit that I left the light on all night. What made me sleep so well was the sound of rain on the corrugated-iron roof, a sound that always has a calming effect on me.

When I woke up I realised I had to go into town for two reasons: to buy an Akamba bus ticket for Friday afternoon and to see the (still disputed, it would seem) source of the Nile – meaning the spot where the waters of Lake Victoria exited to form the Victoria Nile flowing northwards.

When I went to look for a boda-boda I saw that the people camping on the grounds were from Cape Town. A white Land Rover Defender with registration number CA 548601 stood in the parking area. Without even seeing the owner I knew (yet again) that he or she would be white. It's only logical. Nobody expects my brothers from Gugulethu to drive all the way from Gugs to Jinja in greenest Uganda. Nor does anyone expect folk from Mitchell's Plain to do it; after all, they have Green Point right there in Cape Town.

A few seconds later, just as I had expected, a white man, probably in his fifties, started loading his tent onto his white four-wheel drive. You see, some black brothers do own 4×4s, but they never use them for serious off-roading. Their big cars are mostly used to show off in that mine-is-bigger-than-yours manner. They only travel on gravel roads when visiting an uncle who lives somewhere in the deep rural areas.

I took a boda-boda to the Akamba offices where I was told that a Nairobi bus ticket was going to cost me USh43 000 (about US$23). I booked and selected my seat. Since I didn't have enough Ugandan shillings on me, I promised to come back to pay for my seat. Then off I went with the same boda-boda to change money.

About 200 metres from the Akamba offices the boda-boda ran out of fuel. At least that is what I thought, for the engine all of a sudden switched off right in the middle of the road. The taxi behind us managed to brake in the nick of time. I jumped off and the driver pushed the bike to the side of the road.

"Have you run out of fuel?" I asked, thinking: Not this one too.

"No, it's not fuel. Last night's rain water got into the engine."

He started pushing the bike down the road. I must say it was very strange to be walking next to a boda-boda that was being pushed by its driver.

"So what do we do now?" I asked. My thinking was just to pay him for services rendered thus far and get another boda-boda to take me to the source of the Nile via the bureau de change.

"In twenty minutes it will be okay," he assured me.

Since we were already on the outskirts of town, I paid him all the same and set off for the bureau de change after he gave me directions.

I hadn't gone far when there he was, hooting and revving the engine and shouting behind me, "I told you it would only take a few minutes."

No, you said twenty minutes, I was tempted to say. It was, in fact, not even five minutes. So I got back on the passenger seat and he delivered me at Trend Bureau de Change. I paid him the additional fare and thought I would get another boda-boda once I had changed money.

That done and with no boda-boda in sight, I decided to walk to my final destination: the source of the Nile. I was not, after all, in a rush. All I had to do was pay for the bus ticket before jumping sometime after five.

I walked about a kilometre and, after passing Speke Avenue and the Human Rights Council offices, I turned and followed the direction of the arrow on the board where a picture of me had been taken a week earlier. It led to a gate where three gentlemen were relaxing. They told me that I had to pay uSh10 000.

"You are joking, right?" I said.

It turned out they weren't and I had to pay up. At least I got a receipt.

The path to the source of the Nile ran next to a golf course, then down some steps and past a few curio shops. After going down more steps I got to a plaque that commemorated the scattering of Mahatma Gandhi's ashes in the Nile in 1948.

I ended up in a restaurant right on the edge of the Victoria Nile from where I could see the two islands where the water from Lake Victoria pours into the river. It was not good enough; I had to get closer to the source.

One of the disadvantages of travelling alone is that you can seldom share costs, so something like hiring a boat tends to be very expensive.

Not far from where I was standing five Chinese men were negotiating with a skipper. They were quoted USh50 000. I thought I would jump at the opportunity to join them – Chinese or not, Africa's new colonisers or not, contributing USh10 000 to the total cost could work for all of us.

I approached them with the offer but, lo and behold, although I heard them speaking English to the skipper, they pretended not to understand me. Well, I got the message: they didn't want me in the same boat as them. So off they went in their own boat.

Since I'm too old to let small, tiny, little things like that get to me, I walked over to another skipper and enquired how much he would charge me. He quoted USh25 000 for taking me not only to the source of the Nile but also to the obelisk that stands on the spot where John Hanning Speke stood in 1862 at the end of his third expedition.

As I was getting into his boat, the skipper, Friday – yes, that was his name – asked me: "Would you like a life vest?"

"Please," I said.

He looked around and pulled out a fairly decent model from underneath one of the seats and handed it to me with a why-must-you-behave-like-white-people look.

It was a very calm cruise.

It took less than ten minutes to get to what is the official "Source of the Nile": the spot where a stream of water flows from the lake near a natural spring.

However, there is a problem here too. The spring, right on the edge of the lake, is sometimes regarded as the source because, well, it is the beginning of the river. What is not clear is what percentage of the water in the Victoria Nile, as the river is called at this point, comes from the spring and what percentage comes from Lake Victoria. With my unscientific eyes I could see that the lake contributed more. Which then takes us back – regardless of whether there is a spring or not – to the question of the longest tributary to empty into the lake, which has to be "true" source of the river. The remote Akagera (from Burundi)? The "most remote"

Ruvyironza (also from Burundi)? The "true" source Rukarara (from Rwanda)? Who knows?

I spent about a quarter of an hour watching water bubble from the earth and water pour from the lake. I couldn't imagine that you'd see such a phenomenon anywhere else in the world.

Then it was time to proceed to the obelisk. As we were making our way there, I asked Friday with a straight face: "Why do rivers always flow to the sea?"

He looked confused, so I asked the same question in another way: "Why doesn't the water from the sea flow up the river?"

A second later he replied, "Because God wants it that way."

In under ten minutes we were there. I jumped ashore and took the stairs up to the obelisk. I was standing exactly where it is said that Speke had stood in 1862, apparently for hours, after finding evidence – the lake pouring into the river – that Lake Victoria was indeed the source of Nile.

I could understand why Speke stood there for hours. He is reported to have said: "There I stood at last on the brink of the Nile, the most beautiful scene ... nothing could compare." I copied the statement from a toilet wall in Adrift.

Back in the nineteenth century the view must have been even more remarkable because of a waterfall which Speke named Rippon Falls. The falls disappeared in 1954 with the construction of the Owen Falls Dam, which raised the level of the water upstream and "drowned" the falls.

Speke's discovery of the source of the Nile created a lot of animosity between him and his co-explorer and travelling companion Richard Francis Burton. I must admit that Burton strikes me as very peculiar, for lack of a better word. While the two men were getting logistical issues sorted out on Zanzibar before their second expedition into Africa to look for the great lakes they had heard about, Burton spent most of his time measuring black men's penises. Considering that he was British, he probably suffered from an incurable condition called BALPE – Big And Long Penis Envy.

Be that as it may. Speke and Burton discovered Lake Tanganyika on this second expedition into Africa. But Burton got sick and Speke left him behind, discovering Lake Victoria on his own. He returned to England without Burton and announced in a speech to the Royal Geographical

Society that he had discovered the source of the Nile. Burton, who was already very famous when Speke met him, was furious at the upstart when he arrived in London thirteen days later and found that he was being portrayed as a sickly hanger-on who had not contributed much to the expedition. He demanded proof from Speke to substantiate his claim about having discovered the source of the Nile. So Speke went back on a third expedition, which is when he stood on the very spot where I was standing.

I spent half an hour there and I could have stayed for hours, but I had agreed with Friday beforehand that the entire trip would last an hour.

As we were about to leave a man in blue overalls came running up with a big board, which he put down against a tree. It contained all the general information about the early explorations and explorers and the discovery of the source of the Nile that I already knew. However, I read it and even took some photos. I didn't want to give the impression that I did not appreciate the man's trouble.

I must have studied the board for about five minutes. It contained good, accurate information. As I was leaving the gentleman, with a very serious look on his face, said, "Okay, pay five thousand."

I stood my ground. "Why did you not tell me that reading that board was going to cost me money?"

"No, my friend, you have to pay," he insisted.

"Okay, I'll give you two thousand."

"No, my friend, give me three thousand."

"You take this two thousand or you get nothing; I didn't ask you to bring the board for me to read."

He took the two thousand and the matter was settled – to his advantage, I suspect. I was not at all sure that I had not been conned.

A little put out, Friday took me back to where he had picked me up.

On the boat I thought about Speke and Burton and the tragic consequences of their rivalry. You see, after Speke saw the river flowing out of the lake, he sent a telegram to England saying: "The Nile is settled." But it wasn't. Burton, who knew that Speke had not followed the river from its newly discovered source all the way to Khartoum, wanted to know how Speke could be sure that the river he had seen spring from the lake was, in fact, the Nile.

To settle the matter once and for all it was decided that Speke and Burton should hold a public debate. On the day of the debate in September 1864 Speke accidentally shot himself while hunting. An inquest concluded that it was an accident, but many people believed it was suicide.

The pull of gravity

Although it was already afternoon, I could not eat. The anticipation of jumping in a couple of hours' time and the excitement of having visited the "Source of the Nile" were too intense. I had lost my appetite for food.

After buying some souvenirs from one of the craft shops I walked back along the same route next to the golf course. Just before I got to the main gate a young man on a bicycle offered to take me to town. What the heck, I thought, let me take a ride on a bicycle. Apart from the guy at the Kenya–Uganda border, I had not taken a bicycle taxi. As I've mentioned, the boda-boda "taxi service" was started by guys on bicycles at the border – the name comes from their shouting "border, border" to attract customers. Riding a bike was something I had not done in years, and I really liked the idea of being ferried about by pedal power. So I jumped on.

Instead of following the road, the thin, young cyclist took a shortcut through the golf course, which meant going up a gradually ascending slope. The poor guy really struggled to get up that path with all of me seated behind him. I could see and feel that I had lost weight since the beginning of the trip, but it was clearly not enough. He was sweating until his shirt dripped with perspiration.

After a while I felt so sorry for him that I volunteered to walk until we got to the tar road. I got off and he continued to crawl up the slope. When he got his breath back – before he reached the tar road – he said he was fine and I could climb back on. Not even twenty metres further he was struggling again. Before I could volunteer to jump off, he asked me to do so.

I must say the path was not that steep. The cyclist also looked fit – as can be expected of someone who cycled around with loads every day – but he clearly underestimated what it took to carry a heavyweight champion up a hill. We made it to the tar road in the end, he in the saddle and me on foot, and from there it was a relatively flat road all the way to Jinja.

I did not have the heart to continue with him as my boda-boda driver, however, so I leapt off, paid him and did some window-shopping in town. I then took a modern motorised boda-boda to the Akamba office on the outskirts. It turned out that the office belonged to a travel agency. The assistant offered to phone the main Akamba office in Kampala to book my seat while I waited. She said she was going to Nairobi that very afternoon, but assured me that her colleague would be there to assist me when I returned the next day to board the bus at 17:00.

I returned to Adrift Camp just after 15:00. on the same boda-boda. The weather was perfect, a cloudless blue sky with no sign of rain.

The two hours I had to wait for the jumpmaster to arrive felt like twenty. I waited and waited and waited. One thing about extreme sport, once you have decided to do it, is that you do not want to wait. You just want to get it over and done with.

Emmy decided to give the jumpmaster a call. "Well, he's still on his way from Kampala," he told me. "But he says in any case you are the only one booked for a jump today, so he unfortunately cannot do it." Then he quickly added, "But he promises that tomorrow morning there are people who have confirmed to jump. So you can jump with them first thing tomorrow morning."

I felt like sitting down and crying. I had waited the whole day and now I had to wait a whole night. I started thinking that maybe it was a sign to give up the whole idea.

Well, at least I could order a tilapia again – and a Nile Special Beer – while immersing myself in the incredible view of the Victoria Nile at the beginning of its ninety-day trek through northern Uganda, Sudan, Egypt and all the way to the Mediterranean Sea. Slowly the Adrift crew members drifted in with their nice T-shirts. I particularly liked the one with the slogan: *I'd rather be scared to death than bored to death*. Later, another crew member arrived with this warning on his chest: *I am not your mother. Just a raft guide.*

That night I again had a sixteen-bed dormitory to myself. I lay there thinking that, although I had not jumped, it had been a fruitful day. I had finally been to what, since 1862, had been generally considered the source of the Nile, and seen with my own eyes the spring where the Victoria Nile flows from Lake Victoria.

I switched off the lights and fell asleep. This time I didn't keep a light on and I slept like a baby.

"Hey, Khumalo, they are waiting for you. You have to go and jump!" a woman yelled whilst hammering on the door.

I can assure you that this is definitely not the first thing you want to hear in the morning. I leapt out of bed and walked through the campsite to the loo, not because I was scared but because people normally go to the loo first thing in the morning. On the way I saw people standing on the bungee platform. As I was peeing I heard someone being counted down: "Five, four, three, two, one – bungee!" Followed by a scream.

I went down to the bar and was told that I needn't pay beforehand. "Go and jump now! We'll deal with other things later," Emmy said.

From the Adrift bar you have a perfect view of the people who are jumping because the platform is right next to it. I still had to ask somebody to take pictures of me jumping. I hated doing it, but in the end I asked one of the rafting crew who were waiting for their customers to finish their jumps.

I left my camera with a complete stranger before dropping my passport and wallet at reception. Then I walked past the parking area and the security guard who had told me earlier that he had also jumped. He wished me good luck.

This was going to be my third jump in ten years. The previous times I'd jumped from an existing bridge; this time I had to climb up onto a platform. I left my slops on the ground and started climbing. It was frightening in the extreme. As I was going up I could not help but think: Jeez, I have to fall all that distance.

I did not want to look down but I had no choice; I had to see where I was putting my feet. After climbing the six sets of steps and crossing a walkway of about fifteen metres, I was on the platform.

Another guy was about to jump and the jumpmaster suggested that I watch. Well, that was the last thing I wanted to do, so instead I just gazed at the horizon and tried, against all odds, to appreciate the cloudless blue African sky.

The guy jumped and it was my turn.

First, I had to get on a scale: 84.6 kilograms. Great news, but there was no time to rejoice about having lost ten kilograms in less than a month. In fact, there was hardly time to digest the information at all before I had to sit down in a chair so big that you would think it was designed for the royal descendants of Queen Victoria. The jumpmaster introduced himself but I was too scared for his name to register. As I was shifting into the seat he said, "Now is not the time to think because thinking and bungeeing cannot happen at the same time."

I could not agree with him more. A towel around both ankles and then the bungee cord with a 2.5-ton safe working load (only 2 500 kilograms – the weight of an average African elephant would make it snap).

"This thing will never snap," the jumpmaster assured me before asking, "So do you want to jump into the water?"

I didn't answer immediately. I had thought I would love to jump into the lake, but now I was not so sure. The jumpmaster explained, "At this spot, the river is twelve metres deep. So you could never hit rocks or anything of that sort."

"Well, mmmm … yes, I would like to get into the water up to my waist," I said hesitantly.

"Cool! But will you be able to close your eyes and tuck your head under both arms so you do not hit the water with your head?"

"What if I am so disoriented that I either forget or just cannot do it?" I asked, thinking of my first jump when I was so confused that I would never have remembered to hold my arms together.

"Well, if you hit the water head first and with your eyes open, it is going to hurt a lot."

That was very reassuring. But I still insisted that I wanted to be plunged into the water up to my waist.

"You will never hit the bottom, the river is twelve metres deep here," the jumpmaster repeated.

It was time for the most difficult part of bungee jumping. Because both my feet were tied together, I could not walk. So I had to hop, assisted by another guy who urged, "Hop, hop, hop!"

It was even scarier this time because, as I was barefoot, I could feel my toes suspended in the breeze, with only my heels firmly planted on the platform.

They started counting me down. "Five, four, three …" I was poep-scared but knew, come what may, I was going to jump. "Two, one – bungee!"

So I did.

On my first two jumps I had been very disorientated and waited for the bungee cord to pull after I leapt off the platform. As I was going down this time I was aware of exactly where I was all the way down. In fact, I even gauged when I should put my hands together in preparation for dipping into the water.

I touched the water only slightly with my fingertips before the bungee cord pulled me back. As the jumpmaster later explained, a perfect jump uses more cord than when one just drops down. Judging from my body language, he had thought that I was just going to drop off the platform, whereas I made a perfect, far-out jump, which used more of the cord and did not allow me to go into the water.

At Adrift you don't get pulled back onto the platform after a bungee; you are lowered onto a waiting raft with two guys at the ready with a stick for you to grab. After the bungee cord was loosened and I was safely on the raft, they paddled me to the shore. I jumped off and walked, the adrenaline still pumping, up some steps and along a steep path bordered by long grass back to reception.

I was not issued with a certificate, as after my previous jumps at Vic Falls and Bloukrans. And the guy who took my photos had not zoomed in as I had instructed him, so I was just a blip on the screen. Moreover, I still felt some disappointment at not having been immersed in the water. It would have been a perfect christening. Nevertheless, I'd jumped, and that was achievement enough.

I paid my US$50 for the jump and was asked to sign an indemnity form. Better late than never, I thought.

I was still so full of energy and adrenaline that I decided there and then to walk the approximately five kilometres to the bus station later that afternoon instead of taking a boda-boda.

Finish and klaar

The trip was over. I sent my brother and sister an SMS, telling them about the bungee. My sister responded instantly, excited and relieved that I had not only survived the jump but would also be on a plane heading back to Johannesburg within forty-eight hours. My brother, being his usual self (read: nobody can tell whether he is excited or not except when he has had a few drinks with his friends), responded with a terse message: *Ok will talk once you are back.*

I phoned Lulu. I really could not contain my excitement and had to share it with her. She was surprised. I had not told her that I was going to jump because I did not want a lecture about the things that could go wrong. We spoke for a few minutes, knowing I'd be back very soon.

I stood on the balcony of the bar looking at the Nile. It was 9.27 on Friday 31 October 2008 and it was all over. I thought about what I had set out to do and what I had accomplished. Out of six goals I had managed to reach four:

- I had taken a ride on the *M V Liemba*;
- I had stood on the equator;
- I had visited the Kigali Memorial Centre;
- I had bungee jumped at Jinja.

That meant a 66.6 per cent success rate. Not too shabby, hey? In the process I had discovered that:

- it does not get greener than Uganda. Winston Churchill was right – it is the real, genuine "Pearl of Africa";
- it does not get more beautiful than standing at the source of the Nile in Jinja, and it does not get better than bungee jumping off the platform at Adrift Camp;
- it is possible against all odds to get on the *M V Liemba* and travel across Lake Tanganyika;
- the imaginary line that divides north and south is white and runs across a road south of Kampala;

- you can trust people in Africa not to steal your backpack;
- there is a young woman with kissable lips in Kigali who is waiting to be told where the source of the Nile is;
- once a month, on Saturday, there are people in Kigali who find it in their hearts to clean the yards of other people in the name of reconciliation and nation building;
- these so-called discoveries by early explorers were nothing but first sightings by non-Africans; local people knew about the rivers and lakes and waterfalls long before exploring Africa became such a thing to Europeans. So, in reality, there were no discoveries.

The list could go on. And one of my discoveries on the trip – which had absolutely nothing to do with the trip – was that I was going to be a father all over again.

Standing there on the balcony of the bar I realised that there would be no further changes of plan. That afternoon I was going to take an overnight bus to Nairobi where I would spend the day before flying out early on Sunday morning. My flight was going to land an hour after my wife and daughter returned from celebrating my wife's aunt's sixtieth birthday in Umlazi, south of Durban.

Within twenty-four hours of landing in South Africa I would be back at work. It was not a comforting thought. But that was three days away. In the meantime I had to savour the moment. My heart was still pumping uncontrollably, because I had just finished exploring the

Heart of Africa

"We should not find ourselves continuously dependent even on the opinions of those scholars who write about Afrikans without ever having lived with us. We need to produce even more opinion-makers among ourselves than we have."

Es'kia Mphahlele
South African academic and writer, 1919–2008

Acknowledgements

This book would have never materialised if my wife Lulu had not allowed me to go on yet another "expedition". I promise, my sweets, there is only one African trip left.

To my sister Nontobeko Prudence Khumalo for handing me the top-up when I was about to face my own global financial crisis – *Ngiyabonga kakhulu.*

To my other family members, friends and especially my in-laws, from the bottom of my heart I really would like to thank you for … (at the time of going to print, nothing had come to mind).

How can I forget the woman at the South African embassy in Kigali who refused point-blank to write a letter of congratulation for me? I have one simple word for you: *Voetsek!*

Final note: If you want to know something about Sifiso "Bru" Sibisi, to whom this book is dedicated, please read my piece "A confidant who almost was my best man" on the Web at //sihlekhumalo.book.co.za.

Note to the reader

In the course of my journey, I asked myself (and prospective readers of the book I was planning to write) seven questions – see pages 46, 61, 107, 128, 142, 166 and 200.

If you think you have all the correct answers, please drop me an email at sihle.khumalo@webmail.co.za. If all six of your answers are spot on, I will take you out to an exclusive restaurant for a five-course dinner, to be washed down by lots of good wine. The bill will be split in half but you'll be expected to pay the total amount of money owing.